Crime

and

Everyday

Life

FIFTH EDITION

SAGE was founded in 1965 by Sara Miller McCune to support the dissemination of usable knowledge by publishing innovative and high-quality research and teaching content. Today, we publish more than 750 journals, including those of more than 300 learned societies, more than 800 new books per year, and a growing range of library products including archives, data, case studies, reports, conference highlights, and video. SAGE remains majority-owned by our founder, and after Sara's lifetime will become owned by a charitable trust that secures our continued independence.

Los Angeles | London | Washington DC | New Delhi | Singapore | Boston

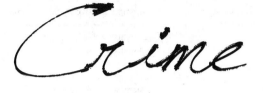

and
Everyday
Life

FIFTH EDITION

Marcus Felson
Texas State University

Mary Eckert
MA Eckert Consulting, LLC

Los Angeles | London | New Delhi
Singapore | Washington DC | Boston

Los Angeles | London | New Delhi
Singapore | Washington DC | Boston

FOR INFORMATION:

SAGE Publications, Inc.

2455 Teller Road

Thousand Oaks, California 91320

E-mail: order@sagepub.com

SAGE Publications Ltd.

1 Oliver's Yard

55 City Road

London EC1Y 1SP

United Kingdom

SAGE Publications India Pvt. Ltd.

B 1/I 1 Mohan Cooperative Industrial Area

Mathura Road, New Delhi 110 044

India

SAGE Publications Asia-Pacific Pte. Ltd.

3 Church Street

#10-04 Samsung Hub

Singapore 049483

Acquisitions Editor: Jerry Westby

Editorial Assistant: Laura Kirkhuff

Production Editor: Jane Haenel

Copy Editor: Terri Lee Paulsen

Typesetter: Hurix Systems Pvt.Ltd.

Proofreader: Victoria Reed-Castro

Indexer: Terri Corry

Cover Designer: Michael Dubowe

Marketing Manager: Terra Schultz

Printed in the United States of America

Library of Congress Cataloging-in-Publication Data

Felson, Marcus, 1947–

Crime and everyday life / Marcus Felson, Mary Eckert. — Fifth edition.

pages cm

Includes bibliographical references and index.

ISBN 978-1-4833-8468-9 (pbk. : alk. paper)

1. Crime—United States. 2. Crime prevention—United States. 3. Social control. I. Eckert, Mary (Mary A.) II. Title.

HV6789.F45 2015

364.973—dc23

2014049340

This book is printed on acid-free paper.

Certified Sourcing
www.sfiprogram.org
SFI-00453

SFI label applies to text stock

15 16 17 18 19 10 9 8 7 6 5 4 3 2 1

BRIEF CONTENTS

DETAILED CONTENTS

———•◦•———

PREFACE TO THE FIFTH EDITION

---•◦•---

The purpose of this book is to help you play a role in reducing crime. To achieve that goal, you need to think clearly about crime and to discern very practical ways to act against it.

We start the book by helping you overcome popular fallacies about crime. Then we offer the fundamentals for thinking about crime in tangible terms. We continue with important examples and principles for crime reduction in real life. Throughout the book we focus on practical ideas and specific crime problems, and what to do about each.

Our book uses plain language and plain thinking. That means avoiding grand theorizing. Instead, we build the book on a middle-range theory—the *routine activity approach*. With the help of the "crime triangle," that approach is easy to learn and remember. We also offer very practical methods for reducing crime, drawing from situational crime prevention.

Instead of studying "criminality" in a broad and general sense, we focus on criminal acts in a more specific way. This book emphasizes modus operandi—who, what, when, where, and how each specific type of crime occurs. We always ask, "What can be done *here and now* to prevent crime from happening?" The answer requires learning how the offender thinks and what the offender wants. Even violent offenders respond to practical changes in the settings where violent acts occur. In explaining criminal events and offender decisions, we offer you a clear perspective for thinking about crime and a practical guide for acting against it.

This is the fifth edition of a book that first appeared two decades ago. The book keeps changing. The current edition is filled with material never presented elsewhere. We offer additional details, refined ideas, and updated references. We add entirely new information on crime multipliers, and on routine activity trajectories as youths develop. We elaborate greatly how juvenile delinquency occurs and how juvenile street gangs emerge. We offer new examples of situational crime prevention, and clarify principles on how to secure residential neighborhoods.

Despite these changes, this edition is shorter than the last. We worked very hard to streamline the writing, saying more in fewer words. We use the first-person singular through most of the book in order to personalize the message and strengthen communication. Our purpose is simple: ***We want you to remember what we teach long after you have graduated.*** Your long-term assignment is the most important one—to find practical ways to reduce crime.

Marcus Felson and Mary Eckert
Austin, Texas
August 2014

ACKNOWLEDGMENTS

We wish to thank the many members of the Environmental Criminology and Crime Analysis group for their longstanding support. We especially thank our colleagues Kim Rossmo and Lucia Summers for personal and intellectual contributions to our well-being. We also acknowledge our colleagues and students at Texas State University.

ABOUT THE AUTHORS

Marcus Felson is the originator of the routine activity approach and of *Crime and Everyday Life*. He has also authored *Crime and Nature*, and serves as professor at Texas State University in San Marcos, Texas. He has a B.A. from University of Chicago, an M.A. and Ph.D. from the University of Michigan, and has received the *2014 Honoris Causa* from the Universidad Miguel Hernandez in Spain. Professor Felson has been given the Ronald Clarke Award by the Environmental Criminology and Crime Analysis group, and the Paul Tappan Award of the Western Society of Criminology. He has been a guest lecturer in Argentina, Australia, Belgium, Brazil, Canada, Chile, China, Denmark, El Salvador, England, Finland, France, Germany, Hong Kong, Hungary, Italy, Japan, Mexico, the Netherlands, New Zealand, Norway, Poland, Scotland, Spain, South Africa, Sweden, and Switzerland. He has applied routine activity thinking to many topics, including theft, violence, child molestation, white-collar crime, and corruption.

Mary Eckert, his wife and life partner, has an M.A. and Ph.D. in sociology from New York University. Her B.A. is from the College of New Rochelle. Dr. Eckert has devoted an active career to applied research in criminal justice and program evaluation. She served as research director of the New York City Criminal Justice Agency, Inc., where she authored many research reports and guided that agency's diverse research agenda, including work on pretrial risk assessment, court-case processing, and evaluating alternative-to-incarceration programs. She also worked for the New Jersey Office of the Attorney General, with a special focus on statistical evaluation of vehicle stops to assist the New Jersey State Police in reducing the potential for racial profiling. Her work has been recognized by the New York Association of Pretrial Service Agencies and the State of New Jersey. She has been an adjunct professor at New York University, Montclair State University, and Texas State University.

To Virginia Raphaelson Felson, who turned 100 years old on October 12, 2014. Stubborn. Independent. Humorous. Fast on her feet. College graduate. Ahead of her times.

———•◦•———

EIGHT FALLACIES ABOUT CRIME

⎯•◦•⎯

I don't believe in grand theory. Instead this book is built on a "middle range theory" that does not try to cover all human misbehavior on a very general level. Instead I offer you a practical understanding of crime and its prevention, organizing information so it will be easy to learn and remember.

That requires controlling our emotions. We are all angered when we learn of suffering crime victims, people wrongly convicted of crimes, or people who destroy their own lives or those of others. But we cannot let our natural emotions prevent us from examining all the facts and thinking clearly about crime.

I have developed the routine activity approach as a middle-range theory to help you study crime without getting lost. It is very practical for policy, too, for it treats the criminal act as a *tangible* event occurring within the physical world. The routine activity approach focuses on exactly how, when, and where crime occurs. In this book I hope to teach you something about crime you do not know already. First, I ask you, as the reader, to overcome these eight fallacies about crime:

1. Dramatic fallacy
2. Cops-and-courts fallacy
3. Not-me fallacy
4. Innocent-youth fallacy
5. Ingenuity fallacy
6. Organized-crime fallacy
7. Big gang fallacy
8. Agenda fallacy

These fallacies keep coming back again and again via the media and in unusual stories people tell that misrepresent what *normally* happens with crime. A Chicago home is burgled. The owner calls police, expecting them to show up with a crime-scene team and to go find the burglar. In reality, big-city police may not show up at all for an ordinary burglary! Or they might arrive after the burglar has been gone for some time. If the victim demands a full investigation, the officer might declare, "Lady, you've been watching too much television."

On television big crimes have big investigations, but that does not represent real life. This book is about crime as it really happens. My challenge to you is not only to learn these fallacies, but to fortify yourself with them and withstand the daily bombardment of dramatic misinformation about crime.

THE DRAMATIC FALLACY

Note that I call my middle-range theory "the routine activity approach." I work very hard to avoid being distracted by dramatic crimes. One semester a student came to me before the first class and asked, "Is this about serial murderers?" and I told her no—this class will emphasize ordinary thefts and fights. She dropped the course. Are you willing to learn about most crime as it really occurs?

Dramatic crimes get more attention because they make a better story. News media know that perfectly well. In fact, plenty of people make money talking about nonrepresentative crime. Included are 24-hour news cable channels that compete with the networks for viewers—CNN, Fox, C-SPAN, and MSNBC—plus many specialized cable channels, such as TNT, A&E, HBO, TBS, and Spike TV.

Even before cable news existed, television and other media would seek strange and violent incidents to keep their ratings high. The media are interested in romantic murders by jealous lovers, shootouts between felons and police officers, and extreme or clever types of murder—whether the events were true or made up for movies or fictional series.

Yet most criminal acts are not very clever or romantic. The *dramatic fallacy* states that the most publicized offenses are very distant from real life. The media are carried away by a *horror-distortion sequence.* They find a horror story and then entertain the public with it. They make money on it while creating a myth in the public mind. Then they build on that myth for the next horror story. As this happens, public misinformation grows, with new stories building on public acceptance of past misconceptions. Thus crime becomes very distorted in the public mind (see Beckett & Sasson, 2004).

These distortions can produce a "moral panic" as stories accumulate and make people increasingly scared—even though the incidents in question are exceedingly rare. I am not denying that horrible incidents occur, and those nearby suffer greatly. But millions of people at great distance suffer vicariously via the news reports, forgetting that their greatest local horrors are likely to come from ordinary car accidents, heart attacks, and strokes that don't even get in the news.

No crime is more distorted in the public eye than murder. The most interesting or elaborate murders are covered. Even worse, much of the public responds as if murder is one of the most frequent crimes. Let's consider the reality based on the Uniform Crime Report (Federal Bureau of Investigation [FBI], 2013b; see Exhibit 1.1).

A simple calculation shows that major violent crimes outnumber the murder category 80 to 1. Total major property crimes outnumber murder by a ratio of 625 to 1. The millions and millions of other crimes outnumber murder by perhaps 10,000 to 1. Clearly the media emphasis on murder is misplaced.

Nor is the coverage of murder circumstances at all accurate. Sherlock Holmes would have no interest whatever in most of these 14,827 murders. Only 12 people were poisoned. Only 8 died of explosives. Only 4 were pushed out a window. Some 35 were killed with narcotics, 13 drowned, and 89 strangled. Two-thirds died of gunshots, but most of the guns were handguns, not assault weapons. There was one sniper death. Just six of the reported murders involved gambling, prostitution, or commercial vice (FBI, 2013b).

Exhibit 1.1 Murder Is a Tiny Part of the Crime Volume

Murder and non-negligent manslaughter	14,827
Total major violent crimes	1,214,462
Total major property crimes	8,975,438
Miscellaneous other crimes in police records	Millions
Other crimes not leading to arrest (based on other data sources)	Millions and millions

SOURCE: Federal Bureau of Investigation. (2013b). Uniform crime reports, Tables 1 and 29.

Most murders are the tragic result of a stupid little quarrel. Indeed, murder is less a crime than it is an outcome. The path toward murder is not much different from that of an ordinary fight, except that, unfortunately, someone happened to die. Murder has two central features: a gun too near and a hospital too far. My brother, Richard Felson (2004, 2013), has written by far the best work explaining how violence emerges from simple disputes. Although some murderers intend to kill from the outset, even they usually have simple reasons not worth televising. More commonly, someone harming someone else does not really know where that harm will lead.

Despite these dramatic exceptions, harm is limited in the vast majority of incidents. Most quarrels do not lead to threats. Most threats do not lead to blows. Most blows do minor physical harm. Most physical harm requires no hospitalization. Most hospitalization is brief and only rarely does it lead to death. This picture is well supported by the National Crime Victim Survey. For example, there are more than four times as many simple assaults as aggravated assaults (Truman & Langton, 2014). Although there is no national repository of calls for police service or 9-1-1 calls, the arithmetic for almost any local police department points to the same conclusion: that disturbances and disputes far exceed in number the actual assaults requiring an arrest, and even these may involve no physical injury whatever.

However, that does not mean people are not upset by quarrels or other small events. Of course we would like a society in which nobody gets mad at anybody else. But we should not interpret murder as our indicator. I am constantly shocked that people use homicide statistics as the measure of overall crime!

The dominance of minor problems is repeatedly verified by the statistics. Property-crime victimizations far exceed violent victimizations. The simplest thefts and burglaries are the most common offenses, and far exceed major thefts of large amounts. Self-report surveys pick up a lot of illegal consumption and minor offenses, but little major crime. The ongoing Monitoring the Future Survey repeatedly asks high school seniors about their use of various drugs (Johnston, O'Malley, Bachman, Schulenberg, & Miech, 2014). Respondents admit to considerable underage drinking, minor theft, and plenty of marijuana experimentation; only a small percentage report using cocaine or hard drugs.

Alcohol abuse remains the major issue! It is also likely that illegal experimentation is sporadic rather than regular. When students are asked about drug use in the past 30 days, these numbers fall to much lower levels

(Johnston, O'Malley, Bachman, & Schulenberg, 2007), and most do not break the rules every day. This principle holds strong: Minor drugs far exceed major drugs, and occasional usage far exceeds regular usage. These drugs do much less overall harm than simple alcohol abuse—always the greatest American drug problem. Misunderstanding the problem has consequences, since it leads the public and its representatives to pick the wrong policies.

You can see, then, that most offenses are not dramatic. Property crime far exceeds violent crime. Violent crimes that do occur are relatively infrequent and leave no long-term physical harm. When injury does result, it is usually self-containing and not classified as aggravated assault, much less homicide. Real crime is usually not much of a story: Someone drinks too much and gets in a fight. There is no inner conflict, thrilling car chase, or life-and-death struggle. He saw, he took, and he left. He won't give it back.

Of course dramatic events sometimes occur in real life. By the time this book is in your hands, another intruder may shoot up a school, and people will then talk about that one event as if it represented all crime. Keep your focus on the plain facts of crime and ignore the dramatic event of the month.

THE COPS-AND-COURTS FALLACY

Many of my students are in law enforcement, and I appreciate their role. But they are not the center of the crime universe. Police, courts, and prisons are important *after* crimes have entered the public sphere, but they are not the key actors in crime production or prevention. Crime comes *first*, and the justice system *sometimes* finds out and acts upon it. The *cops-and-courts fallacy* warns us against overrating the power of criminal justice agencies, including police, prosecutors, and courts.

Police Work

Real police work is by and large mundane. Ordinary police activity includes driving around a lot, asking people to quiet down, hearing complaints about barking dogs, filling out paperwork, meeting with other police officers, and waiting to be called up in court. If you ever become a crime analyst, you will quickly learn that:

- Many calls for service never lead to a real crime report.
- Many complaints (e.g., barking dogs) bother a few citizens, but do not directly threaten the whole community.
- Many problems are resolved informally, as they should be.

The old line is that, "Police work consists of hour upon hour of boredom, occasionally interrupted by moments of sheer terror." But most officers don't experience or deliver that much terror. The vast majority of the 700,000 law enforcement officers in the United States (92%) never experienced any assault during the year 2012. Of those assaulted, one in four was injured, but only 48 died from attack by felons—equal to the number dying by accident (FBI, 2013a). These deaths are very upsetting to other officers and the public. However, the annual risk of dying on duty is only .0000685 or about 7 per 100,000 officers. Such deaths make good television because they are so rare and hence dramatic!

Only a few hundred civilians per year are shot dead by law enforcement personnel. Some police officers have to wait years for moments like those seen on TV. Most seldom—or never—take a gun out of its holster. Most are never shot at and never shoot at anybody else. Only a tiny portion of homicides in the United States are at the hands of police. So what's really happening?

Police are society's agents of daily confrontation. Drunks on the street? Barking dogs? Loud parties at night? Teens hanging around? Couple arguing? Call the cops. Their job is to close down the beer keg just when the party is getting good.

In these encounters, rude behavior can go in many directions: civilians toward civilians; civilians toward cops; cops toward civilians. Police see a lot of rude behavior and hear a lot of rude language, some of it directed at them. Most rudeness does not escalate. But sometimes it does. Police use of force usually amounts to a bit of a shove, or moving the arms behind the back when cuffing someone. Sometimes an offender shoves back, but knives and guns are exceptional in most cities for most police.

To understand policing, understand that most crimes are not reported to the police in the first place. As I noted, police are called more often to deal with barking dogs and loud parties than they are asked to stop a major felony. They handle most events informally with no violence and no arrests.

Police do not even *know* about most crimes that occur during the year. In the 2013 National Crime Victim Survey, only 46 percent of those who said they were victimized by violence also said they had reported the crime to the police

(Truman & Langton, 2014). Self-report studies cited earlier in this chapter turn up even greater numbers of illegal acts that never are reported to police, notably many millions of instances of marijuana consumption, underage alcohol use, shoplifting, private assaults, and billions of dollars' worth of fraud that businesses and citizens leave unreported.

Average citizens often demand more "police presence" in their neighborhood. But they really don't understand their own situation. The *theory* is that police can reduce crime by patrolling—inhibiting wrongdoing by their sheer presence on the streets. The Kansas City Patrol Experiment investigated this point. The experiment discovered that intensified police patrols are *scarcely noticed* by offenders or citizens and have no impact on crime rates (Kelling, Pate, Dieckman, & Brown, 1974). More recent work finds that police can reduce crime, but only if they concentrate police efforts very intelligently (Weisburd & Eck, 2004). Given 300 million people and billions of valuable items dispersed over vast space, there is no practical way for police to deliver blanket protection. Like all of us, the police have to focus their efforts to become more effective.

I live in Austin, Texas, which has 2,300 sworn officers attempting to control crime for

- 840,000 residential population, spread over
- about 350,000 housing units, and
- almost 300 square miles of land.

Perfect 24-hour coverage of every housing unit would require 350,000 multiplied by 24 hours, or 8.4 million person-hours of work. That means that each officer would have to work over 3,600 hours a day! This explains why mass police protection is simply not possible.

Do you really expect police to know that the guy that just left your house is a burglar? Most burglaries proceed with nobody getting caught; when somebody is caught, that's not because the police are there when it happened. Less than 1 percent of offenses end with the offender apprehended in the act by police on patrol. Doubling the number of police in a US city is doubling a drop in the bucket.

Courts and Punishment

For most crimes known to the police, nobody gets arrested. When there is an arrest, most cases are never sent to the prosecutor. Of the cases that go up, most lead to plea bargaining between attorney and prosecutor, not a trial.

Of those that go to trial, bench trials in local police court is much more likely than a full-blown jury trial, as seen on TV. Even people convicted are very likely to avoid incarceration, despite several decades of "law and order" politics. For example, about 3 million household burglaries were estimated in the United States in 2013 (Truman & Langton, 2014). Of these, about half of the incidents were reported to the police. About 1 in 10 resulted in arrests. Only about 1 percent of burglaries lead to a conviction, and fewer still to incarceration. The chance of being punished for a drug offense is much smaller, still.

Within the court setting, very few convictions are based on trials as seen on TV. Most are plea-bargained in meetings between prosecutor and defense attorney, and only about 1 in 50 cases go before a jury. When the criminal justice system delivers punishment, it does so after long delays, typically 6 to 8 months.

That delay is very important for crime policy. People expect way too much deterrence from punishment by the justice system. Psychologists have found that the best way to get someone to do what you want is to reward more than you punish, doing so quickly, often, and mildly. The US criminal justice system does everything wrong:

- It punishes bad rather than rewarding good.
- It penalizes people rarely and sporadically.
- It delivers its decisions and penalties after long delays.

People inside the justice system often find this very frustrating, so when they can finally convict someone they often want to "throw the book" at him. However, extreme penalties delivered late and sporadically have little practical impact. And, remember, they can only be delivered when a crime is known and after an arrest is made.

In contrast, crime itself offers sure and quick rewards to offenders. Don't be surprised that many people continue to commit crimes.

Consider what happens when you touch a hot stove: The pain you receive is quick, certain, sharp, but usually not long lasting. After being burned once, you will not touch a hot stove again. Now think of an imaginary hot stove that burns you only once every 500 times you touch it, with the burn not hurting until six months later. The other 499 times you receive a quick reward. Psychological research and common sense alike tell us a justice system will not work very well if it follows this principle.

My point is not to blame the people in the criminal justice system. They are subject to practical limits just like everyone else. Keep in mind the practical realities for the justice system, and don't expect too much from the clean-up squad.

THE NOT-ME FALLACY

My brother Rich is an outstanding social psychologist, who has shown that social psychological theory and research are highly relevant to crime analysis. *Attribution* is an important principle in social psychology. People tend to forgive their own misdeeds, but not the misdeeds of strangers. They tend to explain away their own misdeeds as situational: "I drank too much at the party because my friends were there." "I had no other way to get home but to drive, and I only had a few drinks." "I wasn't really going that fast considering that there was no traffic." "I didn't have time to find a condom."

On the other hand, people tend to be harsher and more personal in explaining the misdeeds of strangers: "That guy's irresponsible." "Good girls don't do that." "What do you expect of people who live on that side of town?" Note the contradiction: The same deeds are excused for me and my people, even though I blame outsiders for doing the very same thing.

The not-me fallacy is the tendency to think that crime does not apply to me or people in my world, but rather to outsiders. It is consistent with attribution theory, explaining why hypocrisy is so common when people discuss crime.

People tend to hold others, especially strangers, to higher standards than they hold themselves. It is perfectly normal to deny one's own bad deeds or to find situational alibis. Thus people distance moral wrong away from themselves—but are less charitable to people they don't know or don't like. Attribution theory helps us understand why people can participate in crime without labelling themselves as criminals. It also helps explain why white Americans, who consume marijuana about as much as blacks, attribute drug abuse mainly to Americans with darker skins. As juveniles get older and break more roles, they begin to recode their infractions as "minor," to becoming more accepting of their own rule-breaking and that of their friends. Even adults find ways to justify crimes in their own areas, while disparaging the other side of the tracks.

The old cowboy movies had good guys (in white hats with white horses) and bad guys (in black hats with black horses). Indeed, empirical research has virtually destroyed the claim that victims and offenders come from separate populations. You don't have to be bad to do bad. Many people who usually observe the rules may break them from time to time.

If you follow society's rules most of the time, you can conveniently forget your own exceptions. If you commit a few crimes, you can remind yourself of the many you have not committed. If you skip a temptation out of fear, you can persuade yourself that you are morally superior to somebody else.

Or perhaps you never had a chance to break a rule. M. Felson and Gottfredson (1984) found that women's lack of sexual experience early in the 20th century reflected mainly the fact that nobody ever tried. Young women were closely watched by parents and could not easily be alone with a young man. But the vast majority of those women who gained that opportunity proceeded with sexual explorations natural to the species.

Once you know the not-me fallacy, you should remember that active offenders are not that different from the rest of the population. Not only is some offending normal, but offenders themselves have extremely high rates of victimization (Fattah, 1991; M. Gottfredson, 1984). Thus, offenders are often victimized by other offenders, while many victims are really not entirely innocent.

Most people violate at least some laws sometimes. That's why it is so misleading to use such terms as "the bad guys," "the super-predators," or "criminal man." Although overactive offenders exist, they are only part of the picture. We should not credit overactive offenders for all or most crime. Nor should we treat crime motivation as exclusive, since we all have reasons to be tempted.

In 1943, Professor Austin Porterfield gave the same self-report survey designed for the local juvenile delinquents to his own students at Texas Christian University. He learned that the two groups had rather similar delinquency levels. (I return to this work in Chapter 6.) That finding has been strengthened by many self-report studies over many decades. It hardly makes sense to divide the world into good guys and bad guys.

Even more extreme are the studies of sexual fantasies and daydreaming. Several researchers have given the same fantasy questionnaire to sex offenders and college students. Common and frequent fantasies among college students include having sex in public places, sadomasochism, forbidden partners, group sex, and a variety of illegal behaviors (Byers et al., 1998; Leitenberg & Henning, 1995). A human population appears to contain much greater potential for sexual rule-breaking than sex-offending data indicate.

In sum, the general public tends to attribute criminal personalities and tendencies to outsiders, while fancying themselves as above the fray. Their own infractions are recoded in their minds as situational responses or exceptional behaviors. This allows them to divide the world into good guys and bad guys, while assigning themselves, their family, and friends to the first group.

THE INNOCENT-YOUTH FALLACY

The television version of crime often portrays middle-aged offenders. When the young are there, they are usually presented as innocents corrupted by those older. This reflects the *innocent-youth fallacy*, the belief that being young means being innocent.

Are young people really so innocent? Do they really need to be corrupted by adults, or by a foul environment? I have my doubts.

Criminal behavior accelerates quickly in teenage years, peaks in the late teens or early 20s, and declines as youth fades. This has been found in many different data sets, various nations, and numerous eras for which data are available (M. Gottfredson & Hirschi, 1990; Hirschi & Gottfredson, 2000). How could youths be innocent when their relative level of crime participation is so high?

Mischief begins well before the teenage crime period. Archer and Coyne (2005) review a vast literature, taking into account early aggression by normal children. That aggression includes pushing, shoving, and hitting, but also a variety of overt nonviolent attacks. Researchers have used all kinds of clever devices, including cameras and audio transmitters on playgrounds and during classroom breaks—when teachers were out of sight. They also asked victims for reports on verbal and other aggression. Early childhood includes personal rejections of others ("I'm not your friend"). Young kids also cover their ears or refuse to listen when mad, or threaten to exclude others from playgroups or parties. Middle childhood is a bit more sophisticated, spreading rumors, using gossip, backbiting, breaking confidences, criticizing clothes, silent treatment, and various forms of ostracism, group exclusion, recruitment of others against the victim, or embarrassing in public or through abusive communications or practical jokes. In addition, a variety of aggressive and troublesome behaviors occur within classrooms, including disobedience and circumventing adult authority.

I have long believed that our famous "age curve" is misleading, because it implies early innocence. In fact, omission from official statistics does not prove that bad behavior was absent at earlier years. Bad behavior before puberty is handled *informally* by teachers and parents behind the scenes, not usually becoming a public issue. Indeed, legal systems declare young children to be incapable of official crime, and even children past that age are often handled informally. Six-year-olds don't usually have the muscles to do enough harm, and their teachers and parents are much bigger and stronger.

With puberty comes greater size and muscularity, along with sexual capacities. Society can no longer treat misbehaviors entirely on an informal basis, and problems begin to spill into the public sphere. I do not deny the adolescent acceleration in crime and delinquency, but the notion of pre-adolescent innocence is just plain wrong.

In sum, teenage years bring much more misbehavior than earlier years, but it also makes that behavior more consequential. That forces the adult world to do something. Misbehavior begins to enter our statistical flow during adolescence, but that does not prove the prior years to have been innocent.

Nor does it appear that youths are most often corrupted by bad adults. Indeed, most youths are corrupted by other youths. Albert Reiss's (1988) classic review of the co-offending literature makes it clear that delinquency is largely carried out by small groups, usually very close in age. The corruption process is not just a question of a few bad apples or instigators. Rather, it is a process in which youths together have mutual bad influence—as discussed and explained in Chapter 6.

Strangely enough, the innocent-youth fallacy persists after offenders are convicted and imprisoned. It is often said that prisons should keep young offenders separate, or else the hard-bitten criminals will be a bad influence on them. But young inmates already know how to commit crime, or they would not be there. In addition, younger inmates cause *the most* trouble inside prisons. Officials separate prisoners by age to protect older prisoners from young thugs—not the other way around. Juvenile homes are also settings for very serious internal offending, such as frequent assaults by those in their early or mid-teens. Indeed, juvenile homes must keep constant watch to keep the stronger boys aged 12 to 14 from raping the weaker boys, or even the counselors. The public is probably not aware of how often this happens, and does not understand that cutting personnel to save money makes the problem worse.

Some people believe that the real problem is incarceration itself, whether in juvenile or adult facilities. There are excellent *ethical* arguments against excessive or premature punishment (see von Hirsch, 1987). But that does not prove the innocence of youth before incarceration. To understand the impact of any incarceration in practical terms, consider the standard lockup sequence:

1. A youth lives a risky lifestyle among dangerous people,

2. is incarcerated for a certain time, and

3. returns to the same risky lifestyle and dangerous people.

To people who hang out in libraries, the middle stage seems so hellish that it could only have ruined a person stuck there. But a dangerous life before and after can be hellish, too—maybe more so. Again, it is difficult to defend the hypothesis that a largely innocent youth was ruined by the system. Moreover, health tends to improve with incarceration! Offenders use less drugs and alcohol inside, and receive better health care in prison—despite inadequacies and smuggling activities. Again, the criminal justice system—whatever its flaws—is not the center of the crime universe. We have to do our best to run prisons well, but don't expect prisons to make the outside world better.

The innocent-youth fallacy is perpetuated by two basic distortion processes. First, young offenders with innocent faces often remain under the radar screen, so their misdeeds are not yet known by adults or by the justice system. (Facial innocence may also reflect ethnic prejudices, with whites better able to hide their delinquency.) Second, those who get deeply into substance abuse begin to look much older than they really are. A dangerous lifestyle takes its toll on the body. Those aged 18 sometimes look 22; those 22 might look 28; those 28 look 38; those 38 look 58. That helps to reinforce the misconception that bad guys are relatively old. So look beneath appearances and imagery to understand crime.

THE INGENUITY FALLACY

Everybody loves a hero. To have a hero you also need a villain. The ideal villain is not only bad but also highly competent at villainy—crafty, tough, and resourceful. He must be able to adjust to new situations with creativity and skill. Consider Professor Moriarty, the evil and ingenious criminal in an epic struggle with Sherlock Holmes. It would hardly be fair to send the brilliant Holmes chasing after a drunken fool. Our ideas about classic criminals also include the skilled cat burglar who can slip into a third-story room of sleeping victims, quietly pocket valuables, then glide down the drainpipe with nary a worry of excess gravity. Edwin Sutherland (1933) chronicled his interviews with Chick Conwell in *The Professional Thief, by a Professional Thief.* This offender knew how to switch fake jewels for real ones right in front of the storeowner, and had the skill to trick people out of their money, to pick pockets, and to crack safes.

The ingenuity fallacy is the tendency to assume that many or most offenders are highly skilled. I am not denying that there are exceptions, but most crime is all too simple, requiring no advanced skills. Lightweight durables are easy to steal. Empty homes with flimsy locks and neighbors away are easy to break into. It is hardly worth the trouble to crack a safe—not only are today's safes much better, but almost nobody knows how to break into them. The Internet and online shopping make theft of credit card numbers easier and more lucrative. Most credit card thieves are on the lower end of the scale of sophistication (although they might buy card numbers from more skilled hackers).

Embarrassed victims don't want to admit how foolish they were or how easily they were victimized. It's common to tell others a *professional* criminal broke into my house. People who hide the jewels in the cookie jar or the money in the bathroom think that nobody else ever thought of that. Remember that the burglar's mother uses these hiding places, too. If you were looking for someone else's valuables, where would you look?

Most crimes only take a tiny slice of time to commit. Thefts may take 10 seconds or less. An open garage invites a 30-second offense. A burglary needs a minute or two. He makes a mess rummaging quickly, then leaves with some money or jewelry. Robbery also is a quick crime. If someone points a gun at you and asks, "Your money or your life?" how long does it take you to decide? An offender can easily figure out how to get others to comply with his wishes. That's why most crimes involve so little planning, plotting, or creativity (see Chapter 3).

THE ORGANIZED-CRIME FALLACY

Max Weber (1978) described the process of formal organization and rationality on which modern societies are built. A formal organization has written rules, communications, and records. Its employees have official job duties, for which they are trained and recruited. It follows clear and formal patterns of promotion. A formal organization has a definite division of labor and hierarchy, with assignments flowing downward and accountability upward.

Most important, formal organizations stipulate *impersonal* relationships among employees and between employees and customers. That means that every customer gets the same-sized ice cream cone. Every student faces the same rules in seeking financial aid from the university. Everybody has a right to apply for a job opening and to be considered seriously. Even if these rules are sometimes violated, they are the normal operating procedure in business, government, and universities for a modern society.

Do crime organizations fit this model of a formal organization?

On television and in the movies, fictional crime organizations indeed have rules, organized hierarchies, and normal operating procedures. They have regular meetings in wood-paneled rooms, with well-dressed people giving orders down the line. Even their murders seem to be calm and organized.

But in real life, most organized crime is far less formal or routine. The whole idea of crime is to *avoid* going to meetings! In real life, criminal enterprises can be very risky. Offenders have the most to fear from one another, but they also have to worry about police. The formal organization model cannot work for most criminal enterprises. For example, those who traffic in valuable illegal drugs face considerable danger. The leading analyst of this process, Edward Kleemans, explains that illicit enterprises cannot buy or sell commodities via a stock exchange, cannot rely on contract protection, or make easy use of the banking system. They have no way to insure their cargo or to resolve disagreements with attorneys or friendly mediators (Kleemans, 2012; Kleemans, Soudijn, & Weenink, 2012).

One solution is to use violence and intimidation. However, a criminal enterprise cannot survive if it is at war within itself on a daily basis. As a result, illicit business requires building trust between criminals—an uneasy process! Professor Tremblay (1993) explains the problems adult offenders face in finding suitable co-offenders. To accomplish that, organizing crime requires working mostly with long-time friends or family members, with known members of one's own village or neighborhood and one's own social circle or ethnic group, and to stick with the same associates if they have proven reliable. One does not go on the open market in search of co-offenders.

That's why organized criminals cannot work on an impersonal basis. They must be highly personal, picking associates very carefully. Criminal conspiracy is risky, since other offenders can cheat you any time, turn you in to police, and attack or even kill you. And they may decide their share of the loot is greater than you think it should be. In general, ongoing criminal enterprises must minimize the number of co-offenders to avoid betrayal. They must act quickly to escape detection. Thus, the formal organization model is not likely to work in most cases. That's why criminal cooperation is often at a smaller scale than its televised version. Most criminal conspiracies work like a chain letter. Perhaps Joe grows marijuana and sells some to Mary. She distributes smaller packages among five others. They break packages down more for a few more people, and so on. Each of these packages is handed off very quickly. This illegal network may involve many people, but few of them know each other. If one is arrested, only one or two others might be incriminated. Peter Reuter (1998), an economic expert in illicit markets, shows that drugs and gambling have much simpler organizations than their popular image. Don't forget how easy and quick it is to hand someone a package in return for money, to take a bet, or to sell quick sex.

Most crime organization is very rudimentary. A drug supplier meets the person he supplies at McDonald's. Two guys have a drink at a bar and discuss what they need to do later that day. Somebody hides something in the car and crosses the border. A bar owner lets the local prostitutes hang out in return for a kickback. A drivers' license official sells licenses on the side. A purchasing agent buys several thousand desks for the university from the vendor who offers a bribe.

Klaus von Lampe (2011) describes how illegal cigarette smuggling works. Although cigarettes are legal commodities, they are smuggled across borders to evade the very high taxes. It is worth it to smugglers, stores, and consumers to trade in untaxed cigarettes. It occurs through various mechanisms, and it is not very difficult. Nor is it difficult to find small merchants and street vendors to sell them. Although criminal cooperation is essential, it does not require an elaborate or formal organization.

When the Iron Curtain fell and Europe united, there were improvements in prosperity and human cooperation. The border controls were removed. The bad news is that this opened the door for great increases in organized crime across Europe. Illegal trafficking grew not only for cigarettes, but also for drugs, guns, illegal laborers, and movement of prostitutes across borders. Much of that criminal cooperation occurred in networks—one person to recruit the girls in Poland, another to transport a girl or two into Germany, another to work out what house of prostitution each would work in. Not all members of the network know each other or meet in the same room. To quote Soudijn and Kleemans:

> Depending on the number of people to be smuggled, almost anybody can enter this market. Someone might lend his passport once a year to enable somebody else to travel as a look-alike. However, if people are to be smuggled by the dozen every month, a certain kind of organization is called for to facilitate such a large number of people. Such organizations often develop from successful small-scale human smugglers coping with growing demand. (2009, p. 461)

Of course, some crime organizations grow larger and involve more people who know one another. In an extreme case, organized criminals can take over large segments of society, especially when the central government is extremely weak. Examples are found in Southern Italy and some developing countries. But even these more dominant forms of organized crime depend on informal ties and personal trust as they become more hierarchical.

THE BIG GANG FALLACY

Juvenile gangs have a remarkable *image* as cohesive, ruthless, organized groups of alienated youths who dominate local crime, do the nation's drug trafficking, provide a surrogate family, and kill anybody who quits. The most famous gangs are often seen as national or even international. The *big gang fallacy* greatly exaggerates the span and role of juvenile gangs.

I treat this fallacy in much greater detail in Chapter 7. But for now, let me raise these questions:

1. Normal teenagers are highly volatile in their social relations. Why would gang members be any less volatile than other youths?

2. Why would a normal thief want to divide the loot up with a lot of other people, getting a smaller share himself?

3. Do people really like to fight all the time, or to get hurt over and over?

The leading expert on juvenile gangs, Professor Malcolm W. Klein, started by studying gangs face to face (Klein, 1971). He expected to find coherent groups of boys involved in exciting things. Instead, they were extremely boring most of the time. Klein learned that gangs have very loose structures: people fading in and out, and that gangs often disintegrate. Klein described the street gang as an onion, with each part peeling off to reveal another part, then another, until you got to the core. The few core members were more active than the others (i.e., they hung out regularly, doing next to nothing). Yet most members were peripheral—there one day and not the next. Surprisingly, Klein's experience revealed that the social workers *trying* to help boys escape from gangs were *actually keeping the gangs cohesive*. Gangs with no social workers to help them fell apart even more often. Klein's (1995) landmark follow-up book, *The American Street Gang: Its Nature, Prevalence, and Control*, punctures many preconceptions about gangs (see also Klein, Maxson, & Cunningham, 1991). Klein and his associates were not persuaded by the televised version of the gang, or by police press releases.

One of the fascinating features of crime is that so much harm can be done with so little togetherness. A juvenile gang may do evil, but it seldom does *cohesive* evil.

THE AGENDA FALLACY

The agenda fallacy refers to the fact that many people have an agenda and hope you will assist them. They want you to take advice, vote a certain way, or join their religious group. They may be totally sincere, but still they have plans for you. Their promise, usually bogus, is that their agenda will greatly reduce crime in society.

Moral Agendas

Many people believe that declining morality is the cause of crime. Many parents and leaders think you can teach children what's right, then they will simply do it. If they do wrong, that proves you did not teach them the right thing. So if youths do bad things, they must have bad parents and teachers, or they must have learned bad things from bad peers.

That also means that if you set up a program to teach morality, those in the program will be good from then on. Or if the school has kids pray and promise to be good, they will keep that promise. Very wishful thinking.

Researchers have repeatedly proven this morality argument to be wrong. Starting with Festinger (1957) research on cognitive dissonance repeatedly finds that moral attitudes do not simply produce moral behavior. Indeed, prior behaviors can change attitudes as much as attitudes can change behaviors, or more! A study by Judson Mills (1958) found that many people faced with temptation violate their own moral rules. We should not be surprised that hypocrisy is a normal part of human life.

Progressing through adolescence leads to more experience with rule-breaking—one's own and one's friends. Several studies find that such experience leads young people to adjust their moral standards downwards. They become more tolerant and forgiving of their friends and themselves, changing their moral expressions to reflect behavior. (See Rebellon & Manasse, 2007; Engels, Luijpers, Landsheer, & Meeus, 2004; Bruggeman & Hart, 1996). Indeed, illegal behavior has more influence on conventional beliefs than the other way around.

Dennis Wrong (1961) was right. Moral standards do not guarantee moral behavior, nor does immoral behavior prove a lack of moral training. For example, the high murder rate in the United States compared to Canada does not prove that Americans believe more in murder or that they are trained to commit it. If that were the case, why do US laws set such high levels of punishment for murder? Why would US public opinion show such outrage at murderers and other serious criminals? And why would US nonlethal violence rates be lower than those of so many industrial countries, including Canada?

Consider a parallel question: Why do people become overweight? They don't want to be fat. They aren't trained to be fat. They don't need to be convinced. The problem is that we Americans are raised on rich food, can buy it cheaply, and our daily activities burn off too few calories. People don't always follow their own rules.

This is not arguing against trying to instill morality. It's good to teach right from wrong, but you cannot really expect people to follow those rules without being reminded again and again. Each of us knows the rules and that someone might turn us in for breaking them. Morals give Joe a license to watch Peter, and Peter a license to watch Joe. Informal mutual supervision is essential for society to function.

Religious Agendas

Many religious groups feel that conversion to their faith or values will prevent crime and that failure to follow will lead to more crime. Yet the Old South, the most religious region of the United States, also has very high crime rates. The greater US religious observance (compared to Europe) has not given us lower homicide rates. Hartshorne and May (1928–1930) found that young people in religious schools were just as likely to lie and cheat as those in public schools. Bruggeman and Hart (1996) found that 70 percent of religious school students had cheated on tests, offering justifications similar to students in other schools.

To be sure, *some* studies find correlations between churchgoing activity and avoidance of crime. Let me suggest that youths inclined to break laws have trouble sitting still in church, so they don't go. *Some* researchers may find a negative correlation between churchgoing and offending. But the inconsistency of the data on that conclusion tells us to look elsewhere. Churchgoing and crime avoidance correlate for an entirely nonreligious reason: the presence of greater self-control (see M. Gottfredson & Hirschi, 1990). Youths who can sit still and do what parents tell them tend to get into less trouble all around.

But let's give religious institutions credit. They often do a better job of *supervising* people. A close watch on the flock keeps it from straying. Church schools tend to be smaller than public high schools, giving them more effective supervision of youths. They also kick out anybody who behaves too poorly. Smaller church groups can keep close tabs on their flock and thereby remove crime opportunities. Religious groups with quite incompatible beliefs might get somewhere in crime prevention by supervising young people closely. But they have the same problem as everybody else: Turn their heads and their young flock strays; and even the older flock needs some supervision.

Social and Political Agendas

A wide array of political and social agendas has been linked to crime prevention. If you are concerned about sexual morality, tell people that sexual misbehavior leads to crime. If you are a feminist, proclaim that rape is produced by antifeminism. If you dislike pornography, link it to sexual or other crimes. If the entertainment media offend your sensibilities, blame them for crime and demand censorship as a crime prevention method. If you are in favor of a minimum wage as part of your agenda, then why not argue that it will prevent crime? Right-wing, left-wing, or whatever your agenda, if there is something you oppose, blame that for crime; if there is something you favor, link that to crime prevention. If there is some group you despise, blame them and protect others; this is what Richard and Stephen Felson (1993) call "blame analysis" (also see R. Felson, 2001). Joel Best (1999) goes so far as to write about "the victim industry," publicizing its sufferings in order to make claims on society. These are political tactics, not the way to study crime. Many crime reduction claims are far-fetched, even if the proposals are sometimes good.

Welfare-State Agendas

It's very common to assume that crime is part of a larger set of social evils, such as unemployment, poverty, social injustice, or human suffering. That's why some people favor the welfare state, arguing that providing more social programs will reduce crime. Others hate the welfare state and blame it for crime increases.

It is interesting to see partisans on this issue pick out their favorite indicators, samples of nations, and periods of history in trying to substantiate their assertions that rising poverty or inequality produce crime. Yet most crime rates went *down* during the Great Depression. We see all the economic indicators rising *with* crime from 1963 to 1975 (see Cohen & M. Felson, 1979; M. Felson & Cohen, 1981). We see the same indicators changing *inversely* to crime in the past few years in the United States. These inconsistencies tell us that the welfare-state arguments are fallacious.

Consider the crime rate changes since World War II. Improved welfare and economic changes, especially for the 1960s and 1970s, correlated with more crime! Also, Sweden's crime rates increased 5-fold and robberies 20-fold during the very years (1950 to 1980) when its Social Democratic government was implementing more and more programs to enhance equality and protect the poor (see Dolmen, 1990; D. Smith, 1995; Wikström, 1985). Other "welfare states" in Europe (such as the Netherlands) experienced at least as vast increases in crime as the United States, whose poverty is more evident and whose social welfare policies are stingier. Clearly, something was happening in all industrial societies leading to a wave of crime that only recently has leveled off or been reversed.

America's welfare stinginess relative to Europe is often used to explain allegedly higher levels of crime and violence in the United States. It is hard to make international comparisons when laws and police collection methods differ. But we now have a way to solve the problem. In a major scientific coup, Patricia Mayhew of the British Home Office and Professor Jan van Dijk of the University of Leiden in the Netherlands negotiated a worldwide research effort. Thanks to them, a single crime victimization survey was translated and administered in many different nations. Results of that work are now showing that *the United States does not have higher general crime victimization rates than other developed countries.* Nor is violence higher in the United States! In fact, the 2005 victim surveys in 15 industrialized countries (van Dijk, van Kesteren, & Smit, 2008) found this rank order in overall victimization:

1. Ireland
2. England and Wales
3. New Zealand
4. Iceland
5. Northern Ireland
6. Estonia
7. Netherlands
8. Denmark
9. Mexico
10. Switzerland
11. Belgium
12. **United States**
13. Canada
14. Australia
15. Sweden

Note in these cross-sectional data that *some* of the more generous welfare states of Europe, especially in Northern Europe, often have *higher* victimization rates than the United States. Other general welfare states have *lower* victimization rates. Yet Canada and Australia, which have much more generous welfare systems, have *comparable* violence rates. Additional data (van Dijk et al., 2008) on robbery, sexual assault, and assault with force show the United States having relatively modest rates of *nonlethal* violence. The view that the United States is the violence capital is further undermined by research showing that school bullying is virtually a universal problem among nations (P. Smith et al., 1999). British police may carry no guns, but big British kids still beat up little ones (Phillips, 2003).

Nonetheless, the United States has much higher *homicide* rates than any developed country of the world. How can we be moderate in general violence but very high in lethal violence? The presence of guns in the United States makes the difference (e.g., see Sloan et al., 1988; Zimring, 2001; Zimring & Hawkins, 1999). Americans are not more violent than Europeans; we just do a better job of finishing people off.

Welfare systems are largely beside the point for crime reduction. This is not an argument against fighting poverty or unemployment. These are valuable goals in their own right, but don't depend on them for security. Crime seems to march to its own drummer, largely ignoring social injustice, inequality, government social policy, welfare systems, poverty, unemployment, and the like. To the extent that crime rates respond at all to these phenomena, crime may actually increase with prosperity because there is more to steal. In any case, crime does not simply flow from other ills. As Shakespeare writes,

> *The web of our life is of a mingled yarn, good and ill together.*
>
> —*All's Well That Ends Well*, Act IV, Scene 3

Crime has become a moral, religious, and political football to be kicked around by people with agendas. If you want to learn about crime, you do not have to give up your commitments, but keep them in their proper place. Learn everything you can about crime for learning's sake, not for such ulterior motives as gaining moral leadership, political power, or religious converts. If your political and religious ideas are worthwhile, they should stand on their own merits.

CONCLUSION

This chapter has given you a good idea of what you have to overcome to understand crime. You have to resist the most dramatic stories about crime. Stop thinking about the police and justice system as the center of crime. Admit to yourself your own rule-breaking and your human potential to do harm. Resist the verbiage about big gangs and big agendas.

So many misconceptions have crept into your thinking about crime that you must work to purge them. Statistics are thrown at you that don't paint the entire crime picture. The media keep coming back at you with dramatic examples that miss the point. The police and courts are important, but unrepresentative.

Defense mechanisms are strong for denying one's own crime potential. Victims remain in denial about how easily they were outsmarted. Distorted images of crime organization and gangs recur. Ignorant observers link crime to one pestilence after another, or fear the most unlikely events, while forgetting about common risks. Those with axes to grind keep promising that their agendas will stop crime. If you can push aside all of these distractions, you are ready to break down crime into its most basic elements.

MAIN POINTS

1. The dramatic fallacy: The media distort crime for their own purposes, creating many of our erroneous conceptions about crime.

2. The cops-and-courts fallacy: The importance and influence of police and courts as proactive controls over crime are overstated.

3. The not-me fallacy: Crime is committed by everyone, and the "criminal" is not much different from us.

4. The innocent-youth fallacy: Being young doesn't mean being innocent.

5. The ingenuity fallacy: Most crime is simple and most criminals are unskilled.

6. The organized-crime fallacy: Criminal conspiracies are attributed much greater organization and sophistication than they actually have.

7. The big gang fallacy: The span and role of juvenile gangs has been greatly exaggerated.

8. The agenda fallacy: Crime is used haphazardly by a variety of people with moral, religious, social, and political agendas.

PROJECTS AND CHALLENGES

Interview project. Interview anyone who works in private security or retail trade. Find out what offenses are common and how they are carried out.

Media project. Take notes of three different nightly news programs. What crimes or crime statistics do they cover and how? What crimes do they fail to cover? How are the crime statistics represented?

Map project. Find an interactive crime mapping program of a city or police department and create a map of robberies or burglaries for one year. Note how these crimes cluster in space, even on a very local level. (To do this assignment, search online for a city you know or that interests you, then move in on the crime map so you can see variations from block to block. Also try to learn about crime maps at http://www.nij.gov/topics/technology/maps/Pages/welcome.aspx. For extra guidance in creating maps, see works by Boba, 2008; Chainey & Ratcliffe, 2005; Harries, 1999.)

Photo project. Take five plain photographs indicating that a crime might have been committed at that very location. Discuss what makes you suspect this.

Web project. Find some of the sources mentioned in this chapter, or their updates, via the Internet. Look at a table relevant to this chapter and describe it. Look especially at www.popcenter.org.

2

THE CHEMISTRY FOR CRIME

———•◦•———

A s a boy growing up in the 1950s and 1960s, I was lucky to have some really good math teachers. They would first teach us the simplest model, then build on it step by step. Accordingly, I look for the simplest model of crime, share it with you, then build upon it. Let me start with the simplest "mixing" principles, the basic chemistry of everyday crime.

Mixes lead to surprises and sometimes to criminal acts:

- Two teenagers who behave well in the presence of parents get drunk and wild when together.
- A middle-aged man, conventional at work, gets caught somewhere else with his pants down.

Many people are volatile and reactive. Almost everyone has ups and downs, ins and outs, feelings of anger and calm, moods of conformity and defiance, and legal and illegal behavior. Emotional ups and downs are even more common for people who commit a lot of crime (Mallett, Dare, & Seck, 2009). This is why you, as a student of crime, should pay attention to the specific circumstances affecting people at particular times, and how they act together. But even persons who do not commit a lot of crime can sometimes be tempted or disinhibited. Both occasional offenders and overactive offenders are influenced by specific situations.

To understand how that happens, we first have to recognize three different crime situations:

1. *Predatory crimes*, with one person attacking the person or property of another
2. *Consensual crimes*, with two people cooperating to break the law
3. *Fighting*, with two conflicting parties that both act illegally

All three crime types depend on how people mix in the course of a day. That mixing in turn depends on the activities people engage in and the locations where they do so.

RISKY SETTINGS

In the course of a single day, individuals can shift dramatically in where they are and what they are doing. The same people enter and leave a great variety of mixing situations. More than 40 years ago, Professor Roger Barker (1963) developed tools for studying these variations in how people mix and how it affects their behavior. He and his students studied thousands of details of daily life. They first divided a small Kansas town into hundreds of "behavior settings," namely, slices of space and time. Barker noted just what people were doing in each of the settings studied—when and where, in what group sizes, and what ages were together.

Barker's behavior settings ranged from a school history class to guys hanging out on a street corner. Each behavior setting influences individual choices. For example, the same individual would read in the library and play ball on the ball field—different activities in different settings. Compared to today's world, that small town provided teenagers only a few settings for escaping adults for very long. It is very important for criminologists to learn how much time young people spend in different settings, whether parents know what they are doing, what they do in each setting and what happens to them. A setting is a place for *recurrent* behavior at known times. A crime setting is where people converge or diverge in a special way that influences their crime opportunities. Dennis Roncek (1981) studied dangerous places, including bars that set the stage for nearby crime. He even found that living near high schools exposes nearby neighborhoods to higher risk of burglary and other crimes. Brantingham and Brantingham (P. J. Brantingham & Brantingham, 1984; P. L. Brantingham &

Brantingham, 1993, 1999) found that the toughest drinking establishment was the likely origin of nearby crimes, including property crimes and violence (see also Scott & Dedel, 2006).

A bar can set the stage for

- a theft by bar patrons on the way to or from the bar, or by neighborhood boys taking advantage of them;
- a car theft while patrons are inside;
- an ambush, with one patron following another outside and mugging him in a deserted area nearby;
- an illegal sale, such as buying and selling illegal drugs inside or nearby;
- a fight, in which two patrons have a dispute that escalates (see Chapter 4).

Such settings play an important organizing role for everyday life and everyday crime. Most human activities occur in some type of setting, but only certain settings are especially risky for crime (see Clarke & Eck, 2005, Step 15; Clarke & Eck, 2007; M. Felson, 1987). Risky settings include:

a. *Public routes*, especially foot paths, parking facilities, and unsupervised transit areas

b. *Recreation settings*, especially bars and some parks

c. *Public transport*, especially stations and their vicinities

d. *Retail stores*, especially for shoplifting

e. *Residential settings*, especially for burglary and theft

f. *Educational settings*, especially outside or on their edges

g. *Offices*, especially when easily entered for theft

h. *Human services*, especially hospitals with 24-hour activities

i. *Warehouses*, especially those storing attractive goods

Recent work by Andrew Lemieux shows the trip to and from school to be, hour for hour, the riskiest activity (Lemieux, 2010; Lemieux & M. Felson, 2012). In addition, crime risk often concentrates in transportation nodes and storage areas, such as docks and warehouses where valuable electronic products are stored (M. Felson, 1987). This adds to what we learned from Roncek and from the Brantinghams about the impact of high schools and barrooms on local crime. This topic was subsequently renamed "crime hot spots" by David Weisburd and colleagues (Braga & Weisburd, 2010; L. Sherman, Gartin, & Buerger, 1989). The point is that crime concentrates greatly in *particular* settings, and is far from evenly distributed—even within a single neighborhood. To understand this, you should learn the stages of the crime sequence and the basic elements whose presence or absence make crime happen.

STAGES OF A CRIMINAL ACT

A crime incident can be meaningless unless you know more about what led up to it. Suppose one man punches another in the nose. Why did this happen? What led up to the event? What happened afterward? Your task as a student of crime is to think about the behavior sequences of everyday life. You should think about when those sequences set the stage for crime. As you consider everyday sequences, you will better understand how the setting and the people in it get involved in crime.

You can divide the sequence for a criminal act into three main stages (M. Felson, 2006, p. 42).

> Stage 1. The *prelude*: The events that lead directly up to and into the criminal act, such as getting drunk, driving through a neighborhood, or waiting until no one is looking.
>
> Stage 2. The *incident*: The immediate criminal act, such as punching someone, breaking a window, or stealing a purse out of a car.
>
> Stage 3. The *aftermath*: Whatever happens after or as a result of the incident, such as the offender fleeing the scene, fencing stolen goods, or using a stolen credit card.

Notice that other criminal acts are often committed in the aftermath. Thus, a burglary sets the stage for a second crime, fencing stolen goods, and maybe a third crime and a fourth (a topic taken up in Chapter 8). Now that we've covered the sequence of a criminal act and its stages, let's dissect the criminal act into its elements.

FIRST THREE ELEMENTS OF A CRIMINAL ACT

Most criminal acts occur in a favorable setting. Criminal acts have three *almost-always elements*:

- a likely offender,
- a suitable target, and
- the absence of a capable guardian against the offense.

Starting with the likely offender, anybody might commit a crime. Yet the best candidate is a young male with a big mouth who does poorly in school, loses jobs, gets into traffic accidents, and ends up in the emergency room (M. Gottfredson & Hirschi, 1990). Daily life helps some people reach their full criminal potential, whereas others have a stunted criminal growth. Although most active offenders start young, some criminals may be late bloomers. The march of life provides new criminal opportunities, hence changing the pool of likely offenders as time goes on, while making some previous offenders more efficient or less so.

A suitable target is any person or thing that draws the offender toward a crime, whether a car that invites him to steal it, some money that he could easily take, somebody who provokes him into a fight, or somebody who looks like an easy purse-snatch.

"Guardians" should not be mistaken for police officers or security guards, who are very unlikely to be on the spot when a crime occurs. The most significant guardians in society are ordinary citizens going about their daily routines. Usually, you are the best possible guardian for your own property. Your friends and relatives also can serve as guardians for you and your property, as you can for theirs. Even strangers can serve as guardians if they are nearby, and the offender thinks they might turn him in or otherwise interfere with his plans. Some guardians are employees, such as a store clerk or other employee who helps protect against business crime.

With a guardian present, the offender avoids attempting to carry out an offense in the first place. A guardian is not usually someone who brandishes a gun or threatens an offender with quick punishment, but rather someone whose mere presence serves as a gentle reminder that someone is looking. The *absence* of a guardian is very important when offenders and targets are present.

ECK'S CRIME TRIANGLE

You recall the not-me fallacy from the first chapter—the idea that "I'm too good for crime." Yet most people commit some crime sometimes. When will otherwise "good" people do bad things? The answer to that question has to do with temptations, opportunities, and controls. Elaborating from M. Felson (1987), Professor John Eck of the University of Cincinnati devised the basic crime triangle (Exhibit 2.1), another tool for thinking about crime settings. You

Exhibit 2.1 Eck's Crime Triangle

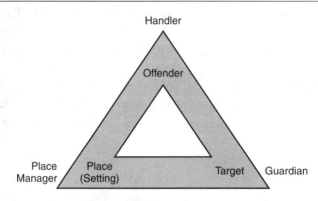

*First, the offender evades handlers. Next, the offender finds a
setting without a manager, and then a target without a guardian.*

can always come back to Eck's triangle if you get lost when studying crime.
That triangle can be applied to anything from loud music to murder.

The small inner triangle gives the three features of each crime problem:
the offender, the crime target, and the place or setting where the crime occurs.
A target of crime is located within that place; it includes any person or piece
of property that attracts the offender's illicit interest. It can include money to
steal, a person to attack, or somebody selling illegal drugs. The offender must
find a place, then a target within it—thus convergence in time and space is very
important.

For that to happen, the offender must evade three types of supervision. The
outer triangle tells us about these three types. A handler supervises potential
offenders; for example, mom, dad, the football coach, and the teachers are
handlers whose presence or controls (e.g., curfew) discourages misbehavior.
A place is supervised by a place manager, whose presence and alertness
discourages crime from happening there.

After evading the handler, the likely offender must find a place containing
a crime target whose place manager is absent or indisposed. Then he must find
a target with no guardian watching it. In sum, the offender moves away from
handlers toward a place without a manager and a target without a guardian.
Pay close attention to place managers. Examples are hotel or store clerks and
apartment building managers. They control the physical environment, set and
enforce rules, oversee behavior, and thus influence crime. A school principal

or mall manager might influence thousands of people and affect whether or not crime occurs. A bar owner with lax policies on underage drinking makes possible more drunk driving, fights, and sexual assaults in and around his bar. Managers are especially important for minimizing illegal drug sales and controlling public drinking. These are often consensual crimes that are best discouraged if places are supervised or managed properly. Remember that both buyer and seller of illegal goods or services want the crime to happen.

In contrast, for predatory crimes, the guardian is probably the most important element. Suppose two teenagers break into your car in the university lot, stealing your property while you're in class. The teens had already escaped their parental supervision and had found a parking lot whose manager had already left the scene. They then find a car whose guardian (you) is absent. Of course, the lighting, video surveillance, or location of parking spaces might also have a bad design. Now you can see why Eck's crime triangle is so useful for organizing a lot of information about crime events.

PREDATORY CRIMES

The very word "crime" brings to mind an image of one person hurting another, with the latter a clear victim. We call such crimes "predatory offenses," but you might be surprised that they are a rather small share of all offenses. Indeed, the FBI (2013b) collects data in two parts. Part I crimes are mostly predatory offenses with victims, including forcible rape, robbery, murder, aggravated assault, burglary, motor vehicle theft, auto theft, and (sometimes!) arson. Annual totals of "major crimes" reported to police are based on Part I. However, the FBI also compiles Part II crimes, many of which lack clear and direct victims. These include drug and alcohol violations, runaways, traffic infractions without accidents, as well as fights in which neither party is an innocent victim.

Predatory offenders are mostly impersonal. Often an offender does not care how the victim feels. Robbers just want the money, and if you give it to them politely, they usually just go away. Yet other predatory attacks are very personal, made by someone mad at someone else. For example, by vandalizing his car a local boy may get even with the neighbor who scolded him. But these noteworthy exceptions do not negate the general rule that the offender is most oriented toward himself, not his victim. Indeed, we prefer the word "target" to "victim" because the offender is often impersonal and practical when carrying out a crime. The *predatory sequence* typically works like this:

1. A likely offender enters a setting.
2. A suitable target enters, too.
3. A guardian leaves.
4. An offender attacks the target.

Some settings are called *crime attractors* (P. J. Brantingham & Brantingham, 1998; P. L. Brantingham & Brantingham, 1999) because they are especially likely to draw offenders. In such cases, the first and second steps are reversed—the targets are already there before the offender arrives. In other settings, likely offenders and suitable targets are around for other purposes, but criminal acts emerge. These are called *crime generators*. Yet such settings can transform into crime attractors in this sequence:

1. A setting hosts normal legal activities;
2. these activities assemble likely offenders and targets, making that setting a crime generator;
3. that gives offenders successful crime experiences in that setting; after which
4. the setting becomes a crime attractor, with crime there getting still worse.

You can readily see why settings are central for crime analysis. That's where the action is. In most settings crime does *not* occur. Even in prime crime settings, crime does not happen most of the time, and depends on what elements are present or absent. Your home is occupied at times and empty at others. Your neighbors are sometimes home, but not always. The bar patrons are rather sober early and drunk later, but are usually not violent. The parking lot is supervised some hours but not others. You can see that a setting is not fixed in time. It transforms itself, altering crime opportunities and outcomes as the day wears on or the night progresses. That process occurs not only for predatory crimes but also for other offenses.

CALMING THE WATERS AND LOOKING AFTER PLACES

Several roles have already been described for people who calm the crime problem. Guardians can prevent property crime and illegal sales. Handlers or peacemakers in particular can discourage fights (see Chapter 4).

Managers also serve to prevent crime settings from deteriorating because they oversee and monitor the settings, such as:

- homeowners and long-time renters;
- building superintendents, doormen, and receptionists;
- bartenders, managers, and owners;
- small-business persons and store managers;
- street vendors;
- security people with focused responsibilities;
- park and playground supervisors;
- train station managers; and
- bus drivers.

A place manager should have a strong incentive to prevent crime there. Owners want to protect their property values. Long-time residents want their home ground to be safe. Businesspeople want customers to come back. Employees want to keep their jobs and be safe, too. Place managers are very important, but they cannot watch everything, everywhere, every moment. Nor are all place managers energetic or careful, and some people hired to watch go to sleep on the job.

Not all place supervision is formal. Crime analysts have also paid a good deal of attention to natural surveillance. That includes ordinary citizens going about their daily lives, whose presence increases security. But mere human presence is not enough for security. We can learn a great deal from Oscar Newman's (1972) classic distinction:

1. Private space
2. Semiprivate space
3. Semipublic space
4. Public space

Private space might include the inside of your home. The area just outside your home—such as an apartment lobby—is semiprivate. That means you have a good deal of control over who goes there. Semipublic space is farther out, such as a yard in front of an apartment building, where the public might not always go but can get to rather easily. Public space, such as a street or sidewalk, is especially difficult for you to control, and hence provides the least security—we return to this topic in Chapter 11. Public space is insecure because, in most cases, there's nobody directly assigned to watch it. But you can never be entirely sure of keeping any space secure from crime. That's why you must pay close attention to crime targets themselves.

Exhibit 2.2   Theft Losses for Two-Door Cars, 2003–2005 Models, United States

Model	Theft Index (*)
Honda Civic Hatchback	236
Chevrolet Monte Carlo	156
Acura RSX	146
Mitsubishi Eclipse	141
Honda Accord	112
Pontiac Grand Am	111
Hyundai Tiburon	102
Toyota Celica	91
Volkswagen Golf	90
Honda Civic Coupe	86
Chevrolet Cavalier	66
Scion tC	63
Toyota Camry Solara	56
Ford Focus	49
Pontiac Sunfire	49
Audi A4 Cabriolet Convertible	48
Volkswagen New Beetle Convertible	42
Saturn ION Quad Coupe	32
Volkswagen New Beetle	28
Hyundai Accent	27
Mini Cooper	24
*Calculated from average loss payments per insured vehicle-year, then indexed to the average for all two-door cars. Thus, an index value of 104 is 4 percent worse than average for two-door vehicles.	

SOURCE: Highway Loss Data Institute, www.carsafety.org. Electronic copy available at http://www.carsafety.org/iihs/iihs-website-search?q=injury%20collision%20theft%20losses. Accessed July 9, 2014.

HOT PRODUCTS

Some products are stolen *much* more than others. Start with cars. The Highway Loss Data Institute (2014; http://www.carsafety.org) shows that specific makes and models differ greatly in their probability of being stolen. Exhibit 2.2 sums up the theft loss data for 2003 to 2005 two-door car models, as reported in September 2006. It shows that the Honda Civic hatchback generates *9.8 times as much theft risk* as the Mini Cooper. The same source above reports (for small cars) eight times as much loss for the Honda SS2000 convertible as for the Mazda Miata convertible. My wife and I have owned some of the least stolen cars, including a Buick LeSabre, with a theft index of 11, while the Chrysler 300 in the same class had a risk over 20 times as great. We also owned a Toyota Prius, with an index of only 13, but our current Camry has higher risk, and the Prius statistics may catch up as the models become more widely used.

Clearly, some products attract the attention of thieves much more than others. Cash, jewelry, and small electronic goods are more likely to be stolen *in burglaries* than most items in the house. A wider variety of items is stolen *from stores*.

According to the National Retail Security Survey, in recent years, those products most stolen from stores have been magazines, shirts, jeans, items with the Hilfiger or Polo label, CDs, videocassettes, beauty aids, cigarettes, batteries, condoms, sneakers, Nike shoes, hand tools, jewelry, and action toys (Hayes, 1999). B. Smith's (2013) dissertation established the concentration of shoplifting on certain products, based on a very large and detailed retail data set.

Past studies have compared retail value per pound of most stolen goods (see Cohen & Felson, 1979; M. Felson & Cohen, 1980). Washing machines are worth several hundred dollars, but only about $5 per pound. They are not usually stolen. In contrast, electronic consumer goods are high in value per pound and attractive targets of crime. Clarke's (1999) pamphlet, *Hot Products: Understanding, Anticipating and Reducing Demand for Stolen Goods*, tells us a good deal about which items are most likely to be stolen. That and other sources help us understand an important issue in the chemistry of crime: What features of crime targets make them so inviting?

Items That Invite Theft

The property offender wants to steal something valuable, enjoyable, and available. He wants to be sure he can remove it from the property. As he removes it, he wants to be able to conceal it. After he removes it, he wants to have a way to dispose of it, perhaps selling it to somebody else.

Clarke (1999) rearranged those words to form this acronym for goods "CRAVED" by thieves. Hot products tend to be

Concealable,

Removable,

Available,

Valuable,

Enjoyable, and

Disposable.

Cash solves all six problems, so it will be a hot product as long as we are still printing it. Jewelry is often desirable, too, for it is easily concealed on one's person. A very common car is easier to conceal than an unusual model (such as a Rolls-Royce) that is easy to spot. Small items and those on wheels are the easiest to remove. Light televisions are more vulnerable than the heaviest models. If thieves had to carry the car on their backs, there would be no car theft.

Items produced in great numbers and placed near a door are most likely to be stolen because they are available (Clarke, 2002). Valued items to young thieves might be popular CDs, but not Beethoven. Old-style maternal minivans are almost never stolen because young car thieves do not want them. Offenders are more likely to steal products that are fun to own or consume. They tend to enjoy alcohol, tobacco, expensive clothes, fancy shoes, DVDs, or condoms. Thieves also prefer items easy to dispose of, as indicated in Chapter 9 on moving stolen goods.

Hot Products Are Affected by Their Settings

Hot products are affected by the setting that contains them, as indicated in Chapter 11 on local design against crime. A household burglar targets both the home and the goods inside it. Many burglars assume that something good is inside, paying attention to the building in making their decisions. The offender considers tall bushes that could conceal entry and exit and may take into account the proximity to the street and driveway, enabling illicit removal. The offender also considers the environment and whether people are in the building, which is why residential burglaries happen predominantly during the day when the residents aren't home. Subsequent chapters of this book will go into more detail on how settings affect offender decisions, which also then provide tools for preventing crime.

Stores that hide their cash-counting operations in an upstairs office gain some protection by not tempting people needlessly. Being out of sight also helps protect some illegal transactions from prying eyes. Access is the ability of an offender to get to the target and then away from the scene of a crime. With enough effort and sufficient tools, every offender can get to every target, but the whole idea of crime is to get things the easy way, acquiring few skills and applying little effort over a short time. Easy access is essential for ordinary crime. Many offenders are probably even more concerned with their exits than their entrance, wanting a safe getaway. Flashing money, leaving valuables out, making obvious the lack of locks, putting valuables by the front window where people pass by, living on a busy street, inviting too many people to see your new stereo, putting a shiny new car on the street, letting the hedges overrun the back windows—all of these can generate extra crime risk.

Targets Vary by Offender Motive

Legal definitions of criminal acts often hide human differences. For example, auto thieves differ in their motives and hence in the targets they pick (Clarke & Harris, 1992):

- A joyrider takes a trip for fun, picking a flashy and fun car.
- A "traveler" chooses almost any car that's convenient and drives home.
- A felon steals a car to perform another crime, picking a fast model.
- A parts shopper selects a common model three to five years old for which parts are in demand.
- A "shipper" takes a luxury car to sell abroad.

As motives shift, so do targets.

When Heavy Items Are Stolen

We noted earlier that washing machines and other heavy appliances are worth a lot of money but are too heavy for the average thief to remove quickly. These exceptions illustrate how relative these concepts really are. Washers, dryers, dishwashers, and similar appliances are sometimes burgled from rural homes, vacation homes in the off-season, or construction sites. In these three cases, pickup trucks are probably common, making the burglary easier to conduct and less likely to stand out.

As a general rule, the weight of items burgled increases as one goes farther from the city center. Inside the city, burglars are more likely to work on foot, doing their best to carry off money or jewels. In suburbs, more burglars use cars and can remove televisions or other electronic goods. In rural areas, with pickup trucks at hand and guardians away, offenders may find it easier to load up with whatever they want. At construction sites, burglars may look like, act like, or overlap with construction workers and have the equipment and trucks needed to uninstall and drive away with new appliances (Boba & Santos, 2008; Clarke & Goldstein, 2002).

More generally, wheels help steal heavier items. Cars, motorcycles, mopeds, and bicycles face high risk because they provide their own getaway. A family returned from vacation to find that someone had broken into their garage, taking the two cheaper bikes but leaving the expensive one that had no air in the tires. On some college campuses, bicycles are often stolen. In nations such as the Netherlands and China, where bicycles are a primary form of transportation, their theft is endemic, in part because it's so easy.

Theft Trends

To learn which targets offenders crave, find out what's popular among youths. What brands of shoes are in style? What video games are in demand? What clothing labels are in current fashion? What items are getting lighter? Has the packaging changed? Are items being stored where they are more subject to theft?

Changes in goods and money are very important for crime rate trends. Cohen and M. Felson (1979) showed that one of the major causes of the mushrooming crime rates in the United States after 1963 was the proliferation of lightweight durable goods that were easy to steal. Knutsson and Kuhlhorn (1997) in Sweden and Tremblay (1986) in Quebec, Canada, demonstrated that easier use of checks and credit cards without careful identification produced a proliferation of fraud. Americans using far less cash helped to produce the declining US crime rates since 1990 (M. Felson, 1998). You can see that the CRAVED model tells us a great deal about theft variations and trends. These practical features also apply to targets of violent crime and how offenders select these targets.

THE GENERAL CHEMISTRY OF CRIME

Each crime type has its particular chemistry. Crimes also have a common chemistry. For each setting, consider its presences and absences, its entries and exits, and how these make a particular crime likely to occur. Even solo drug abuse depends on the absence of anyone to interfere. Some settings favor one offense but not another; for example, a crowd drives away most offenders but invites pickpocketing. Some settings enhance many types of crime. Scholars have shown that blocks containing bars or high schools have more crime (Roncek & Lobosco, 1983; Roncek & Maier, 1991). Other work uses the medical term "hot spots" to show that a small number of addresses (such as a large retail store or a tough bar) generate many more than their share of calls for police service (L. Sherman et al., 1989). Even within a high-crime area, most specific addresses appear to be quite safe, whereas a few addresses generate most of the problem.

To understand where many types of crime risk occur, Brantingham and Brantingham (P. J. Brantingham & Brantingham, 1998; P. L. Brantingham & Brantingham, 1999) offer three terms:

1. *Nodes*: settings such as homes, schools, workplaces, shopping or strip malls, and entertainment areas. They provide particular crime opportunities and risks. A node that favors one type of crime might not favor another, but specific crime risks differ greatly among nodes.

2. *Paths*: leading from one node to another, also offering crime opportunities and risks. Not only do paths conduct more people per square foot—hence providing offenders, targets, and guardians—but also lead people to nodes that might involve them, one way or another, in crime.

3. *Edges*: places where two local areas touch. Crime is often most risky here. At the edges of an area, outsiders can intrude quickly and then leave without being stopped or even noticed. For example, college students might find their cars broken into when they park at the edge of campus. Those who can only find parking at the edge of a high-crime area suffer greater property or even personal risk.

Finally, some human categories face the greatest general risk of crime victimization, including young males, especially if they are single, living alone, drinking a lot, and staying out late. Those who are past victims or are themselves frequent offenders also face extra victimization hazards (Hindelang, Gottfredson, & Garafolo, 1978; see also Fattah, 1991; Kennedy & Forde, 1990;

Lasley & Rosenbaum, 1988). If you put together hot products, young males, people living alone, heavy drinking, late hours—at risky nodes or along edges of areas—you have created the ideal chemistry for crime. But this is just a generalization; in this book, you will learn details that vary from that theme.

CONCLUSION

As you read this book, you should look at life from the offender's point of view. The offender sees targets and considers whether guardians are absent. The offender picks suitable settings from his own point of view. The offender is the one who perceives an insult, gets in a quarrel, and then gets into a fight, so his viewpoint is the one you need to consider to understand how that happens.

Yet offenders are but one element in a crime, and probably not even the most important. Predatory crimes need targets with guardians absent. Illegal sales depend on settings where buyers and sellers can converge with place managers absent. Fights thrive on audiences and troublemakers without peacemakers. Offenses depend on quick entry and exit. Targets most craved by offenders are concealable, removable, available, valuable, enjoyable, and disposable. We shall demonstrate in the course of this book that *opportunity is a root cause of crime* (M. Felson & Clarke, 1998). Everyday life tempts and impairs potential offenders, influencing their decisions about crime, as the next chapter considers in detail.

MAIN POINTS

1. A setting refers to activities that recur at known times in the same place. Some settings are important for crime.

2. A criminal act has three main elements: a likely offender, a suitable personal or property target, and the absence of a capable guardian against a crime.

3. The crime triangle depicts

   a. the offender evading handlers,

   b. finding places without managers, and

   c. targets without guardians.

4. A guardian is usually not a police officer or security guard but, rather, an ordinary citizen.

5. A crime with one person hurting an innocent victim is a predatory crime.

6. Much more crime risk occurs in and near public routes and recreational locations. Nodes, paths, and edges help us think about such risk.

7. Offenders "crave" hot products and targets of violence for specific reasons.

PROJECTS AND CHALLENGES

Interview project. M. Felson and Clarke (1998) believe that opportunity is the root cause of crime. Interview any retail store owner, manager, clerk, or someone who worked in a retail store about what gets shoplifted. What role do they say opportunity plays? If you yourself worked in a store, supplement the interview with your own experience.

Media project. Find a detailed newspaper account of any plain crime and describe the prelude, the crime incident, and the aftermath. Draw from this chapter to make sense of the account.

Map project. Draw the floor plan of a retail store and consider the vulnerable places for shoplifting based on layout and types of goods.

Photo project. Find four different places on campus most suitable for a crime to occur. Photograph each one and then describe it.

Web project. Use the Internet to gather information that helps you elaborate any point in this chapter. Especially use www.popcenter.org.

3

OFFENDERS MAKE DECISIONS

—•◆•—

A careless decision is still a decision. A foolish decision is still a decision. A decision that hurts you later is still a decision. My task as a crime theorist and your task as a crime analyst and student is to figure out how the offender thinks and decides, what he considers or ignores.

THE DECISION TO COMMIT A CRIME

Three big theoretical steps help us understand how offenders make decisions:

- Jeremy Bentham (1907) explained a basic principle that every individual seeks to gain pleasure and avoid pain.
- Nobel Laureate Herbert Simon (1957) taught us the principle of limited rationality. Real people only keep in mind a few specific goals when making a decision. People don't think of everything.
- Cornish and Clarke (1986) explained that offenders are not much different in their decision making from everybody else. They seek to maximize their benefits, minimize their risks, and limit their own difficulties.

Clarke and colleagues not only modernized how we think about offender decisions but also how to control crime by reducing the offender's benefits, increasing his risks, and making the crime more difficult to carry out. Our later chapter on situational crime prevention is based on his work.

r seeks to gain quick pleasure and avoid imminent pain. decisions that are concrete—depending on specific setting, ive—while staying out of immediate trouble. Offenders are .... too careful nor totally spontaneous. A crime decision is often made a split second before acting, or a few minutes earlier. In sum, offenders think, but not too much.

Casual Decision Making

Most criminals take a rather casual approach to crime. The point of crime is to get things without having to work hard and without much dedication; thus, most crime is quick and easy, and most offenders are unskilled at crime. That does not mean they are stupid, merely that they do not usually put forth a lot of effort. Nor do they need to.

Nor are they extremely daring. Of course, "daring" is a relative term. Most active offenders are daring enough to break the law and to risk serious personal consequences. But they usually go for the easy pickings. They are daring in comparison to non-offenders but usually avoid the worst risks. Yet when an offender thinks an offense will be extremely rewarding, he might take a strong drink and go for it. In other words, the most active offenders are daring compared to non-offenders, but they still avoid the worst risks.

How Much Planning?

Consider the ordinary robber. Martin Gill (2000a) gathered some of the best information we have from British commercial robbers. Gill asked 15 basic questions to assess how careful they had been in robbing particular banks, stores, post offices, or other establishments. He asked offenders—among other things—whether they had visited the target earlier, kept the target under surveillance, worn a disguise, chosen the specific day and time, considered its location, and paid attention to its security measures. Most commercial robbers had taken very few of these steps.

Consistent with Gill's British robbers, Feeney's (1986) interviews with California bank robbers found that most did not make intricate plans and had never been in the bank prior to robbing it. One in five almost stumbled into a robbery while carrying out another crime, or acting on sudden impulse. Exhibit 3.1 illustrates how little planning these robbers did. Only 3 of 112 robbers reported

Exhibit 3.1   Planning by California Bank Robbers

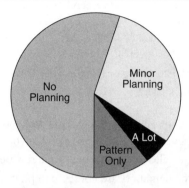

SOURCE: Calculated from Feeney, F. (1986). Robbers as decision makers. In D. Cornish & R. V. Clarke (Eds.), *The reasoning criminal* (pp. 53–71). New York: Springer-Verlag.

doing a lot of planning. Feeney gives examples of offenders driving along with passengers who were totally unaware that a robbery was about to happen. Many a robber even surprises himself.

This does not mean, however, that robbers do not make any decisions. It merely shows that they do not act with great care, nor do they need to when a robbery target is easily available. This general view of robbery is confirmed by other studies (Altizio & York, 2007; Petrosino & Brensilber, 2003; Scott, 2001; R. T. Wright & Decker, 1997). So we are left with offenders who think a bit about a few things, avoiding the worst risks.

Offenders in Their Own Words

If you interview an offender, he may show general bravado. If you then ask him about a particular crime, he won't want to self-incriminate. Or he may feed you a sob story in hopes of getting out of jail. He may deny guilt or claim a bad childhood. And it may be true, but it won't get you any closer to know-ing about crime. The best way to get a straight answer is to ask the offender specifically how a crime is done—exactly how to break into a car, shoplift a store, or rob a bank.

Paul Cromwell and his colleagues learned a great deal about the modus operandi for burglary (Alarid & Cromwell, 2006; Cromwell, 2012; Cromwell & Olson, 2004; Cromwell, Olson, & Avary, 1993). Their main method was simply to drive around with local burglars, peppering them with questions on the spot, giving them no time to make things up (see also Hearnden & Magill, 2004; Schneider, 2003). The researchers asked questions that could be answered without fluff:

- Why do you pick this street?
- Would you break into this house? Why not that one?
- Would you go back later?

Most of these burglars said they wanted to break into low-risk homes that were easy to enter. They start by looking to see if anybody is in the house and the ones next to it. Three clearly empty houses in a row put the middle house at greater risk because the neighbors are not there to prevent the crime. Burglars first look for activity, after which they might probe by ringing doorbells or knocking on the door to see if anybody is there. They drive around a little to find the easy pickings. The idea is to look and act quickly.

As we noted earlier, an offense can be almost spontaneous without being irrational. Even without real planning, an offender responds to cues in the immediate setting and decides what to do (see Wortley, 1997, 1998). Even an offender with a plan may discard it if the cues tell him to do so. Environmental cues are the crucial link between individual choice and the immediate settings that impel or constrain choices.

When Does Crime Pay?

Most offenses pay in the very short term, namely, on the day they are committed. In the long run, most offenders suffer enough bad experiences to justify our conclusion that crime eventually fails them. Bodies deteriorate, other people counterattack, and one is left with a bad resume for later life. That ought to provide sufficient motivation to go clean. Offenders almost certainly suffer more from the consequences of their own lifestyles than from the actions of public officials.

This point is echoed in excellent research by Pierre Tremblay and his colleagues, who studied whether and how much crime pays (see Morselli & Tremblay, 2004; Morselli, Tremblay, & McCarthy, 2006; Tremblay & Morselli, 2000; Tremblay & Pare, 2003). At least some people stick with crime for several years before they pay the price or have to quit. But most ordinary criminals don't get rich at it. Many offenders peak at age 16 or 17, after which they turn to more conventional pursuits.

The costs paid by offenders are usually not delivered mainly by the justice system! Indeed, offenders tend to be more afraid of one another than of the police or prosecutors. Active offenders themselves have very high rates of victimization, plus a tendency toward injury and health problems.

OFFENDERS RESPOND TO EVERYDAY CUES

As noted above, the everyday environment external to offenders guides their illegal acts by giving them cues—enticing them to commit a crime, or scaring them off. Offenders make decisions in response to these cues.

Not everybody responds exactly the same to any given environmental cue. Mary may be more timid than Jane, or not really attuned to a crime opportunity. Not only do people vary, but none of us is a machine. Thus the very same person may be enticed by a crime opportunity on Tuesday but not on Wednesday. Crime is highly situational, depending on who we are with and what we are doing at the time.

Everyday settings vary moment to moment in their degree of temptation or control—the cues they emit—hence the degree of choice they provide. Constraints on individuals shift quickly as events unfold. The next sections explore these variations and shifts, even within a very short time span.

Settings Offer Different Choices at Different Times

To understand how temptation and controls shift so quickly, consider the cue-decision sequence:

1. Someone enters a setting
2. **containing some cues that transmit temptations and controls**;
3. after quickly noting and interpreting these cues,
4. he or she decides whether to commit a criminal act.

The boldface type alerts you to how settings vary in the cues they emit. These cues often come from or are created by guardians, managers, and handlers discussed in Chapter 2. Some settings are overbearing in their controls, whereas others have hardly any at all. For example, in some settings, several people are watching their property, making it difficult for the offender to steal it, whereas in other settings, nobody is around to discourage the would-be offender.

Yet temptations are themselves very uneven. Some settings provide strong temptations, such as money lying around; others offer nothing to entice a crime. In other words, some times and places offer an individual both temptation and room to resist it. Other times and places offer either little temptation or plenty of temptation but not much chance to succumb to it with impunity.

We can best evaluate personal responsibility by taking situations into account. Imagine two boys who are equally responsible, but one is placed into a tempting situation, while the other is sitting at home. Despite their personal similarity, their situations differ greatly at the time. That's why parents and other adults often try to remove youths from tempting situations, or to minimize problematic contexts.

This is not to deny that individuals vary. But let me challenge you with the following statement. I believe that within-person variation far exceeds between-person variation. That is, each of us varies greatly in what we can and might do if the circumstances arise. Each of us could be surprised at our own weaknesses, could find creeping temptations to drink, to get into a fight, or to violate sexual rules. Indeed, the power of self-control itself rises and declines in different situations, as the next section indicates.

Options Shift

Richard Felson[*] describes the potato chip principle: No one can eat only one potato chip. The key decision, therefore, is to avoid eating the first one (see Baumeister, Heatherton, & Tice, 1994; Henry, Caspi, & Moffitt, 1999; Webster, 2005). The principle tells us that blame and control may vary as a person goes through even a few minutes of life. This applies to crime in very serious ways. Consider the disinhibition sequence:

1. A young man drinks some beer with friends.
2. He gets "high" and drinks still more.
3. Then he smokes some marijuana, getting "higher."
4. Some of the boys commit a burglary.

An early decision sets the stage for what happens later. One drink leads to another. A misdemeanor can lead to a felony (see Chapter 8 on crime

---

[*]Brother of the senior author, Marcus Felson, and author of the world's best research on violence.

multipliers). It may get harder and harder to pull away from and resist trouble. But if you ever get arrested for burglary, do not tell the judge to let you go because you were intoxicated. The legal system blames you anyway. The judge probably will get mad and tell you, "If you can't handle alcohol, don't start drinking it." To quote the stern but astute father, "You shouldn't have been there in the first place. If you had listened to what I told you, you wouldn't be in trouble now." Just as that father focuses on the points of maximum self-control to assign blame, the son emphasizes the moments of minimum self-control to escape blame. You need to look at both points in order to understand crime fully.

We all could make a decision that nearly enslaves us for some time afterward. Then a flash of freedom arises, a crucial juncture for the next decision. Moving through life, a person never has complete freedom or complete constraint, but the degree of constraint shifts by time, place, and setting. Even in the course of a day, one has more pressures and constraints here and fewer there. For example, when home with parents, one is pressured against getting drunk; while out with peers, one's pressures may go in the opposite direction. Yet a person still deserves blame for picking bad friends, placing oneself in dangerous settings, or abusing substances. That's why "precriminal situations" (Cusson, 1993) are so important for crime, as well as for drawing blame for bad outcomes. Like photons shifting into matter, blame takes quantum leaps in the course of everyday life.

Cues Are Needed to Assist Self-Control

We are all born weak, but parents and teachers try to teach us self-control to help us resist various temptations. High self-control helps people study, do their jobs, stay away from the bottle and the refrigerator. Self-control helps you keep your mouth shut when the boss, customer, spouse, or teacher says something you don't like.

Those low in control have trouble regulating their minds, mouths, or actions. They also commit more crimes, have more accidents, drink and smoke, and make a mess of school, work, and family relationships (Britt & Gottfredson, 2003; Hirschi & Gottfredson, 2000; Junger & Marshall, 1997; Pratt & Cullen, 2000).

However, self-control is not just an individual trait. Real people vary from one situation to another, shifting over the course of a day. Most of us need reminders to follow the rules over the course of a day. Society delivers these reminders in various settings. That keeps the offending population smaller and the others at bay. Thus, teachers and parents remind youths to follow the rules, and citizens remind one another to stay out of trouble.

One Marshmallow or Two

In the 1970 Stanford Marshmallow Experiment, Walter Mischel offered each small child a choice of one marshmallow *now* or two marshmallows *later*. Those children who were better able to defer gratification—that is to resist the quick marshmallow and wait for two—tended to have greater success in later life (see Mischel, 2014; Mischel, Shoda, & Rodriguez, 1989). These findings are generally consistent with M. Gottfredson and Hirschi (1990), who link criminal behavior to low levels of self-control.

Suppose, however, that the experimenter stops monitoring the marshmallows. A child could now take *both* marshmallows without repercussions. In these new circumstances, even the child with more self-control might go for both. Indeed, providing easy crime opportunities without sanctions allows a wide variety of youths to participate in crime, even those who subsequently succeed rather well in society. The correlation between self-control and delinquency should be duly noted, but not exaggerated. As youths get older, they often learn what they can get away with.

This point is reflected in over 80 years of research on deceit, starting with Hartshorne and May (1928). These studies consider various forms of lying and cheating on tests, and demonstrate that otherwise normal members of society often break rules along the way, especially when they think that they will evade detection or noteworthy punishment.

ODD AND BIZARRE CRIMES

Even when an offender's motive has an abnormal twist, basic human tendencies show through. Rossmo (2000) has studied serial killers with bizarre sexual tastes, who are also very routine in how they pick up victims and discard bodies. LeClerc and colleagues (LeClerc & M. Felson, 2014; LeClerc, Wortley, & Smallbone, 2011) have studied child molesters, showing that they are very ordinary in some respects—trying to use normal settings to find and cultivate their victims. These researchers interviewed quite a few sex offenders, asking them how they did their crimes. Offenders with a strange sexual fetish nonetheless develop their habits in the course of daily life, and find practical ways to get what they want.

Those who crave sexual release with children or young teenagers can also be pragmatic. James M. Mannon (1997) considers how easy it is for stepparents to gain access to stepchildren, priests to choirboys, and child care workers to young children. Offenses usually occur in settings with guardians absent and unable to intervene. Family members are also more vulnerable to intimate victimization when isolated from those who would protect them (see Davis, Maxwell, & Taylor, 2006; R. Felson, Ackerman, & Yeon, 2003; R. Felson & Outlaw, 2007; Wortley & Smallbone, 2006; Zolotor & Runyan, 2006).

The essential point is that the crime triangle *also* applies quite well to bizarre and unusual crimes.

CONCLUSION

You can see that settings change choices by providing temptations and controls. These are mediated by various tangible cues that tell people what they might get away with. People make decisions accordingly. They are somewhat constrained, but not necessarily all day or all week. The constraints shift from one setting to another. Studying tangible settings and cues helps us understand whether and when people will make illegal choices.

MAIN POINTS

1. Offenders make decisions seeking to gain pleasure and avoid pain. Even so, they respond to the settings that limit their choices. An offender is neither too careful nor totally spontaneous or without reasoning.

2. Most offenses pay in the very short term, namely, on the day they are committed. In the long run, most offenders suffer enough bad experiences to justify our conclusion that crime eventually fails them.

3. Offender freedom to decide is greater at some moments but less at others. Settings offer different choices at different times. Offender

choices can shift within a particular setting, in that one bad decision can lead to others down the pike (see Chapter 8 on crime multipliers).

4. Environmental cues are needed to assist self-control. Most of us need reminders to follow the rules. A reminder is nothing more than a cue designed for people who have a good deal of self-control and are basically inclined to follow the law.

5. Criminal acts often seem senseless or even bizarre, but offenders still make decisions to commit them, and use their daily routines to find targets or victims.

PROJECTS AND CHALLENGES

Interview projects. (a) Interview a fellow student about settings inviting or discouraging illegal action. Do not ask questions about personal involvement that would put that student at risk. (b) Interview a bartender, former soldier, or high school teacher about techniques for making the peace.

Media project. Read one of Elmore Leonard's thrillers. Then write a summary of how one of his characters blundered into something much worse than he bargained for.

Map project. Sketch a map of a convenience store from above. Put into the sketch five features that might influence someone's decision to rob it or not. Number these items in order of likely importance to the thief. Justify your numbering.

Photo project. Photograph three settings that would be very suitable for a burglar and three that would be unsuitable. Discuss why.

Web project. Use one of the police crime maps to find an area with a lot of auto theft and another area with very little. Then use *Google Street View* to look at and compare the two areas.

⊰ 4 ⊱

HOW VIOLENCE ERUPTS

———⊶•⊷———

T wo guys get into a quarrel over something stupid. Their dispute escalates. Finally one of them hits the other and somebody gets hurt. This seems to be an entirely irrational sequence of events, but is it? Violent decisions are included among the crime decisions I discussed in the last chapter. It may surprise you that one of the best ways to study how disputes escalate is to carry out experiments at universities.

MAKING STUDENTS ANGRY IN A LAB

Psychologists at universities have conducted a variety of experiments in which they seek to create disputes and to make people angry. In a typical experiment, a student subject walks into a room where he finds another student sitting. The other student insults him, perhaps saying, "That's an ugly shirt you are wearing." The other student is really working for the professor, who is sitting behind a one-way mirror watching the situation. Will the subject answer the insult and escalate with a worse insult?

In general, a young male is more likely to answer and escalate if insulted by *another young male*. A young man is less likely to insult a woman back, least of all an older woman. (I think young men have long been insulted by middle-aged women—their teachers—and are quite used to it.) The most important finding is that young males respond worst to perceived insults by other young males.

Remember to look at this from the viewpoint of the person experiencing an insult, regardless of whether you think he is right or wrong in his perception. His viewpoint counts the most. Does he think he was insulted and does he feel he must answer?—that is the question.

Now you can vary the experiment in a number of ways:

- Add an audience, so the subject is insulted in front of others
- Vary the ages and sex of the audience
- Add a peacemaker, who tells him to ignore the insult
- Add a troublemaker, who tells him to stand up to the other guy
- Give the subject some alcohol to drink before you insult him

When these experiments are carried out we learn that subjects are much more likely to answer and escalate when there is an audience for the insulting experience. They are also more likely to escalate when a young male is insulted by another young male in the presence of still other young males—a recipe for trouble. Comments like "Don't pay any attention to Joe" or "You guys knock it off" generally suffice to quiet the waters. On the other hand, some members of an audience may act as troublemakers or provokers. Statements such as "Are you going to let him say that to you?" tend to encourage escalation. Thus, a peacemaker can quiet things down and a troublemaker really can escalate the situation by saying the wrong thing at the wrong time. Alcohol can reduce inhibitions and escalate verbal aggression in the university lab, but also outside the lab.

IN REAL LIFE

Tedeschi and R. Felson (1994) review a substantial literature justifying the points I made in the last section (see also R. Felson & Outlaw, 2007). But they also showed that these principles apply *outside* the laboratory in real-life incidents. Barroom settings, for example, have patterns of aggression, and disputes arise and escalate more often when young males drink together. This gives us a policy handle, reminding us to be careful about heavy-drinking bars and all-male settings. It tells us also that barroom regulation has a major role in violence prevention.

The barroom literature shows that bars generate more aggression with heavy drinking, especially when the barrooms are large, disorganized, and dominated by males who are given more to drink when already drunk. Barrooms are quite a bit worse when they bring together small groups from different places.

This occurs when one group of guys go to a large bar and then clash with another group from another part of town. All-male groups of strangers are especially volatile. Very large bars create more problems. Bar mismanagement and bad design is an important factor—I take this up later in the current chapter, then return to the issue in discussing how to design and manage safer bars (Chapter 10).

FIGHTS VS. PREDATORY ATTACKS

Fights are violent interactions involving two or more persons in the same conflict role. Most fights emerge from quarrels in which neither party is fully innocent. Often they are equally guilty, or almost so. They frequently have a preexisting relationship, but sometimes strangers or near-strangers get into a fight.

True, one guy might have thrown the first punch, but if the other guy insulted or taunted him, it is hard to call that a predatory crime. Fighting words and a fighting response may incriminate *both sides* in the eyes of a local judge or police officer. Typically, the police take the winner of the fight to jail and the loser to the hospital.

The *escalation sequence* typically works like this:

1. One party perceives an insult from the other.
2. He responds to the insult and escalates the confrontation.
3. That answer evokes a similar escalation.
4. Someone throws the first punch, and so it goes.

Of course, the lab experiments I mentioned above stop short of a physical fight, sticking to the first three steps for research purposes.

In a fight, the audience is especially important, for it enhances the embarrassment of being insulted and compels a response. If someone in the audience acts as peacemaker and face-saver, escalation can be averted. Later in this chapter I further discuss barroom disputes and escalations.

VIOLENT DECISIONS

The robbery decision might be the easiest violent decision to explain: "Your money or your life" might not be polite, but at least it makes sense with what the robber wants. Other types of violence are sometimes not so easy to explain.

In their book *Violence, Aggression and Coercive Action* (1994), James Tedeschi and Richard Felson conclude that all violence is instrumental. They deny that any violence is "expressive," and reject the old distinction between instrumental and expressive violence. They take great care to show how various types of violence have a purpose in the immediate situation.

Suppose three 14-year-old boys throw a rock at a middle-aged man, cutting his arm. His neighbors conclude that "This is senseless violence. These kids did not get one cent for what they did." But the youths probably have a purpose. They may be punishing the man for yelling at them the other day. They may be putting on a show, proving how strong they are. Tedeschi and R. Felson (1994) show that various principles of social psychology can explain this and other violent incidents quite easily. Violence requires neither a unique theory nor an elaborate one. Unfortunately, many of the people who write about violence are so upset that they cannot calm themselves down enough to analyze it well.

What if two guys get into an argument? They get madder and madder, until one hits the other. Is this irrational violence? Regrettably, the words "rational" and "emotional" are often seen as opposites, implying that a person cannot make a decision while angry. Nothing could be farther from the truth. Angry decisions are part of life. That does not mean an emotional person reasons carefully or for long. Nor are emotional decisions likely to be wise or good for the long run. But they are still decisions. (On this point, see Bouffard, Exum, & Paternoster, 2000; Harding, Morgan, Indermaur, Ferrante, & Blagg, 1998.)

Perhaps we can invent the term "minimal rationality" as a reminder that decisions need not involve wisdom, good sense, or good results. A decision made in a split second for the wrong reasons, even while angry, is still a decision no matter how foolish it appears in hindsight.

Even violence by athletes has a structure. They seldom attack the officials or the most muscular opponents. They almost always drop bats and sticks first. They punch, but don't kick. Athletes are well aware which acts of violence draw the worst punishments and stop short. They also pay attention to whether the officials are looking, but sometimes they get carried away and end up with a more serious suspension than they bargained for.

Drawing from Tedeschi and R. Felson, there are three types of motivation for a violent act:

Motive I—One person uses violence to force another person to do something he wants. *Example: Making someone give you money or sex.*

Motive II—One person uses violence against another to restore justice, as he perceives it. *Example: Punishing someone for being unkind to a woman, or for stepping in line ahead of others.*

Motive III—Assert and protect your self-image. *Example: Punch someone for insulting you in front of a group of people—the example used earlier in this chapter.*

As we shall see in Chapter 10, these goals often make violence highly amenable to situational prevention. Much of that prevention is related to alcohol. But why does alcohol help fuel disputes and their escalation into violent action? Alcohol gives people big mouths and big ears. While drinking, a person is more likely to make aggressive statements that provoke counter-attacks and escalation. Alcohol makes bigger ears by getting people to hear things that were not said. The key to crime analysis is *always to look at the offender's viewpoint, even if the offender is drunk.* In the case of violent crime, the question is whether somebody *perceives* an attack on themselves, not whether they are acting like a reasonable person.

I mentioned how robbery is the easiest violent crime to explain. A simple robbery starts out with the robber demanding your money and using or threatening force to get it. The robber is simply getting you to comply with his wishes—receiving your money without an argument (Motive I). But if you challenge the robber in front of his co-offender, he may harm you to assert and protect his own identity (Motive III for violence). That is why it is best not to have a big mouth when someone is pointing a gun at you. It's also best not to go around giving people grievances against you; somebody might decide to restore justice (Motive II). Fights between drunken young males usually occur as attempts to assert and protect identity (Motive III). Road rage is often an effort to meet the second goal, restoring justice, or perhaps combining Motives II and III. Domestic violence could meet all three purposes (see R. Felson & Outlaw, 2007).

Although predatory violence is generally oriented toward the first motive—gaining compliance—predatory offenders will sometimes seek to protect identity or restore justice. For example, youths angry at the store owner who yelled at them may rob him not only for loot but also to retaliate and punish. Remember, all these evaluations are based on the *offender's viewpoint.* To understand violent or nonviolent crime, we cannot be distracted by our own moral outrage, or by the legal code, or by objective facts about what a person *ought* to think of others. If the guy in the bar hit you because he *thinks* you insulted him, the fact that he heard you wrong is entirely beside the point. Thus, nonacquisitive violence also has a purpose. Punishing others for what you think is bad behavior is also a purpose. Saving face for yourself after someone else has diminished your reputation is also a purpose. Hence, social psychological purposes are just as important as money—maybe even more important for explaining violence.

Moreover, violent actions are often carried out in practical ways. R. Felson (1996) explained that "big people hit little people," and more generally offenders find victims who are relatively smaller, or enlist help from co-offenders when the victim is able to defend. Rana Sampson's (2002) review of the bullying literature establishes that weaker youths are more likely to be "picked on." None of this sounds "irrational."

IT MIGHT NOT WORK OUT WELL

Yet people often have regrets later about their violent decisions. An offender hits someone who hits back harder. Another offender restores his self-image for a moment, then spends a month in jail. Another wins a fight but is punished by the loser's friends. He thought he was advancing his own interests, but it didn't work out that way.

Consider the headline in the newspaper, "Cab driver murdered for one dollar." The news story implies that the robber knew he had only a dollar and killed him to get it. Probably something like this happened: The robber entered the taxi hoping to wave a gun at the driver and take home a few hundred dollars for a few seconds' effort. It went badly. The driver did not comply and even insulted the robber. The robber got mad and shot him, then grabbed his wallet, only finding a dollar within, and then was picked up by police, ending up with a long prison term. We cannot infer the offender's intention from the outcome.

Barroom Impacts on Violent Escalations

As I stated earlier, a good setting for examining the escalation of disputes in real life is a barroom. You will see many more references to barrooms in this book, since they are often crime generators and even crime attractors, and are very amenable to design (see Chapters 10 and 11). Although they vary greatly, some barrooms create the worst-case conditions for conflict to emerge and escalate. It is not just that people are drinking. Many barrooms assemble numerous young males. You recall from earlier in this chapter that young males are more likely to escalate a dispute than other social categories. In addition, barrooms have an audience for a dispute, which makes it harder to shrug off an insult. Since potential peacemakers are themselves drinking, they might not be able to calm things down. In addition, barrooms create disputes between customers and their own staff, who may refuse entry to underage youths or try to shut a drinker off or kick him out. Often bartenders are themselves the problem, acting with excess verbal or physical aggression against patrons, instead of as peacemakers. (For the sources of information contained in these sections, see Homel & Clark, 1994; Homel, Hauritz, Wortley, McIlwain, & Carvolth, 2007; Scott & Dedel, 2006.)

Problems are especially likely with very large bars where guardianship and place management are much more difficult. In addition, such bars can assemble *clashing groups of young males*. After each group of friends arrives they encounter other groups they don't know. A youth who is bumped in front of his peers may lose face and an escalation is more likely.

In studying discos and other nightclubs, researchers observed brushing, bumping, knocking, spilling drinks, pushing, shoving, hitting, and fighting (Homel, 2001; Macintyre & Homel, 1997). Conflicts were enhanced when activities were too dense inside nightclubs, or when their tables, pillars, and design caused people to bump into each other. Disk jockeys played a role in watching the crowd and calming them down when necessary. In later chapters we come back to the environmental design issue, but the point for now is that barroom contingencies can cause patrons to become more peaceful or less. Disputes can emerge much more often in some bars, and escalation can be prevented or enhanced, depending on situational features.

So, if we look at other bar settings we see fewer disputes, especially ones that escalate. Those bars that mix different ages and are close to parity between males and females often have minimal problems, especially if they are not too large and avoid drinking contests or other trouble-enhancers. Bars with regular customers have fewer problems than those with sporadic assemblages. Thus the outcomes are extremely varied from bar to bar and even from night to night. Recent work by Steve Geoffrion illustrates these points very well.

Geoffrion is a graduate student at the University of Montreal who formerly worked in a large bar drawing from two large universities. He arranged for bouncers to write detailed narratives of each incident of aggression and incivility that occurred in the bar. He gathered and analyzed this information (see Boivin, Geoffrion, Ouellet, & M. Felson, 2014). Problem events and escalations were far from random. They shifted over the course of a night and varied by day of week. Tuesday nights offered cheaper drinks and drew large crowds of heavy drinkers from different areas, producing extra problem events. Long weekends also had extra aggression. This confirms what we have been saying, that barroom problems display some systematic variation, while responding to serving policies and supervision by bar personnel.

The Role of Barroom Staff

If I am sitting next to you at the bar and accidently knock over your beer, a skilled bartender should quickly replace the beer for free and wipe up the mess. The dispute is quickly contained and the bar remains peaceful. Scott and Dedel (2006) review and detail the evidence that barroom personnel can contain aggressive behavior. Experienced bartenders do better than neophytes, and trained bartenders outperform those who are untrained. Staff can function as guardians (protecting victims), handlers (modifying behavior of offenders, especially regular customers), and place managers (in a way, their main job).

Scott and Dedel compile several strategies by which bar personnel can defuse aggressive incidents, including

- removing the audience (getting aggressors away from onlookers),
- employing calming strategies (using verbal and nonverbal skills), and
- depersonalizing the encounter or offering face-saving possibilities.

In Chapter 11, which deals with local design, I review quite a number of other tactics and strategies for reducing barroom violence. In Chapter 6, I consider adolescent settings where drinking-related problems may also occur.

CONCLUSION

Note how closely the real-life outcomes in barrooms coincide with the artificial laboratory situation. Aggression can escalate or not. People might respond to insults, but can also shrug them off. Other people can fire them up, or else cool them down. Situational factors have considerable impact on whether a dispute will explode or not.

Dispute-related violence is quick and quirky. How ironic that the most serious of crimes requires the least consideration. A shoplifter or burglar needs a minute or two, but someone can punch you in the nose in a flash. As you shall see in later chapters, crime prevention experts have used the situational features of disputes to dampen escalation and keep people from blundering toward violence.

MAIN POINTS

1. Violence is not irrational but involves goals and quick calculations, even when the offender is very angry.
2. Small disputes can escalate into something much bigger.
3. Disputes are more likely if young males perceive insults from other young males.
4. Being insulted in front of an audience makes things worse.
5. Peacemakers and provokers can, respectively, make a situation better or worse.
6. Bars assembling large numbers of young males create extra problems, including clashing groups.

PROJECTS AND CHALLENGES

Interview projects. (a) During off-duty or slack hours, interview a bartender about specific methods used to prevent conflict from developing and escalating. Ask about shutting off those drinking too much, how to refuse those who are underage, and how to calm people down. What does he or she do when someone spills a drink? (b) Interview anyone with experience in a sport that involves a fair amount of violence. Find out the decision factors and settings that invite violence, as well as those that discourage it.

Media project. Find a media account of two conflicts in baseball or some other sport, one that escalated and one that did not. Consider decisions the players or officials might have made and how the escalation might have been avoided.

Map project. Draw the inside of two bars and consider which one is more likely to have people bumping into each other and other conflicts.

Photo project. Take a picture of five crowded settings and discuss which ones would probably generate more conflict and escalation.

Web project. Search the web for sites that discuss conflict. How many of them treat conflict as irrational and how many, in some sense, as rational and/or structured?

◄ 5 ►

BRINGING CRIME TO YOU

———◄•◦•►———

You have learned about some of the cues that evoke crime or discourage it. These cues emerge from the structure of everyday life. That structure takes different forms from one historical era to another, one nation to another, one locality to another. The current chapter helps you understand that variation and its consequences for crime. That understanding depends on asking two key questions:

1. How do people and things move about every day?

2. As they move about, do people come into contact with things to steal, people to fight with or to attack them, or offers of illegal goods and services?

Everyday life thus sets the stage for people to break laws, hurt each other, and even hurt themselves. Yet everyday life varies a good deal by the size and distribution of population and by how many people one encounters in the course of a single day.

A university is only one part of the world, but it offers a variety of settings that help me make my point. A large American university campus is an historical anomaly that mixes the various stages of history.

1. Like a village, college students are often on foot and are in frequent contact with others they recognize, living in apartments or dorms divided into small units.

2. Like a town, bicycles extend the range of daily travel and activity and increase the number of people who can converge on a given spot.

3. Like a city, buses integrate the larger campus with a much larger local population.

4. Like a suburb, autos extend still farther the daily commute of students and staff, linking a larger campus to a metropolis.

If you live on a diverse campus with all these traits, you are experiencing the history of human settlement covered in this chapter. As I present that history to you, consider its impact on your life today, including any crime risks you have to face. If your campus is not like this, at least try to imagine the four stages described below and what they mean for crime.

FOUR STAGES IN THE HISTORY OF EVERYDAY LIFE

The four stages in the history of everyday life stem from the transportation technology of each era (see M. Felson, 1998; Hawley, 1971).* These stages help us understand the growth of crime and the forms it takes.

The Village

During this first historical stage, most people traveled on foot, and their daily range of activity was less than 4 miles. With most villages having fewer than about 250 people, daily interaction was entirely local and people knew each other. Strangers could seldom assemble in large numbers. What few things people owned were custom-made and easily recognized if stolen. Local crime was unlikely, but villagers suffered from marauding bandits and highway robbers.

The Town

When horses were domesticated, people could travel about 8 miles a day. Local populations could exceed 10,000. Most townspeople would still recognize one another by name or have a friend in common. Local crime was limited, but horses made speedy raids possible. Horses and wagons themselves became targets for crime. Overall, towns provided considerable security.

---

*This analysis neglects the nomadic and hunter-gatherer states of human existence.

The Convergent City

After nautical technology advanced, ships transported voluminous and valuable goods to leading port cities. Their docks and warehouses provided important crime targets and fed a tremendous crime wave (Colquhoun, 1795/1969). These cities grew greatly in size, even then spawning such dangerous slum neighborhoods as the rookeries of London (P. J. Brantingham & Brantingham, 1984). But that was just the beginning. Railroads, powered by fossil fuels, fed even more people and goods into even more cities. Elevators sent buildings upward, while steam-powered factories—operating around the clock—concentrated workforces. Compared to village and town stages, the convergent city drew far more strangers into mutual contact, with greater risk of property and violent crime.

The Divergent Metropolis

Automobiles allowed people to travel farther and wider than ever before. No longer limited to train tracks, they filled the areas in between. The ability to supervise space and property declined. Autos themselves provided vast crime opportunities—theft of cars, parts, and contents; use of cars to carry out felonies; passenger exposure to personal victimization; crimes in streets and parking areas; and more. Later, we will discuss some modern adaptations of these four stages of urban history, going beyond the divergent metropolis. But first, let's consider the convergent city further.

LIFE AND CRIME IN THE CONVERGENT CITY

The convergent city provided not only crime opportunities, but also sources of control.

Safe Aspects of the Convergent City

The convergent city might have seemed risky compared to the village and town stages of the past. But its crowds of pedestrians also provided natural surveillance of streets, discouraging overt physical attacks most of the time. Street vendors, including newsstands, enhanced this surveillance.

(See Chapter 11 for further discussion of people on the street providing natural surveillance.)

Initially, convergent cities were slow to transport people, with horses and buggies producing terrible congestion and ongoing concerns about where to step. However, this changed as public transit became mechanized. Subways, streetcars, commuter trains, buses, and taxis moved people around in the convergent city. These vehicles funneled crowds into work, school, shopping, and entertainment districts. People came into contact with large numbers of total strangers.

Public transit systems in convergent cities fill up very little public space considering the number of people they moved about. A single urban train line could carry as many commuters as a six-lane highway of today. Subway cars took up much less parking space than automobiles. Thus, convergent cities had a chance to design and control space to minimize urban crime.

Risky Aspects of the Convergent City

Despite the fact that pedestrian crowds in the convergent city would discourage some crime, they still posed threats through exposure to strangers (Riedel, 1999). Pedestrian crowds make it easy to pick pockets and slip wallets out of purses. Grab-and-run attacks on merchants' wares were also common. Crime in general is a stop-and-go activity (M. Felson, 1998), and convergent cities helped a thief get back into the flow of foot traffic for a quick exit. Public transport could also assist the offender in a hasty departure (see Clarke & Smith, 2000).

Even if train cars and buses were relatively safe inside, they generated crime in important ways. Their stations and bus stops were not always safe. Long subway platforms, built to handle the worst crowds, also assisted offenders by making surveillance difficult. Old systems had many nooks, blind stairwells, and shadowy places, making the offender's task easy (LaVigne, 1996). It is fairly safe right by the station, which has enough foot traffic. But areas a block or two away from the station have too few people around for constant natural surveillance and are the most dangerous: offenders can wait there for stragglers (Block & Block, 2000; M. Smith, 2005; M. Smith & Cornish, 2006). Furthermore, side streets and alleys are not frequented by crowds. After the Industrial Revolution, many cities had late shifts of factory workers; that meant that offenders could find the right time and place for attack.

The convergent city afforded settings for public drinking, often in crowded taverns with high risks of bumping and fighting inside. Taverns could dump crowds or individuals onto the street in a drunken stupor. Those drinking in streets or on stoops could create problems for themselves and others. Initially, alcohol problems were greater in rural areas, where the grains were grown. But better roads brought alcohol into the city, which was least able to manage it because of the crowds.

Convergent cities provided excellent opportunities to mismanage parks, street corners, and other public places. With drunken young males hanging out, crowds could turn from a source of supervision to a font of trouble. Even three or four drunks together could be rather hard to handle. At the same time, the entertainment districts in cities of the past had street crowds combining people of various ages, not all drunk. You can see now that convergent cities provided sources of both security and crime. All of life is trial and error.

In every stage of life, people seek to prosper and to keep others from seizing their gains. Couples want to raise a beautiful daughter, but they also want most men to leave her alone. Urban life offers prosperity, unfortunately with a lot of insecurity. But people keep trying and sometimes find solutions.

The Urban Village: A Low-Crime Area

In 1961, Jane Jacobs published a classic book, *Death and Life of Great American Cities*. Her thesis was that the old urban neighborhoods, despite a bit of grime, were actually good places to live and raise children. She was adamantly opposed to the urban renewal projects that bulldozed these neighborhoods and replaced them with high-rise public housing. She felt that the old neighborhoods were built for pedestrians and that life on the street created not only a vibrancy of a living city but also a relatively low crime rate. She anticipated that high-rise buildings and streets built for cars but hostile to pedestrians would destroy neighborhood life and ultimately undermine the city as we knew it.

About the same time, Herbert Gans (1962) invented the term *urban village* to describe areas within the convergent city where people could find rather secure daily life and face-to-face interaction. Combining the ideas and observations of Jacobs and Gans, an urban village provided

- stable ethnicity,
- stable residency,
- homeownership—even if homes were tiny,

- narrow streets and wide sidewalks that are easily monitored, and sometimes
- new migrants recognized from a shared past in Europe or the same part of America.

In the urban village, middle-aged adults—not the toughest youths—controlled urban spaces. Women had more power than met the eye, keeping the men largely out of trouble. People knew each other and could not get away with much. Owners and long-time renters together watched over the area (note the discussion of place managers in Chapter 2). New entrants had social ties to those already there. Streets were well supervised. The paint may have been shabby sometimes, but the streets were clean. And you did not have to be rich or even middle class to be safe.

The security of the urban village was not based entirely on love or the milk of human kindness. It depended also on nosy neighbors who were suspicious of outsiders and willing to ask them, "What the hell are you doing here?"

To understand why stable residence is important, take a look at Exhibit 5.1, which compares short-time residents to those living at the current address five years or more as of 2005. Short-term residents suffered six times the risk of robbery victimization as those who lived there longer. Stability and home ownership, plus the other factors mentioned above, made urban villages safer than the rest of the convergent city.

Exhibit 5.1   Robbery Victimization by Number of Years Lived at Current Address, United States, 2005

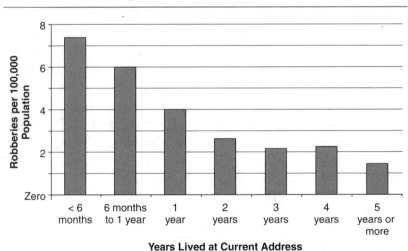

SOURCE: Bureau of Justice Statistics (2006).

The convergent city was and is a very exciting place. It produced Broadway musicals and jazz improvisation. It produced many of the greatest people with the most vitality. It offered the greatest museums in history, many of which survive today. Many convergent cities are found around the world, but the American version went into a period of decay and dispersion to suburbs. Whatever our nostalgia for it, the convergent city produced congestion, noise, annoyance, and some types of crime. Its high density ensured that you could hear ambulances and police sirens day and night, and that other people's problems would impinge on you. A visit to Manhattan is all you need for a quick reminder that a city can get on your nerves. Although the larger city offered chances for boy to meet girl and provided ongoing entertainment districts, young singles were too poor to have their own apartments and had to go home to Mother. More settings were then under control of middle-aged people, especially women. Boyfriends and girlfriends could not easily go home for the night and had trouble finding a place to do what's natural for mature males and females together. Even after marriage, most couples had to live at home for at least a while. For very tangible reasons, crime rates were relatively lower in convergent cities of the past than in the metropolis as we know it today.

Prosperity and growth changed that world. The twin searches for affordable real estate and peace of mind help explain what followed.

CRIME AND THE DIVERGENT METROPOLIS

A great transition has occurred in the past 50 years: the convergent city gave way to the divergent metropolis. This transformation was set in motion by events that occurred before the transition began. Many people contributed, but three noteworthy events help explain best what happened.

Three Inventions With Real Consequences for Crime

Although social change is always complicated, three important inventors helped produce the divergent metropolis and life in America as we now know it.

- Henry Ford invented the modern assembly line. Producing cars by the millions, Ford made them available to the masses.
- Serving in the navy during World War II, William Levitt learned how to put up wartime buildings quickly. After the war, he applied these lessons to invent mass-produced suburban housing. In building Levittown on a former potato field in Long Island, New York, Levitt organized the opposite of a moving assembly line, with specialized workers moving from one site to the next.

- In 1919, Dwight D. Eisenhower was a 29-year-old officer for an army truck convoy crossing the continent. The trip was so slow and inefficient that he never forgot it. Thirty-seven years later, as president of the United States, Eisenhower signed a bill that inaugurated the interstate highway system.[*]

- Daily life in modern America was transformed because the auto industry built so many cars, the home industry so many suburbs, and the highway system so much access. These three innovations also produced the major crime opportunities of today. Cars and suburban homes provided millions of new targets for crime and conveyances for offenders. Highways provided crime access and evasion of control at a level never before seen.

It Did Not All Happen at Once

With housing and roads, the metropolis could and did develop. First, bedroom suburbs grew along travel corridors into the central city. But these suburbs began with low crime rates. Youths did not yet have autos, suburbs had not grown together, mothers were outside the labor force, and shopping malls had not developed. With the dispersion of jobs and shopping to the suburbs, and the other conditions reversing, suburbs became much more suitable for criminal activity. In time, suburbs had more to steal, more people to steal it, and easier transport for those most likely to do so. People got home later and had less time to watch over youth or property.

The divergent metropolis developed through an intricate *unpacking process*, carried out over many years, which involved several components.

- Dispersing homes and other buildings over larger lots, wider roads, and vast parking areas, all at lower heights. These were increasingly difficult to protect from criminal entry.

- Dispersing people over a greater number of households, with fewer persons living in and supervising each—including young individuals, young couples, and divorced persons with their own places to live.

- Spreading people over more vehicles as they travel and park. That subjected parked vehicles and drivers walking to and from parking spots to high risk of attack.

- Disseminating social and shopping activities away from home and immediate neighborhood. As strangers, people became ready targets of crime or perpetrators.

- Spreading vast quantities of retail goods over a wider expanse of space, with fewer employees to watch them, thus inviting people of all ages to shoplift.

- Assembling millions of dollars' worth of cars in huge parking lots with virtually nobody to watch them.

---

[*]Arguably, Eisenhower had more impact on society than any other peacetime president of the 20th century. However, we can hardly brush aside the dramatic domestic influences of Presidents Roosevelt and Johnson.

Ironically, we think of cars as private, yet they require much more *public* space than does public transit. That space is then difficult to control and thus invites crime to occur at higher rates. More generally, the divergent metropolis brought offenders and targets closer together in locations unsuitable for supervision.

The Great Metropolitan Reef

The earlier development of the divergent metropolis followed main road arteries and formed a patchwork of development. The metropolis grew like an amoeba, surrounding and absorbing each nearby town, allowing people to live at suburban densities while using automobiles to make up the distance. In time, the areas between the lines and patches filled in with additional development: residential, shopping, factory, and office. Growth continued outward, and towns grew together. In time, even metropolises themselves begin to fuse into a single organism, a vast suburban sprawl at moderate- or low-metropolitan density.

Thus, the divergent metropolis becomes part of a Great Metropolitan Reef. Each new piece of suburb fastens onto this "metroreef" like coral, building outward and connecting inward. The metroreef not only grows like coral but also functions like a coral reef after growth has taken place, with organisms moving about the reef continuously and diffusely. The same freeways that allowed quick access for shopping, work, and friendship also made many types of crime easier, including burglary, fencing stolen goods, or assembling a group of drunken youths. The suburbs were no longer a refuge from urban problems. Malls provided many crime opportunities formerly associated with the central business district of the convergent city. Indeed, metropolitan specialists sometimes talk about *edge cities,* the commercial districts outside the center. You can see once more that our old categories can barely keep pace with human inventiveness.

POPULATION DENSITY, SHIFTS, AND PATTERNS OF CRIME

Patterns of crime are not so easy to study in a metropolis, where people and things move around so much. Once it was believed that crime rates vary directly with population density. In other words, criminologists expected to find more crime in high-density cities than in low-density cities. But it is not so simple. Comparing victimization in different cities D. Decker, Shichor, and

O'Brien (1982) found fantastic differences between cities in how population density related to each type of crime (see Exhibit 5.2). Cities with high population density tend to have much less burglary and household larceny than cities with low density. Motor vehicle theft, however, goes up somewhat with population density. Robbery and larceny with contact (often similar to it) go up a good deal with a city's population density. Here's the puzzle: why does density correlate +.57 with contact larceny but −.77 with household larceny? It is puzzling to see these signs going in opposite directions. To solve the puzzle, consider the modus operandi for each type of crime.

A detailed study of 1,284 burglaries (Winchester & Jackson, 1982) found that detached houses have almost three times the burglary risk as flats (apartments) and eight times the risk as long terrace apartments. The latter provide

Exhibit 5.2   Correlations Between Population Density and Different Crime Types Over Several Urban Areas

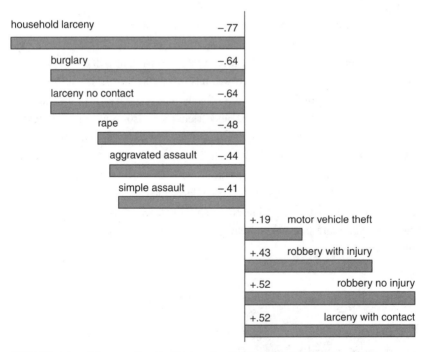

SOURCE: Adapted from Decker, D., Shichor, D., & O'Brien, R. (1982). *Urban Structure and Victimization.* Lexington, MA: Lexington Books, Table 4.1.

us an interesting natural experiment, since they only allow entry in the front, having no rear or side windows or doors. Clearly, burglars pick housing types carefully enough to escape the eyes of neighbors. Importantly, high-density residences are the hardest to break into, and those in low-density areas are the easiest targets. The detached houses of low-density cities and suburbs offer

- entries on all sides,
- more space between, and
- trees and bushes to block the view of doors and windows.

Burglars like more windows and doors to enter, well-spaced houses, and blocked sight lines.

And Then There's Car Theft

Why, then, does motor vehicle theft go up a bit with population density (i.e., they have a moderate positive correlation)? Although there are fewer automobiles per capita in dense cities, they are parked in more risky places. Drawing from Clarke and Mayhew (1998), Exhibit 5.3 shows the risk of auto theft per million hours parked in a particular type of spot. Generally, a car is safest from theft when you are at home, less safe when you are working, and least safe when you are doing something else. If you park somewhere to shop or for leisure activities, watch out! Indeed, if you park in a public lot for these purposes, your risk is almost 190 times as great as parking in a personal garage.

Exhibit 5.3   Auto Theft Risk in Different Places People Park

Garage at home	2
Driveway or carport	40
Street outside home	117
Public parking lot	454
Thefts per 100,000 cars parked 24 hours, British Crime Survey	

SOURCE: Adapted from Clarke, R. V., & Mayhew, P. (1998). Preventing crime in parking lots: What we know and what we need to know. In M. Felson & R. B. Peiser (Eds.), *Reducing crime through real estate development and management* (pp. 125–136). Washington, DC: Urban Land Institute.

In many European cities, as well as dense American central cities, people have cars but no private garage, carport, or driveway. Giving up a parking spot means both having to park farther away from your apartment and increasing the risk that someone will steal your car or its contents. In contrast, low-density areas provide personal garages and opportunities to park right near the home or office. You can now understand why rising population density brings less burglary but more auto theft with cars parked on the street. Conversely, lower density suburbs have more residential burglary, but the cars are safely parked in enclosed private garages.

Density Shifts Quickly in the Course of a Single Day

In a modern society, population density shifts very quickly from one spot to another. An office area packed with people on weekdays is abandoned later in the evening and on weekends. A shopping area largely empty during school hours is dominated by teenagers after school, and then changes when adults come home from work. As these populations shift, so does crime. With population density shifts come related shifts in crime opportunities.

All crime is local. The minimal elements of crime converge locally. The physical and social components of crime are fluid in the course of a day, a week, and a month, posing quite a challenge to crime analysis.

Density variations are great in modern life, and different density levels produce alternative crime opportunities. When people move from central cities to suburbs, they might escape from crime at bus stops or in streets, but they face new risks in everyday suburban life. When they go to work, burglars have a chance to check out their houses, and while they are at work other offenders have an opportunity to look over their cars.

Research is beginning to document how daily population shifts influence crime patterns (Andresen, 2011; Andresen & Jenion, 2010; Herrmann, 2012). Crime maps become very different when considering the *ambient population*, namely, the inflows and outflows of people working daily or having nighttime recreation. The crime map near schools is very different after school on school days, compared to weekends. The crime map shifts from early evening to late night. Areas with lots of nightlife have especially sharp changes in crime risks and types during the daily cycle.

Especially interesting is Remi Boivin's (2013) study of crimes in 506 census tracts in Montreal, Canada. His results show that local burglary and assaults by strangers are determined mainly by the influx of visiting population, *not* by the residential population. That suggests that many of our local theories of crime based on nighttime residents hardly tell the story for many crimes and many parts of the city. Instead we need to focus on flows of activities influencing crime risks—the main point of the current chapter and indeed this book.

A GREAT PARADOX: CENTRAL CITY PROBLEMS VERSUS SELF-REPORT EVIDENCE

A great paradox in criminology is that

A. Police and victim data show certain of the central city areas have more crime, especially violence, than the suburban rings around them.
B. Yet self-report surveys show that central city youths are about the same as suburban youths in basic offending patterns.

Observations of shoplifters in action also show that the crime is not dominated by one social group (Dabney, Hollinger, & Dugan, 2004). So are different social groups greatly different or slightly different in their crime tendencies?

One reason for this discrepancy is broached in Chapter 6, where I discuss the time that youths spend escaping parental supervision. I suggest that enough central city youths evade parental controls earlier in adolescence, and stay longer in peer group activities. That serves to push up the overall community crime levels, even though central city and suburban youths tend to be quite similar in mid-adolescence.

Shaw and McKay Gave Us a Start

On the other hand, the worst places have a lot to teach us. They provide a natural experiment: how can society concentrate crime opportunities to maximize misbehavior? Burgess (1916) and White (1932) were well aware that local areas could greatly enhance delinquency.

Shaw and McKay (1942) were most famous for showing this in their studies of "delinquency areas." They noticed in particular that these areas had many abandoned buildings, declining industries, and out-migration of people who got a better job, along with in-migration of new groups. Each new group developed high crime rates as it entered the "worst" part of town. Shaw and

McKay were not always precise when writing about "social disorganization," but they gave us an important starting point for precision by specifying that abandoned buildings assisted criminal behavior. We know much more today to help understand how central city areas deliver extra crime opportunities.

The Lack of Place Managers Gives Crime an Advantage

Recall that Chapter 2 discussed the significance of place managers for preventing crime. Earlier in this chapter, we considered how urban villages provided place managers, namely, more homeowners and long-time residents. But on the other side of the tracks, there are few homeowners or long-time residents to watch over people, places, and things. Apartment buildings cannot afford doormen. Many public housing projects are found here; although some may be well designed and managed, many are not. (See Chapter 11 on local design against crime.) Park and playground supervisors have long been cut out of city budgets, with parks too often taken over by thugs.

Industrial Land Use Assists Crime

Mixing residence with industry generally makes it more difficult to keep young people away from delinquency (Burgess, 1916; White, 1932). That's even truer when central city industries have gone bankrupt or found greener pastures, leaving a shell of abandoned industrial sites ideally suited for crime to occur. Prostitutes use these sites for strolls and assignations; drugs are sold and used in and near them; boys hang out, get drunk, or fight there; and remaining items are stolen and sold, feeding substance abuse. Industrial properties also provide escape routes to offenders. That makes this turf virtually impossible to police.

How can police in old industrial areas corner and arrest an offender who has 8 or 10 escape routes? Similarly, customers for illegal goods find convenient entry and exit, also with little risk of arrest. Other industrial areas provide parking lots for local youths to plunder during daytime hours, with good spots to chop up cars at night.

Exposure to Skidders

Skidders are people who go downhill in life, perhaps because of drugs or alcohol. But they may also have suffered a variety of diseases, mental illness, accidents, war injuries, or anything else that interferes with their prospects in life. Skidders very likely end up poor and may be easy for offenders to pick off. Some may become offenders themselves, but whether that happens or not skidders contribute to higher crime rates in poor neighborhoods simply by providing local offenders with excellent crime targets.

Sometimes we forget skidders when analyzing how poverty relates to crime. Many people who are poor today were not poor in origin. Thus, middle-class people or their children can end up on the other side of the tracks if they become alcoholics or drug abusers, sick or injured, or otherwise fail to succeed by traditional standards. Homeless runaway youths may come from middle-class homes. As we study more, we learn more about exactly how poverty and crime can be linked.

More Cash, Less Credit, and Things to Steal

Poor people often have poor credit. That means they carry more cash relative to their income than middle-class people. They are also more likely to use a check-cashing storefront than a bank, then walk down the street as easy targets. Poor people also spend a smaller share of their income on investments, home equity, real estate, or other commodities that are hard to steal. With cash in their pockets and lightweight electronics as their best luxuries, they provide more adequate crime targets than you might guess from their income. Meanwhile, wealthier persons keep most assets unavailable for direct theft, burglary, or robbery.

In short, society delivers a lot of crime opportunity to low-income areas. That explains why it is possible for more crime to be in these areas without necessarily requiring that poor people have more criminal inclinations than other people.

CONCLUSION

The divergent metropolis serves to unpack human activities. It disperses people over more households, more metropolitan space, more vehicles, and more distant activities. In the village and town stages, it was easier to keep crime low. The convergent city provided new crime opportunities but confined these to certain main locations; it also devised the urban village to contain crime. In contrast, the divergent metropolis weakened the supervision of space and provided even more crime opportunities. Those fleeing city for suburbs were not anticipating the vast increase in purely public space that makes the divergent metropolis less secure than meets the eye.

Society is a living and learning organism. Each of these four stages—the village, the town, the convergent city, and the divergent metropolis—blends into its successor. Villages are absorbed into towns and towns into cities. The convergent city and divergent metropolis blend together. Thus the very small-scale incidents we call criminal acts occur within a large, living, and changing system of activities.

MAIN POINTS

1. The history of everyday life can be summarized in four stages, responding to the transportation technology of the time. They are the village (on foot), the town (horses), the convergent city (ships, railroads, etc.), and the divergent metropolis (automobiles).

2. Transportation technology is the driving force of change in everyday life. As transportation modernizes, more people are brought into daily contact. That contributes to rising crime rates in many ways.

3. Even though the convergent city has more crime than do towns, its urban villages combat crime with more personal contact and stability. Crowds on the street often produce safety, at least when sober. On the other hand, convergent cities expose individuals to strangers, provide unsafe physical environments, and facilitate offenders' quick escape.

4. The "urban village" is an area within the convergent city where people can find rather secure daily life and face-to-face interaction.

5. Three important changes helped produce the divergent metropolis and life in America as we now know it. The auto industry built so many cars, the home industry so many suburbs, and the highway system so much access that daily life in modern America was transformed.

6. The divergent metropolis, with its reliance on cars, generates more crime than the convergent city. Cars not only make good crime targets but also lengthen trips and lessen control over targets and offenders alike.

7. The great metropolitan reef is the development of a seemingly endless suburban sprawl at moderate- or low-metropolitan density.

8. Population density shifts and their impact on crime vary. Auto theft and burglary depend on very different densities and settings.

9. Lower-income areas often draw more crime because they have fewer place managers, including homeowners or long-time residents to watch over people, places, and things. Industrial settings assist crime especially when they have been abandoned. Formerly middle-class persons—skidders—contribute to the crime problem in poor areas. People who are poor have more cash in their pockets and lightweight electronics as their best luxuries, thus providing more adequate crime targets than you might guess from their income.

10. The flows of daily activities and supervision of such activities are central for understanding crime risks.

PROJECTS AND CHALLENGES

Interview project. Interview an elderly person about what village, town, or city life was like in the past. Ask especially about such topics as street life, people knowing neighbors, and activities of women.

Media projects. (a) Pick out five detailed media accounts of specific offenses for which nobody was caught. Avoid outlandish or unusual examples if possible. How did each offender probably take advantage of the surrounding area and setting? (b) Obtain a literary description of life in a large city of the past, one without automobiles and relying on streetcars or other old modes of transportation. Do a thought experiment about how theft would occur in such a city and the forms it would take.

Map project. Using Google Maps or Google Earth, access a satellite photo of a local parking lot and the building(s) it leads to. Put one asterisk (*) at the spots where the car itself is most likely to be stolen. Put two asterisks (**) where the car's contents are more likely to be stolen.

Photo project. Use the Street View in Google Maps to capture images of some buildings from past stages of history. What stage produced them? What tells you that? What features of the buildings invite or prevent crime?

Web project. Find websites that describe streetcars and trains from the past, how they were used, and what they did to daily life.

6

TEENAGE CRIME

———•◦•———

The public is *so* misinformed about teenage crime. The innocent youth
fallacy described in Chapter 1 is only the tip of the iceberg. Here are
some of the myths:[*]

> *Myth 1:* "Schools themselves are dangerous." In reality, most risk occurs *on the
> way to or from school*, not usually inside the building. Putting officers inside
> school buildings misses the point.
>
> *Myth 2:* "Teenagers with jobs commit less crime." In fact, teenagers with jobs
> (hence extra spending money) *get in more trouble than those without jobs*!
>
> *Myth 3:* "After-school activities keep youths out of trouble." These activities are
> not dependable for reducing youth crime, for reasons discussed in this chapter.
>
> *Myth 4:* "The D.A.R.E. program reduces drug abuse." These programs are good
> politics, and make parents happy. But research keeps showing they fail to reduce
> crime or drug abuse.
>
> *Myth 5:* "Youth crime is mostly done by gangs." The next chapter goes into this
> myth.
>
> *Myth 6:* "Minority youths do most of the youth crime." Except for more serious
> violence, *crime participation during teenage years is similar among major social
> groups*!

---

[*] For a summary of D.A.R.E. program findings, see Center for the Study and Prevention of Violence,
Institute of Behavioral Science, University of Colorado at Boulder, CSPV Position Summary,
Fact Sheet 1, 2010, http://www.colorado.edu/cspv/publications/factsheets/positions/PS-001
.pdf, accessed October 7, 2014. For the other findings, see citations in the rest of this chapter.

On the last point, you might recall my discussion in Chapter 1 of how the self-report survey began. Professor Austin Porterfield (1943, 1946) gave the very same self-report survey to both local juvenile delinquents and his own undergraduate students at Texas Christian University. The study asked respondents about illegal acts they had committed. He found *little difference between his middle-class students and the local delinquent population* in basic self-reported delinquency participation—a finding often replicated since. In modern societies, keeping youths out of trouble is not just a problem on the other side of the tracks. It is a general problem that includes middle-class youths, too. As you shall see, youths on the other side of the tracks might start getting into trouble at younger ages, and then continue to older ages. But modern society has a general youth problem, ranging well beyond low-income areas.

PERSPECTIVE ON YOUTH CRIME

Where did this general problem come from? The next section searches for an historical perspective to help answer that question.

Historical Role for Youths

Youths throughout much of human history had valuable roles for procreation and physical work. Start with procreation in Biblical times, when marriage at ages 10 to 14 years old was common, and babies arrived early and often. Yet most people then lived on limited protein, so their adolescent growth spurt and sexual maturation did not occur until ages 14 or 15, two or three years older than what happens in today's world. That left little time for *premarital* pregnancies. Nonetheless, young couples in premodern times got quite busy at procreation and continued with it. Despite the delayed puberty, early procreation and large families were common throughout most of human history, particularly because rural societies needed young people to work the land.

The energy and muscle of youth were more valued before modern machinery had been developed. Without machinery driven by fossil fuels, you have to use your own muscle or try to divert water, wind, and animal energy. I once visited a traditional farm and tried to chop a load of wood, to make apple cider by hand, and to do other traditional chores without machinery. I stopped as soon as possible. I can remember the rural women in the North Carolina mountains scrubbing clothes in the creek and tilling their gardens by hand.

In this traditional world, youths are highly valued for their energy and muscle, and most people are busy with the struggle for existence.

Yet misbehaving youths are hardly new to history. Drunken soldiers and sailors over the ages, wild and wealthy youths in ancient Greece and Rome, students in the historic European universities outside of parental control—all of these exceptions occurred. But most of the population was not involved. An ongoing and prevalent local youth problem emerged mainly with metropolitan and modern life. I explained much of that process in the previous chapter, but it cannot be fully understood without addressing the changing role of youths.

Modern Role for Youths

The role of youths in today's society is very different today from most of human history. The vast increase in protein in modern societies leads to sexual maturation around age 12. That maturation brings early muscularity, but the economy has little use for muscles. Machinery has replaced muscle. Fossil fuels have supplanted human energy. Extended schooling fills ages formerly spent working in home, farm, or factory.

Thus, modern society delays the onset of full and traditional adult roles. If puberty occurs at age 12 and marriage at age 28, that leaves a 16-year period without traditional family roles. Educational requirements and sporadic labor force participation at young ages further disrupt entry into full adult roles. *That leaves modern youths without a satisfactory or stable position in society and undermines society's ability to keep them out of trouble.* Many young adults work their way through all of this, but not always easily. The growth of cities and suburbs helps youths get around and thus evade adult supervision.

As women joined the workforce, they were less able to supervise children or their residential neighborhood.

- Modern mass transit made it easier for youths to evade adults.
- Automobiles dispersed both victims and young offenders across a wider area, while providing excellent targets for attack.

This transformation in routine activities produced the crime wave of the 1960s and 1970s, but it also set in motion a variety of efforts to regain control. Some of these efforts are discussed in later chapters on situational crime prevention and designing out crime. But in this chapter we consider the more direct actions that decrease or increase crime participation among youths in particular.

Crime Risk Varies Greatly by Activity

To be sure, modern youths have conventional responsibilities and are under society's control to some degree. They exit home early and usually go back home at night. They go to school. They often have part-time jobs and then full-time jobs. They even hold one another to society's conventions, and follow rules more often than not. But when they break those rules, it usually happens in or near youth settings.

That's why, to understand juvenile crime, *it is essential to learn how young people spend their time*. This has long been accomplished with the time-use survey—asking people about their use of time or to fill out diaries for a day or longer. These surveys have a 90-year-history (see review in K. Fisher & Gershuny, 2013) and are used around the world to study what people really do with their daily lives. That allows us to study how much time young people spend in different settings, and how that changes as they get older. I found the time-use survey was very important for developing the routine activity approach. The crime wave in the 1960s and 1970s occurred because people changed their use of time—where they were and what they were doing. As daily life dispersed people away from family and household settings, the opportunity for crime proliferated.

With new time use information about youths, we are on the threshold of a revolution in routine activity research. Today's electronic media, mobile phones, GPS, and apps help us to trace daily activities and their location in much greater detail. These data are already coming in, showing dramatic shifts in population in the course of a single day, along with quick changes in crime participation risks. The old theories and methods are quickly becoming obsolete. However, some of the old methods helped a lot.

Time and Crime Rates

Arithmetic is the most important branch of mathematics. A crime rate is calculated by dividing the "crime numerator" by the "exposure-to-risk denominator." Although conventional crime rates simply use the residential population as the denominator, I began to do something different in the original routine activity paper. For example, to measure how risky street life was, I divided the number of victimizations in streets by the *amount of time spent in streets* (Cohen & M. Felson, 1979, Table 1, Panel D). That allows a fair comparison between a street-specific victimization rate to a home-specific victimization rate. (See Boggs, 1965, for the origins of that idea.)

Exhibit 6.1 shows dramatic differences. Hour for hour, risk from strangers is 45 times higher in the street than at home. Even for nonstrangers, assault risk is much greater on streets than at home. These results have been amplified by Andrew Lemieux's dissertation research (Lemieux, 2010; Lemieux & M. Felson, 2012), showing that the greatest dangers occur in transit—traveling to and from school, work, and leisure settings. For example, time going to or from school is over a dozen times riskier than time spent shopping. Lemieux's dissertation research showed these results to be even stronger when looking only at persons aged 15–19. Their victimizations per 10 million person-hours in each activity were

Home activities	34
Attending school	85
Leisure away from home	160
On the way to or from school	448

Exhibit 6.1   Risk of Assault (by Strangers and Nonstrangers) by Time Spent at Home and in Streets

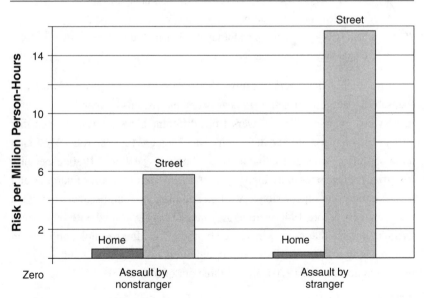

SOURCE: Calculated from Cohen, L. E., & Felson, M. (1979). Social change and crime rate trends: A routine activity approach. *American Sociological Review, 44,* 588–608.

You can see that *hour for hour*, the school journey is more than a dozen times more risky than home activities, and more than five times as risky as attending school itself. These powerful findings justify detailed research on teen activities and risks.

Teenage Routine Activities

In the 1980s I developed a set of questions to find out about the time adolescents spend with peers and away from the watchful eye of parents. It was a reminiscence study asking respondents 18 years old and older to think back to age 17, and then answer questions about their time use. Although the study is subject to recall error, it asked specific questions about youth activities, producing powerful results.

The respondents and interviewers loved the survey, perhaps because of the underlying flavor of sexuality and gossip. Our survey team asked them

- what time they had to be home on Friday and Saturday nights;
- whether their parents noticed when they came home late;
- how many nights a week they were out;
- whether any adults were around or nearby while they were out;
- whether they drove around with other teenagers at night;
- about afternoons, chores, and who was home then;
- whether they had to be home for family dinners; and
- whether they had ever engaged in sexual intercourse.*

This then led to a publication (M. Felson & Gottfredson, 1984) that focused on "adolescent activities near peers and parents"—mentioned briefly in previous chapters. The answers from different generations indicated that society had changed greatly, making it easier for teens to break rules. We found a major shift in teenage routine activities between 1940 and 1980, especially for girls. Youths spent more nights a week away from the gaze of parents, and had less afternoon supervision as well. In addition, the reminiscences indicated that teenagers before 1940 were largely unable to ride around with other teenagers, a practice that greatly increased by the 1970s. For example, only one in four males age 17 before 1940 rode around often with other teens, and only one in six females. By the 1970s, almost three out of four did so.

---

*Unfortunately, my detailed routine activity questions were never added to the crime victim surveys, although some simpler items are sometimes asked.

This transformation in daily teenage life had consequences. In the earliest cohort, relatively few girls had sexual intercourse by age 17, mainly because no guy had ever tried. The activity patterns in the oldest generation provided young men and women much less chance to be alone together, so they had to discover sex later.[*] Although that sample was not large enough to study crime victimization, we made our routine activity opinion very clear: *youthful rule-breaking depends upon the convergence of peers in the absence of parents.*

Linking Teenage Time Use to Crime and Delinquency

Wayne Osgood's research has strongly supported that hypothesis (Haynie & Osgood, 2005; Osgood, Wilson, O'Malley, Bachman, & Johnston, 1996). Youths participate in much more crime while spending time together with parents out of sight. Osgood uses the term "unstructured peer activities," but the main point is that youths converge without parents. Osgood's empirical findings fit right into the crime triangle presented in Chapter 2. Recall that the potential offender needs to evade the "handler"—especially parents—in order to commit a crime. Evading parents applies not only to high-risk teenagers, but even "average" teenagers face greater risks in similar settings.[**]

More recent research reinforces this dramatically. Sonja E. Siennick and D. Wayne Osgood (2012) learn that the risk of hanging out for crime and delinquency stems from hanging out *as an activity*, not the nature of adolescents' companions. If correct, that research will greatly alter how peer effects are interpreted. Peers influence one another by sharing settings in the short run, not because they have bad influence in the long run.

---

[*] Interestingly, my generation (the post–World War II baby boomers) was the youngest generation in this survey. We were quite a bit more liberated than our parents. This trend in routine activities of youths may have continued. For example, pediatricians and child researchers are increasingly concerned that continued declines in shared family meals undermines nutritional health of children (Hammons & Fiese, 2011). However, most of this change probably already occurred some decades ago.

[**] I do not accept the argument made by Wikström, Oberwittler, Treiber, and Hardie (2012) that the most moral youths are unaffected by time spent in unstructured activities. That finding was attained by preselecting youths who had no offenses or almost none, due to a complex index process. Those youths had zeros under all circumstances. For more on that study, see M. Felson (2014).

Even stronger support for the routine activity approach to teenage offending is emerging very recently in Europe. I re-calculated data from Peterborough, a British city, in order to draw Exhibit 6.2 (Wikström et al., 2012, pp. 330–331). Respondents reported on the *crimes* they committed in certain activities, as well as how much *time* they spent in those activities. They committed 57 crimes per thousand hours spent in unstructured peer-oriented activities, but only 2 crimes for the same share of time spent with family. Hour for hour, unstructured peer activities are 28 times more risky, or 2,800 percent worse from a crime viewpoint. American researchers are moving very much toward the same conclusions. *Scholars from the Netherlands and Belgium are finding even stronger results* when taking into account more information about where teenagers get together and where they go (Bernasco, Ruiter, Bruinsma, Pauwels, & Weerman, 2013; Weerman, Bernasco, Bruinsma, & Pauwels, 2013). Hoeben and Weerman (2014) found that unstructured socializing *especially increases youth offending when it occurs in public places.* You can see why it is so important to study how, where, and when teenagers converge.

Exhibit 6.2   Crimes Teenagers Commit per 10,000 Hours in Each Setting

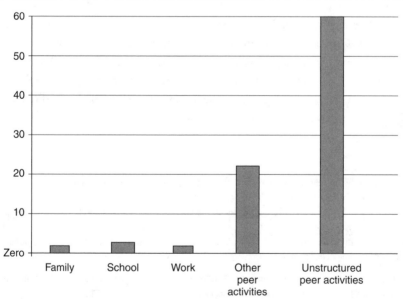

SOURCE: Wikström, Oberwittler, Treiber, & Hardie (2012); calculated from Peterborough, UK, data, pp. 330–331.

Adolescent Convergence Settings

One of the greatest advances in situational analysis occurred before mobile phone apps could help researchers. In the 1950s and 1960s, Roger Barker and colleagues (Barker, 1968; Barker & Wright, 1951, 1954) studied everyday life by dividing a small town into all the behavior settings that people occupy during daily life (as I noted in Chapter 2). Barker's behavior setting has three magnificent features:

- It includes *informal* settings, such as in front of the gas station where the guys hang out. Also formal ones, of course.
- It allows for the *same place* to shift gears, becoming a *new setting*. The History class at 10 a.m. gives way to the English class at 11 a.m. in the same room.
- It allows for the *recurrence* of a setting even if the names and numbers of the players change. Thus from 3 to 5 p.m. there's a hangout in front of the gas station every school day, but the *specific* youths who go there will vary day to day and hour to hour.

Hence behavior settings persist in a world where activities shift quickly. It is the ideal unit for studying informal behavior and exposure to risk of crime participation. Behavior settings are especially relevant for teenagers, who are often quite a bit more volatile than adults in where they go and what they do. Barker observed everyday behavior, also paying attention to the teens hanging out in front of the store or on the back steps of the high school. Barker learned that an informal behavior setting favored by teenagers recurs day after day, *even if the specific participants may shift*. Thus informal settings provide some structure in the absence of adult organization.

Youth settings are especially important because so much crime and delinquency is carried out in small groups (Andresen & M. Felson, 2010; Reiss, 1988; Warr, 2002). "Offender convergence settings" are places where offenders spend time before or after committing crimes (M. Felson, 2003). Thus a certain mall or corner might have a handful of teenagers hanging out every afternoon, even if they are not always the same ones. In the gang chapter (following this one) I discuss whether youth hangouts and gang hangouts are different.

Professor Gisela Bichler and colleagues (Bichler, 2010; Bichler, Christie, & Sechrest, 2011; Bichler, Malm, & Enriquez, 2014) mapped some of these convergence settings and provided us with empirical confirmation of the basic idea. She asked 2,563 Southern California delinquents where they hang out, and then calculated how far they traveled to get there. Surprisingly, there's very little mapping of teen hangouts. That's why I added some projects at the end of this chapter where you can teach yourself more about this topic. Perhaps future researchers will supplement what we know about where youths meet informally and how that sets the stage for crime at nearby settings.

School Proximity Effects

Schools play an important role in the youth convergence process. A typical American high school assembles over a thousand youths, then dumps them out together onto the streets, funnels them into the same school buses, and drops them off at the same bus stops or dumps them out on the street at the same time. This process sets the stage for quite a number of problems in the vicinity of schools or the routes home, especially on school afternoons. Snyder and Sickmund (2006) showed dramatic differences in the hourly crime patterns on school days vs. weekends. On school days, school-age youths get in more trouble in the afternoon when school lets out—or perhaps the hour before they are supposed to be free. On weekends, in contrast, school-age youths get into more trouble in early evenings. Classic work by Dennis Roncek established that secondary schools produce crime nearby (Kautt & Roncek, 2007; Roncek & Lobosco, 1983).

Just as the vast majority of offenses committed by teenagers are minor, most of the crime near high schools and teen hangouts is also minor. However, more serious offenses are also influenced by youth journeys from school. Chris Herrmann's 2012 dissertation found major shifts in robbery hot spots in the Bronx between school days and weekends. On school days, robberies concentrated between the school and the subway station. Weekend concentrations were entirely different from school concentrations. Many of these patterns show up in *overall* crime maps, but it is not so easy to map *individual* youths.

TEENAGE ZIGZAGS

In November 2013, Professors Frank Weerman, Pamela Wilcox, and Christopher Sullivan presented important new research findings to the annual meeting of the American Society of Criminology. Their study interviewed teenagers *every two weeks* about their activities, friendships, and delinquency. (Most studies of teenagers only interview them every year or two, and some wait five years before re-interviewing.) Their study of 155 teenagers in one Kentucky high school is uniquely equipped to study the short-term dynamics of peers, activities, and behavior. They taught us what we all should have known anyway—that *teenagers are highly volatile in their activities, friendships, substance abuse, and criminal behavior.* Their social networks and friendship patterns in one interview were quite different two weeks later. Their reports of crime and delinquency area also varied greatly.

These teenagers *clearly do not follow smooth trajectory* as they move through a single year, much less their entire adolescent period. Quite the opposite! Even though alcoholism and substance abuse can eventually become habit forming (hence regularized), for most youths drinking and smoking marijuana is a sporadic activity. Their zigzag pattern depends on who is around and what peers they are hanging out with that week. We cannot even depend on the same crime instigators, since delinquent leadership is itself highly volatile (Warr, 2002).

The "Crime Trajectory Illusion"

Teenage zigzags give crime researchers nightmares. We are supposed to come up with good predictions of offender behavior, but offenders keep confounding us. If you don't believe me,

- Take a look at any criminal's official criminal history and you won't see much of a career or a smooth curve, or
- Go back to the original data files going into "criminal career" research, and you will see highly uneven behaviors in the raw data about most youths.

Many researchers use mathematics to smooth out these variations. Mathematics offers us wonderful tools, but we should be careful how we use these tools. Curves may *look* smooth, but that doesn't mean the real youths are themselves so dependable when you look at the original data. Is there any way in which youths change smoothly while moving through adolescence?

Routine Activity Trajectories

The "routine activity trajectory" depicted in Exhibit 6.3 focuses on the most *dependable* change during adolescence—the increasing time spent with peers in the absence of parental or adult control. From early to late adolescence,

Exhibit 6.3   The Routine Activity Trajectory in Adolescence

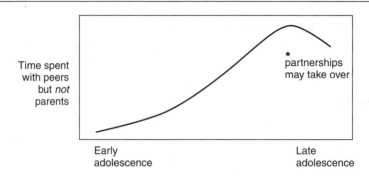

evasion of parental supervision is a growing and cumulating fact of life for most adolescents, who grow increasingly independent from parents (Douvan & Gold, 1966; Noom, Dkovic, & Meeus, 2001). As they progress through the teenage years, youths *tend* to commit more crimes and to experiment with alcohol and illicit drugs. They also get into trouble farther from home (Andresen, Frank, & M. Felson, 2014). However, these *events* are sporadic, even though the *more general autonomy* is incremental.

To put it another way, autonomy from parents grows rather smoothly, but specific incidents are sporadic even as they become more likely to occur. The best way to understand that point is to think about traffic accidents—as youths *routinely* spend more time in automobiles they tend to have more accidents, but any one accident is still a surprise.

Thus *adolescence combines dependable and volatile features.* Crime, delinquency, traffic accidents, sexual encounters, new friendships, arrests, victimizations—these are volatile features. Events erupt from time to time. These eruptions occur within a larger and smoother set of changes toward increased evasions from parental controls, resulting from the upward curve in peer group time.

We should not measure parental supervision by taking the word of parents, who often give themselves high marks. Teenagers have considerable capacity to evade. They might skip school, lie about schedules, or otherwise escape parental scrutiny in afternoons or evenings. Most of these evasions occur for social reasons, and the resulting crimes are largely incidental to the time spent with peers.

Over time teenagers may find girlfriends and boyfriends. As their partnerships stabilize and gain increasing influence, peer dominance *may* give way to partnerships. Eventually partners form their own households and families, which normally depress peer dominance. However, the volatility of partnerships, even in late adolescence, leads me to put an asterisk in Exhibit 6.3. The point is that time spent with peers (without parents) may give way to time spent with partners (without peers or parents), but that process has its ups and downs.

Standard changes during adolescence can be summed up as

- a relatively smooth overall trajectory with increased time with peers absent parental supervision or dominance;
- in late adolescence, formation of sexual partnerships reducing time spent with peers without augmenting time with parents;
- a zigzagging experience with specific personal friendships; and
- episodic involvement with crime and delinquency.

How can changes over adolescence be smooth and episodic at the same time? The answer to that question comes from the nature of adolescents, who have strong social needs without strong organizational tendencies. The more time they spend together, the less we can predict exactly what will happen. In contrast, the more time they spend under control of parents and other adults, the more readily you can predict what they do. As their autonomy from adults grows steadily, they continue to zigzag in specific friendships, in partnerships, and in crime participation even though their basic shift follows a rather smooth trajectory. Of course, this is a very general pattern. Some youths develop stable relationships early, and some people never seem to do so. To analyze the process, think of three Ps: parents, peers, and partnerships. Ask which one is dominant and how that dominance changes over adolescence.

Parental Trials and Errors

A parent's dream is depicted in the top bar of Exhibit 6.4. It shows the dominance of peers for a very limited period during later adolescence. In this dream, parents have extended their control for a good deal of adolescence. The adult nightmare is represented in the bottom bar, with peer groups dominating through most of the youth period. In the worst cases, parental influence gives way to peers at ages 10 and 11, proceeding through the 20s.

Exhibit 6.4   How Long Does Peer Dominance Last?

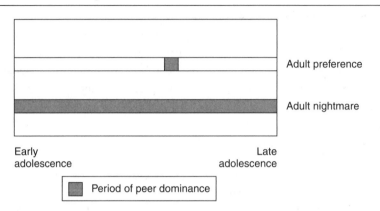

Exhibit 6.4 implies something very interesting:

- Two boys with exactly the same criminal tendencies may differ greatly in the amount of crime committed over time. One of the two boys might have greater success in evading parental supervision at a younger age, and continue with peer dominance through later adolescence.

- Two neighborhoods whose youths have exactly the same criminal tendencies may differ greatly in crime rates. One of the two neighborhoods might have less ability to depress peer dominance at the beginning or end of the youth period.

You can see that a focus on adolescent time use helps us comprehend crime better than focusing on arrests or delinquency directly. Sometimes we learn more by taking a step back to look at the larger picture.

Parental Efforts to Delay Peer Dominance

Many adults have tried to thwart the peer takeover. Two basic methods are used: fostering afternoon activities and arranging for jobs for youths. Both of these efforts have often failed or even backfired.

Denise Gottfredson and David Soulé (2005) summarize the afternoon activity research as follows:

> [O]ne undesirable side effect of grouping youths together for schooling or for after-school programming is an increase in crimes against persons. This effect is greatest during the school day, when youths can potentially encounter other youths with whom they have "beefs" or during which time any number of irritations might arise that lead to fights or other interpersonal crimes. (p. 118)

The research on jobs for youths gives even worse results. High school students who have jobs get involved in *more* crime, not less (Apel, Bushway, & Brame, 2007; Brame, Bushway, Paternoster, & Apel, 2004; Runyan, Bowling, & Schulman, 2005; Staff & Uggen, 2003; J. P. Wright & Cullen, 2000). Perhaps their jobs give more opportunities to steal and more money to spend to evade parents.

I suggest that adult ideas about supervising teenagers might not be practical enough. That is, they might not take into account that assembling teenagers can itself be criminogenic. Thus we cannot assume that all teenage sports activities will have the same impact on crime and delinquency participation. The answer to this question may come (in the near future) from Evelien Hoeben and Frank Weerman (2014) of the Netherlands Institute for the Study of Crime and Law Enforcement (NSCR). These researchers are checking how teenage sports activities vary in parental proximity. They kindly let me have a peek at their preliminary data. Six teen sports differ greatly in the amount of parental supervision, and crime activity varies exactly as one might expect. Perhaps future research will help us sort out when parental efforts to supervise teenagers work or fail, and why.

CONCLUSION

In general, modern society leads to less control. It is a mistake to interpret this as a "cultural change" or "moral deterioration," or "bad child rearing." Rather, it represents a shift in the tangible features of everyday life. Bodies, products, technology, and transportation have also changed, undermining adult control over teenagers. However, youths are not in trouble every moment of the day or in every location. Their offending and victimization alike are highly concentrated in certain behavior settings characterized by peer dominance and parental absence. That information helps us improve our perspective on the innocent youth fallacy (discussed in Chapter 1). Youths have a wide range of possibility, even within a single day. They are capable of compliance with adult wishes, as well as evasion of those wishes. They have a lot of volatility but are not strictly random. Trouble is most likely to occur when peers are present and parents are absent. The extension or contraction of the *period* of peer dominance is essential for understanding the arithmetic of individual and community crime and delinquency. Those communities that are able to narrow that period will end up with considerably less overall crime, even though their youths dabble in delinquency, at least for a while.

MAIN POINTS

1. A major transformation occurred in the United States and numerous industrial countries, affecting the roles of youth, and hence their crime and delinquency.

2. Biosocial change in adolescence came from a protein-rich environment that shortened the onset of puberty and had profound implications for both the productive and the reproductive roles of teenagers, because work roles shifted in exactly the opposite direction.

3. Changes in the American occupational structure to highly specialized jobs requiring more years of schooling and experience means that young, strong adults have fewer opportunities for work.

4. Changes from the 1960s onward, in particular when more women went to work, meant that the lives of teenagers were transformed with the lack of supervision.

5. Modern life puts young people in a bad position, taking away their historical roles in work and family life. However, it puts them in a good position for escaping parental supervision.

6. Automobiles greatly enhance the ability of youths to escape parental controls. That causes crime to disperse over a wider area, while providing good targets for illegal attacks.

7. Schools help to control crime and victimization of youths, but they also facilitate problems by bringing many youths together and then releasing them simultaneously at particular times and in particular areas.

8. Managing the time of teenagers becomes a major problem for society. Many ill-considered and ineffective control methods are still offered and believed effective by people who think little about the timing and location of adolescent activities. Jobs and recreation for youths can easily fail to reduce crime, and may even make things worse.

PROJECTS AND CHALLENGES

Interview project. Interview three high school students about how they use text messaging and cellphones to escape parental controls.

Media project. Look at media treatment of young people as offenders 20 years ago and today. Has it changed?

Map projects. (a) Map a secondary school and major nearby housing areas. Emphasize the main paths those teenagers on foot take home in the afternoon. (b) Map an entertainment area or district where young people often go. Map bars, attractions, hangouts, and so on. Predict trouble spots.

Photo project. Photograph a path often taken by teenagers. Take a photo every 10 feet; array these photos into a sequence with discussion. Note any litter, vandalism, or signs of burglary. Note where problems have not occurred.

Web projects. (a) Find websites that deal with school bullies and bullying. What do they say about dealing with the problem? Is their case persuasive? (b) If you are a user of a social networking website, think about the dangers of youths sharing too much information about themselves and accepting strangers as friends. How can parents help prevent and monitor their children's activity on these sites?

7

BIG GANG THEORY

———•◦•———

M uch of the public (and even many police) fail to see juvenile gangs for what they are—a giant effort to intimidate. That effort includes a lot of fakery. I am not denying that gangs harm the community and society, but I am trying to put that harm into perspective. That means addressing the big gang fallacy noted in Chapter 1.

In popular image, a juvenile street gang is a steady and stubborn group of young thugs. Miller (1982) defined the gang as organized, with identifiable leadership, well-defined lines of authority, and acting in concert. That makes the juvenile gang sound like a formal organization, with members *more* organized than other youths! Neither the logic nor the evidence supports *that* image of the juvenile gang. Nor does the image of a highly organized youth gang fit what you learned in the previous chapter about the volatility of youths.

WHAT ARE GANG CRIMES?

It isn't even clear how to distinguish gang crimes from other youth crimes, such as those discussed in the previous chapter. Many police departments specifically code "gang crimes" in their computer files, but what does that really mean? I am going to describe some crime events. In your opinion, which of the following is a "gang crime"?

Example 1. Two boys were added to the police gang list two years ago. There's no evidence on whether they are still active in the gang. They burgle a house together.

Example 2. Two boys who are definitely current gang members pair up to sell drugs to strangers, but don't share their profit with the other gang members.

Example 3. Three boys who are definitely current gang members break into a house together, dividing the loot into three shares, but not sharing with other gang members.

Example 4. One gang member and one non-gang member steal a car together and are arrested.

Example 5. A gang member gets into a fight with a non-gang member over a personal matter unrelated to the gang.

Any of these incidents may well be included in the "gang crime" statistics. Police are very slow to remove the gang designation from their computers, so their list of "gang affiliated" youths includes many who no longer hang out with the gang guys. Moreover, any youth who commits a crime with a gang member is likely to be added to the gang list, even if he is not really a member. Nor do police always know the petty little reasons that people get into fights or what they do with loot. You can see why the gang impact on crime is often inflated.

FUNDAMENTALS

Unfortunately, juvenile gangs get too much credit for bad deeds, organization, leadership, unity, and enormity. *Big gang theory* is my term for the exaggerated view that youth gangs are highly organized, cover a lot of territory, and dominate local crime. I do not deny that gangs are a real problem, but big gang theory goes way too far. To understand the gang, we should neither sanitize nor demonize it. My goal is to dissect the problem, not to pound the table. In the last chapter, I spoke about convergence settings for teenagers and their trajectory away from the influence and guardianship of adults to the influence of peers. These are important points for understanding the formation of gangs.

Gang members and non-gang members do not necessarily hang out at different settings. They can be at the same corner or in the same school, interacting socially and criminally. We know that gang members and nonmembers have overlapping activities—legal and illegal. However, much more needs to be known about the degree of overlap and interaction. This may vary by size and duration of gang, and whether the gang faces an outside threat that enhances its cohesion. Unfortunately, police and other adults might miss the nuances that teenagers themselves know. Thus a teen hangout with some gang members present might appear to adults as a gang setting, when that is only part of the truth.

Although I learned most of what I know about gangs from experts (especially Klein, 1995; Klein & Maxson, 2006), I have quite a different perspective than many of them. I don't see juvenile gangs in terms of friendship or social identity, but rather as primarily a protection service that promises to intimidate one's enemies. Thus much of this chapter runs counter to the usual gang literature, even though I draw most of my raw material from that very same literature (Klein, 1992, 1995, 2004, 2005; Klein & Crawford, 1967; Klein & Maxson, 2006).

Intimidation as the Defining Feature of the Gang

A juvenile street gang offers its members a special service—a promise to scare others. The defining and driving force behind a juvenile street gang is its ability to intimidate through numbers and a threat to fight outsiders. That central feature *distinguishes* the gang from the stamp club, the marching band, or the simple friendship group. The gang offers this special service to members for a reason: many youths confront a real problem from living in a dangerous local area—or even from having to go to high school with other youths.[*] Young people are especially vulnerable to personal and property attack, and many feel a need for protection that simply cannot be provided by parents, teachers, or police.[**]

A gang promises youths a specific solution to their security problem. A gang's distinguishing feature is that it helps them intimidate others, especially outsiders. Although gangs may also offer companionship and group identity, that is not their distinguishing feature (see Colvin, 2000; S. Decker & van Winkle, 1996). In fact, they intimidate so much that they even get credit for crimes they did not do!

---

[*] This is one more example of a fundamental rule: always look at crime from the offender's viewpoint if you really wish to understand what's going on.

[**] I wonder whether youths feel especially safe at convergence settings where fellow gang members hang out.

Gangs Get Too Much Credit

Contrary to popular belief, most youths in "gang areas" are not so clearly "under gang control." Professors Klein and Maxson (2006) teach us that

- a majority of youths in gang areas are not gang members,
- a majority of crimes in gang areas are committed by non-gang members,
- gang members' *share* of local crimes exceeds their share of the local youth population,
- gang members commit more than their share of violent offenses, yet
- most of the crime committed by gang members is nonviolent and ordinary.

Thus a gang area might have only 10 percent of youths belonging to gangs, but this minority might commit 20 percent of local crimes and 30 percent of local violent crimes. The police might well designate even higher percentages of violent crimes as "gang related," and the public might think the gang did it all.

The gang problem is bad enough—we don't need to exaggerate it. Like other youths, gang youths are unfocused offenders, largely aimless, committing a variety of ordinary offenses. The image of the gang exaggerates their bad reality, scaring everybody in the process. Gangs don't try to reassure people, since scaring them is the main service they provide.

THE PUZZLE

Several decades of juvenile street gang research and media coverage have produced a lot of confusion. In this section I explain some of that confusion, and later try to sort it out.

The Gang Membership Problem

In 1959, Professor Lewis Yablonsky opened up a can of worms. He concluded that gangs are "near groups," with diffuse, limited, and shifting relationships. In 1968, Professor Gerald Suttles found considerable turnover in gang membership. Other researchers have confirmed that gang "membership" is unstable and unstructured. Participants drift in and out over the months, enough to destabilize the group. Moreover, gang "members" commit crimes as often with nonmembers as with one another. Scholars discovered that gangs are not very cohesive.

On the other hand, gang cohesiveness can appear suddenly if an outside threat intervenes. Incursions by outside gangs, real or imagined, cause a gang to come together. Police interventions often backfire, causing the gang to become more cohesive and to survive longer. But juvenile gangs in general are not very coherent or organized. Is there any glue at all holding them together?

Efforts to Find Gang Structure

Some scholars see gangs as a loose social network, not a clear-cut organization, but that does not answer the question about what makes them cohere. Professor Malcolm W. Klein (1995) offers a very interesting answer. Even a loose gang has a rather smaller set of "core members"—those who stay in longer and hold the group together. However, researchers find that core membership is itself unstable—the core members this month might shift next month. Moreover, core members often commit crimes with non-core members and even with non-gang members!

Gang Terms and Names Are Very Confusing

To make it even worse, people use the "gang" word in too many ways, and I can't stop them. The word has been applied to groups of juveniles, but also to motorcyclists, skinheads, and prisoners; organized crime; organized drug sellers; and more. Gang experts (see Klein, 2004, 2005) try to help us sort this out by distinguishing three types of gangs:

1. drug gangs,
2. prison gangs, and
3. juvenile street gangs (also known as youth gangs).

Confusing these three types of gangs is a bad idea. We can understand that some members of one of the above also in time belong to another. But that does not make the three identical. We cannot expect the same behavior inside and outside prisons. We cannot expect 12-year-old youths to interact freely with those who are 17, or those age 24.

The current chapter emphasizes juvenile street gangs, and that's what we mean with the word "gang" in this chapter. Juvenile street gangs alone are confusing, because

- gangs appear and disappear;
- gang "members" join and quit;
- members and nonmembers interact and even commit crime together; and
- different gangs use the same or similar names, giving the *impression* that they are one and the same.

It's interesting that new gangs are born in a big city every year, but they might be gone the next year. Very few gangs survive long enough for fame; but famous and long-lasting gangs or gang names get more attention and affect community perceptions of all gangs. Why do gangs have to be so messy?

Big Gangs Are an Illusion

Sometimes gang observers draw a local map showing how a few huge gangs control large swaths of the city. If you keep questioning them, they admit that each "big gang" is really a bunch of little gangs. Perhaps two hundred different gangs in the Los Angeles region are classified as "crips." These gangs cover a vast area, and range from the "Altadena Block Crip" to the "Most Valuable Pimp Gangster Crip." But what does that really mean?

Many people think of a huge gang with many little branches. *Big gang theory* makes a more dramatic story for the media, and most local people—even many police—believe that story. Government agencies provide more funding to fight a big gang than to oppose a bunch of little groups of local toughs. It is easier to blame your problems on something colossal, rather than a group of very local boys intimidating others. Unfortunately, rumor reinforces the dubious impression that many gangs are one.

The 200 so-called gangs noted above do not usually see one another, so how can they be one gang? Gang experts tell us that many gangs using the "crips" name are rivals and even fight one another—despite having "crips" in their title. I believe that the colossal gang is largely an illusion—many independent gangs just using the same name over wider space and longer time. That implies that such terms as "crips," "bloods," and "latin kings" are really common nouns pretending to be proper nouns. If these are just synonyms for the word "gang," they should not even be capitalized.

There are French-speaking bloods and crips in Montreal, Canada, and Dutch-speaking bloods and crips in Amsterdam. Do the Los Angeles and Chicago gangs have multilingual ambassadors? Or are these just people borrowing a name from the mass media? So what is going on with the juvenile street gang?

THE REASON FOR A GANG

Most of us want to hide our nastier side and convey a more polite image to outsiders. Gang members are the opposite. Most members are pleasant or at least innocuous on a daily basis, and are likeable enough for gang workers and researchers. They are peaceful most of the time. But they do not want you to know this! Small gangs portray themselves in big terms for good reasons.

The Quest for a Nastier Image

In a crime-ridden area, or among tough-acting youths, there are very good reasons to intimidate others physically. Because intimidation is useful, many people would like to do a better job of it. But it is very hard to intimidate others when walking down the street alone. Rare is the boy so dangerous and obnoxious on his own that he can fend for himself in a tough neighborhood. Therefore some boys try to form protective alliances. Ideally these allies should walk down the street together for mutual protection, but that is not always possible. That's why some boys develop a common warning signal that tells enemies that an attack on one is an attack on all.

A youth walking alone on the street, by wearing gang colors, hopes to gain an extra ability to intimidate. He hopes others will be convinced that he is tough. If the gang colors do the job, he won't even have to fight very often. Others will be convinced by his colors that

- since he is in the gang, he must be tough and dangerous;
- the gang might hear his distress call, and swarm to assist him now; or
- the gang will retaliate later on his behalf. (B. Jacobs, 2004)

At younger ages, it makes sense to go around in a pack, relying on immediate strength in numbers. But a pack is no longer sufficient for protection after youths are old enough to roam wider, and later into the day and night. A gang tries to solve the problem, helping intimidate adversaries by drawing assistance from those not always present. Without a gang, you have to stand on your own two feet. With a gang, you can seek a free ride on the toughness of others, even when they are not on the spot. Thus, gang colors help each member appear more dangerous than his naked reality.

The Reason for Colors

Unlike organized crime, which prefers anonymity, street gangs seek visibility. A juvenile street gang is a simple alliance, using clear and common warning signals. A clear color tells others, even strangers, to leave you alone. You are announcing your membership in hope that predators will be afraid to bother you. The main purpose of gang colors is to link the bearer to a larger group of ruffians, real or imagined. That's why they pick deep blue or red, not powder blue or pink. Nor do they pick gang names that are warm and friendly. Gang membership might provide identity or friendship as a byproduct, but that's not the main point for joining. The purpose is to link oneself to a larger group that knows how to fight and will do so for you.

Enhancing a Nasty Image Even More

I do not assert that intimidation is the only feature of juvenile gangs or their members. But intimidation is the gang's distinguishing feature, along with the use of specific signals to accomplish it. A group that did not intimidate would not be referred to as a "gang." In other words, you join a juvenile gang hoping to convey danger and power greater than yourself. You hope others will be afraid to attack you because you have dangerous friends. You wear a gang color to scare off foes; this might serve you well, at least for a while.

Now we begin to understand why gangs pick nasty names. Seldom do they call themselves the cherubs, or the angels, or the exemplars. They pick names that are famous for aggression and danger. A name that includes "crips" or "bloods" or "latin kings" conveys the idea that you are not just a handful of local boys, who borrow these famous symbols in hope of scaring off their rivals. That's why a group of boys in Omaha, Nebraska, might select such names as bloods or crips to convey the notion that they have a national following. In fact, they do not know the California gang members whose names they might imitate. Even within Los Angeles, the bloods in one neighborhood do not normally know the bloods down the road. They are not usually coordinating, but they are sharing the same symbols because they have the same problem to solve—a need to intimidate others for their own protection and perhaps for crime purposes.

Most of us would dislike bad media coverage, and would resent being blamed for crimes we did not commit. But from a gang viewpoint, that's all good news since it enhances their nasty image and their capacity to intimidate. Mass media inform the general public about gang signals and names, linking these to the nastiest possible image. Local boys simply need to borrow these signals; then others may start complying with their wishes.

I define a juvenile street gang as "a very local group of youths who intimidate others with overt displays of affiliation." These displays depend on mixing fakery with reality. To understand the juvenile gang, don't believe completely its story about itself, or the story told by others in the vicinity or by the media. The myth and reality are woven together—that's the point of it. The gang's exaggerated reputation influences how current gang participants behave and draws reactions from those around them. It also can undermine the very security they had hoped to attain by joining a juvenile gang.

Gangs Can Backfire Badly for Members

Initially, gangs are formed for defensive purposes, and might even do members some temporary good. But over time, gangs set in motion

- retaliation from rival gangs,
- unfavorable attention from police, and
- growing entanglement in the justice system.

If gang membership draws more problems, that defeats the purpose—to keep members secure.

The gang's strength is its ability to exaggerate its power and reach, providing an intimidation service to participants. But events can reveal a gang's true weakness—that it cannot deliver sufficient protection. A gang must make its members seem more obnoxious to others than they would be alone. Eventually they have to fight, and that might not turn out well. A gang that ceases to communicate fear, or that delivers occupants into more danger than it repels, no longer can serve them well, and might soon evaporate. Most gangs do just that.

The basic gang participation dilemma is quite severe. On the one hand, each member draws security from the larger group. But each member also draws antagonism because he is identified with that same group. Thus, displaying gang membership becomes risky. Gang members are subject to harm by parents, schools, police, rival gangs, and maybe one another. Sometimes gang colors protect from adversaries and sometimes exactly the opposite. Youths have strong incentives to wear blue in the heart of the territory of the blue gang, but to hide those colors in other territories or at the edges. The risks and advantages can easily shift from hour to hour, depending on what groups are most in proximity—police, parents, rival gangs, or one's own. I do not deny that gangs do extra harm to themselves and their communities. But I suggest keeping that harm in perspective and not taking at face value the images they convey or the rumors about them conveyed by others.

Gang Policy and Crime Prevention

It's easier to despise the whole gang rather than each member. By telling yourself that the evil resides in the gang, you can convince yourself that each young person is basically good. I dispute the second point. I see human beings as very mixed—capable of good and bad deeds. Youths are sometimes nasty enough to create a security problem for one another. Indeed, the more general teenage crime problem produces an incentive to join a juvenile gang—which promises members a solution for their security problem. Moreover, proximity of *another* dangerous gang adds an incentive to form your own.

That incentive cannot be depressed by angry public officials or nasty media attention. It only backfires. A sensible gang policy should have four main features:

1. Stop publicizing the gang's evils or what you have done against it. Take down the anti-gang posters. That just makes gangs appear strong, enhancing their ability to intimidate, survive, and multiply.

2. Focus on reducing *general* local crime rates in gang areas and increasing security—*especially on the way home from school*. That lessens the incentive to form or join gangs. Situational prevention and designing out crime—discussed in later chapters—have important indirect impact on gang potential.

3. Suppress places, not people. Chapter 11 discusses re-designing spaces and places so they cannot be taken over for the wrong reasons. Without a hangout, a gang will tend to fizzle naturally.

4. Every six months or less, erase the term "gang member" from individuals' police files and policemen's minds, unless there's real evidence that a gang still exists, and that the "members" still "belong." Try not to exaggerate the gang's impact in your own mind. And try not to give gangs credit for ordinary crime in the vicinity or to classify "gang violence" without thinking about what it means.

Squads of social workers and SWAT teams fall into exactly the same error: enhancing the gang's nasty image, hence augmenting its service to members. Gang prevention should avoid publicity about gang nastiness.

Police will tell you, "We're the biggest gang in town," and that has some truth. Police signal their membership. They seek to intimidate. They want you to know they can call on the others if you give trouble to one of them. However, the police-as-gang strategy does not work so well in suppressing juvenile street gangs—whose coherence often grows with suppression. Police can better protect society by outsmarting juvenile gangs—dividing them up and removing their hangouts.

CONCLUSION

"Gang crime" is usually just ordinary local crime carried out in groups of two or three youths, who do not share the loot with the whole gang. Gang colors and names are used to intimidate others, conveying a nastier image than any member could convey alone. Widespread media coverage, police attention, and neighborhood gossip help scare the public and reinforce intimidation, keeping gangs alive longer. Just as gang protection often backfires for members, gang suppression often backfires for the community.

MAIN POINTS

1. Despite many years of effort, scholars have been unable to find what structures juvenile street gangs.
2. A gang uses the same color and broadcasts membership.
3. This helps gang participants scare off enemies, gain compliance from victims, and discourage bystanders from interfering or turning them in.
4. Gangs mix real intimidation with exaggeration; the latter serves a practical purpose.
5. Unless you have real evidence to the contrary, assume that gangs in different areas do not know each other, even if they share a name or color.

PROJECTS AND CHALLENGES

Interview project. Talk separately to two students who claim to live in a gang area or go to a high school with gang members. Find out their image of the gang, then determine how much of that image came from (a) what they heard from others and (b) their own direct experience. Discuss whether they might be misinterpreting (b) based on (a).

Media project. Contrast three or four of the points I made in this chapter to the image that mass media give on those same points. Use media searches to verify your comparisons.

Map project. Go to the maps in the *National Gang Threat Assessment: 2009* (National Gang Intelligence Center, 2009). Discuss whether you think the implications are true or misleading.

Photo project. Take 10 photos of people from any source, showing them to 10 people. Ask which person or persons are most and least intimidating; then discuss the results.

Web projects. (a) Use web sources to learn the different ways that the "gang" word is used to study groups committing crime. Also look at the use of the gang word in the National Gang Intelligence Center (2009) publication. (b) Use web sources to find out how much money local governments have gotten from the federal government in the United States, after declaring a gang problem.

8

CRIME MULTIPLIERS

————•◦•————

Crime has multipliers. Sometimes, violence breeds violence. Sometimes, burglary leads to fencing stolen goods. Sometimes, a minor amount of alcohol gets someone into big trouble. One crime can feed into another (see a full treatment of this topic at M. Felson, 2006).

Let me prove to you how important a crime multiplier is. Suppose someone breaks into your home and takes your diamond ring. That's the first crime. He sells it to a fence (the second crime); and she buys it knowing it is stolen (the third crime). She re-sells it to somebody else (the fourth crime). The burglar who did the first crime uses the money gained to buy illicit drugs (the fifth crime). Thus the break-in has a multiplier of 5.0. My general point is this: if a community can prevent 100 burglaries, it might prevent 500 crimes in all! On the other hand, if we allow 100 additional burglaries, the total crime level might go up by 500. Crime multiplies by at least eight mechanisms:

1. One crime requires another
2. One crime disinhibits another
3. One crime advertises another
4. One crime entices another
5. One crime sets up another
6. One crime escalates into another
7. One crime starts a victim chain
8. One co-offender attacks another

As you go through these, try to count or estimate how many crimes will follow from the first one. Remember that most people don't pay taxes on illegal gains, so each property crime implies tax evasion, too. More examples are discussed below.

ONE CRIME REQUIRES ANOTHER

Many stolen goods cannot be used directly by the offender. That requires trading or selling them to somebody else. Nor can the fence use all the stolen goods received, and really needs to re-sell them in order to stay in business (see Chapter 9). So burglary often requires additional crimes. The close linkage between crimes goes beyond burglary.

Ingesting a small quantity of illegal drug seems simple, but it virtually requires other criminal acts, such as buying the drug and possessing it. Illegal drug manufacturing often requires illegal procurement of controlled substances beforehand, and illegal transport of those drugs after they are made. Indeed, an illegal drug process might well set in motion a chain of at least six or seven illegal acts. Thus, multiple crimes are almost implicit in the process.

An illegal act, no matter how small, immediately compromises the offender's position. *Virtually all offenders have a strong incentive to cover up the first offense*, and that might require committing a second one. A burglary starts out nonviolent, but the offender has a reason to assault someone who discovers him or threatens to turn him in. The simplest theft gone awry can lead to a struggle and even a serious assault. Something so small as a traffic violation can lead the guilty party to speed away to avoid detection, or even to fight police.

ONE CRIME DISINHIBITS ANOTHER

Illegal substances often disinhibit people, after which they commit crimes they would not have committed. But there's more to it. A legal substance such as alcohol can be used to an illegal excess, or in an illegal place—then serving to disinhibit another crime. In addition, the person who might have discouraged a crime when sober might not do so if drunk or disengaged due to illegal substance use. A study of bars in Hoboken, New Jersey, found that many bar personnel are themselves drunk on the job (Maurer, 2010, reporting on research by James Roberts). When the place managers are drunk, it doesn't matter much that they are present.

ONE CRIME ADVERTISES ANOTHER

Drug corners and drug markets are known in the community. Each crime there advertises another for the offender. Even an illicit solicitation might not work this time but can bring the customer back the next time. Many other examples of offender advertising can be found. Perhaps deterrence theory works better for offenders than for the justice theory. An offender can punish a victim without consulting attorneys or judges. One beating intimidates those who hear about it and advertises one's dangerous reputation. Based on Chapter 7, I suggest that juvenile gangs rely on one crime to advertise the potential for another; that might help them to gain compliance with their illegal demands.

ONE CRIME ENTICES ANOTHER

I've noted more than once the overlap between offender and victim populations. Offenders hang out too much with other offenders, and are themselves often victimized. Part of that is the sheer expenditure of time in risky settings. Offenders also have proceeds of crime that entice another offender to attack them. Thus prostitutes, after collecting their cash from the customer, find themselves robbed by somebody else. John Eck (1995) details how drug sellers and buyers alike face high risk of victimization, since they have cash and drugs in hand. A good share of home invasions are simply home robberies of drug dealers (Heinonen & Eck, 2012). The invader makes an appointment to buy or sell drugs, and then forces the victim to lead him to the loot and turn it over. Criminals themselves have very high rates of crime victimization, partly because their crimes entice others to commit crimes against them.

Repeat victimization is a topic receiving a lot of attention (Farrell, 1995; Grove, Farrell, Farrington, & Johnson, 2012; Pease, 1992; Weisel, 2005). Very often burglars go back to the same home and break in again in a few weeks. Perhaps they are happy with their success the last time. Perhaps they hope the victim already replaced the missing items, with help of insurance. In any case, it appears that one crime entices a repeat against the same victim. There is also increasing evidence of "near repeats," where offenders satisfied with their success in the first burglary then break into the house next door, or two doors down.

ONE CRIME SETS UP ANOTHER

A burglar enters a house, thinking only about loot. But he finds a young lady there alone and, with no prior planning, rapes her. This is an example of one crime setting up another, despite the offender's lack of initial intent. This malicious serendipity is a common component of sexual assault (LeBeau, 1987; Warr, 1988).

It applies to other situations. A burglar finds a business to break into, then engages in vandalism while he's at it. Assailants have been known to pick the wallet off the victim, even though a property crime was not the initial plan. A prostitute can slip the wallet from the unaware customer's pants dangling on the chair. A drug dealer can blackmail the customer. An auto thief finds a credit card in the car and uses it.

In some cases, the subsequent crime was not planned. For example, the burglar did not plan on somebody being home and the resulting assault. But youths who shoplift alcohol or cigarettes probably planned the initial theft with subsequent illegal use already in mind. And so we see that many crimes occur as chains of events, with planned and unplanned links.

ONE CRIME ESCALATES INTO ANOTHER

Most disputes that escalate do so within a short period of time, such as a minute or two. However, some disputes involve a cycle of retaliatory crimes that are distinct. An example is if one person attacks another, but two weeks later the victim runs into him and gains revenge—perhaps in a new dispute, perhaps not. The point is that one violent crime can lead to retaliation and perhaps escalation. Even an innocent victim might take the law into his own hands and retaliate at another time. In extreme cases, feuds develop between families or inter-gang violence develops and persists, reflecting escalation from a smaller crime (again, see Chapter 4).

George Kelling's (1999) work on broken windows and police discretion reflects a concern for escalation of minor crimes and disorderly behavior into major disputes and shootings. Allowing minor offenses and disorder to thrive (while focusing on more dramatic crimes) opens the possibility for escalation. Property crime is not exempt from interpersonal conflict or escalation. Arguably a third of property crime incidents emerge from interpersonal disputes, often when a former couple goes their separate ways, with one of them taking the television without asking. And many violent disputes start with an argument over things.

ONE CRIME STARTS A VICTIM CHAIN

One of the more subtle and interesting facts about crime is that a victim becomes a thief. Jan van Dijk (1994) is a leading criminologist in the Netherlands, where bicycles are commonly owned, ridden, and stolen. For many Dutch people, a bike is a necessity for everyday transportation; almost everyone knows how to ride a bike. It is not uncommon for someone whose bike was just stolen to steal someone else's. This sets in motion a van Dijk chain reaction, as depicted in Exhibit 8.1. First, **A** steals **B's** bike. Then **B** steals **C's** bike. Next, **C** steals **D's** bike. Finally, **D** steals **E's** bike, but **E** is left out in the cold. This happens, too,

Exhibit 8.1   van Dijk Chain Reaction

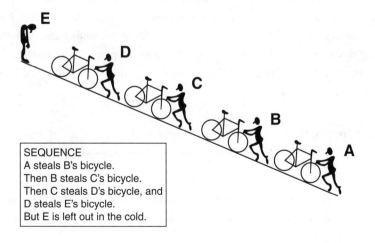

SEQUENCE
A steals B's bicycle.
Then B steals C's bicycle.
Then C steals D's bicycle, and
D steals E's bicycle.
But E is left out in the cold.

in entertainment districts. One person comes out of the bar to find his bike gone, so he then steals someone else's, and so on. Although it's a simple example, the important point is that each crime can generate many others.

van Dijk chain reactions occur in the United States with certain auto parts or car stereos. Other chain reactions can be set in motion when a worker picks up a tool belonging to another worker. If you look around in your own environment, you may see that van Dijk chain reactions are common at universities, where bicycles, required textbooks, and student computers disappear regularly.

ONE CO-OFFENDER ATTACKS ANOTHER

Many crimes are carried out by co-offenders, who then may have a conflict of interest over how to divide the loot. Other crimes lead to betrayal or a perception of betrayal. Among offenders there are usually no courts to settle disputes and no legal rules to follow. That means that offenders are themselves likely to fight when they have a dispute. The police use their conflict of interest against them, trying to turn one against the other—especially after the arrest process has begun.

CONCLUSION

We often find that one criminal offense sets up a chain of criminal events. In most cases, heavy involvement in crime is a slippery slope for the individual. More crime can breed a lot more crime down the road. On the other hand, society can gain from an auspicious spiral, because preventing one crime can easily thwart another. Removing crimes tends to set in motion a chain reaction of crime reductions. Crime multipliers are very important, and I would like to know a lot more about them.

MAIN POINTS

1. Crime multipliers tell us how many crimes follow from the first.
2. Crime multiplies by eight mechanisms, summarized by these verbs: *requires, disinhibits, advertises, entices, sets up, escalates, start*s, and *attacks.*

3. Even minor offending and disorder can lead to major offenses.

4. Even victimization can lead to offending.

5. Even property crimes can be dispute related and escalate into worse.

6. Fortunately, reducing one crime can help reduce several others.

PROJECTS AND CHALLENGES

Interview project. Interview three victims of theft or burglary to find out what was stolen. Estimate whether the offender was likely to need a fence to unload the loot.

Media project. Check for news reports to see whether they actually name the streets where vice arrests have occurred, providing free advertising to the offenders.

Map project. Map the location of busy local bars, and check which types of crime are located near them and which are not. Can you discern whether the bars set the stage for some crimes, but not others?

Photo project. Do some historic research to find famous feuds in history, and put together a photo-slide essay on the crimes and retaliations they generated.

Web project. Search for websites dealing with repeat victimization, reporting on what you learned.

9

MOVING STOLEN GOODS

————◦•◦————

A thief can do this with the loot:

- Use it himself.
- Trade it for other contraband.
- Sell it directly to others.
- Sell it to a go-between, who sells it to the public.

If the thief or burglar uses the stolen item himself, he has to like that particular CD, or the clothes must fit. If the thief trades it off, he has to find someone who wants it and has something to trade for it. If he sells it for cash, he has to wait around or find a buyer. The easiest solution is to find a go-between to take the loot off his hands and pay him quickly. That shifts over the slower process—selling—to someone else.

But the go-between does not pay well, so the thief may have to steal $100 worth of goods to get $5 or $10 cash. This formula explains the thief's problem:

The thief's profit equals

the original value of the loot

minus the markdown for damage while stealing it

minus the markdown because it is used

minus the markdown because it is stolen

minus the markdown for the rush to get rid of it

As the farmers say, it mostly goes to the middleman. Sutton's (1995, 1998) classic research finds three types of stolen goods handlers: those who fully know the goods are stolen (a "fence"), those who half know, and those who really do not know (see also Sutton, 2004; Sutton, Schneider, & Hetherington, 2001; Tremblay, Clermont, & Cusson, 1994).

The thief can try to get around stolen goods handlers by just stealing cash. But victims often watch their cash more closely than they watch their goods. Some thieves try to bypass the fence or other go-between by setting up a table at the flea market or going around selling the stuff. Yet the whole idea of crime is to get quick money for less work. Go-betweens keep crime moving, with important help from the public itself.

THE THIEF AND THE PUBLIC

When selling stolen goods, a thief depends on the public. People must be interested in the loot. Cromwell, Olson, and Avary (1993) raised this issue more than 20 years ago by asking "who buys stolen goods?" Do not dismiss that interest as secondary. In fact, evidence is growing that the demand for these goods drives property crime, more than the other way around.

Exhibit 9.1   The Wheel of Theft

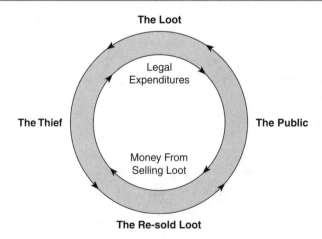

The Wheel of Theft

Thieves and the public are linked in a market, even if it is not quite the same as the market for toothpaste. Exhibit 9.1 depicts a very special sequence for crime, the Wheel of Theft.

1. The thief steals the loot from the public.
2. Then sells the loot back to the public.
3. Then gets money for it.
4. Then spends that money as a consumer.

The money flows clockwise in the inner circle, whereas the loot flows counterclockwise in the outer circle. Exhibit 9.1 neglects go-betweens for stolen goods, who could be slipped into the eight o'clock position. We could envision an extra wheel depicting the market for contraband purchased by the offender with his crime profits. Indeed, we can envision a series of wheels, like in an antique clock, with illegal goods and services being traded or spun in an intricate web of shady activity. That web gives an impression of organized crime, except that not all participants need to meet in a single place. The Wheel of Theft helps you understand the nearly invisible hand of criminal behavior and its significant consequences for society.

The Public Interest

The Wheel of Theft shows how much the offender depends on the public, and the public draws from the offender. Finney, Wilson, Levi, Sutton, and Forest (2005) provide empirical evidence for this symbiosis based on the British Crime Survey 2002–2003. Some 21 percent of the public admitted being offered stolen goods in the previous five years. Given that some people would probably not admit this, and that many stolen goods are not known to be so, the public likely purchase many more stolen goods than they admit or even realize. About 35 percent said they thought their neighbors' homes contained "a lot" or "quite a few" stolen goods, 52 percent thought "not very many," and only a minority (13%) thought their neighbors had no stolen goods at all.

Roughly 13 percent of males 16 to 25 years of age admitted having bought stolen goods. A much higher percentage (41%) said that someone had offered them such goods. Again, because people tend to avoid admitting unsavory facts, the real numbers are surely higher. Some surveys also indicate higher numbers than these.

When offered stolen goods, males are no more likely than females to accept them—at least by their own account. On the other hand, males are more than twice as likely as females to receive illicit offers. Thus, in the end, males purchase more stolen goods without showing signs of being morally different. We need to always ask not only whether people respond to temptations, but also whether they are exposed to temptations.

Eighty-three percent of respondents saying they were offered stolen goods also reported having turned down the offer. However, the more offers they get, the more they are likely to accept. Those offered stolen goods once resist the temptation 91 percent of the time. Of those offered a few times, 80 percent resist. Of those offered stolen goods often, 80 percent also resist. Stolen goods offers drive stolen goods purchases. That's why Sutton's "market reduction approach" is so important for crime prevention. Shrinking the stolen goods market would give thieves fewer outlets and less incentive to steal. Their markups would decline, and they would have to work too hard at crime to make it pay. They would be turned down more often as they tried to unload the loot and would have to take additional risks of being turned in.

This British survey cleverly asked which of the goods purchased in the prior year were new versus used. They asked about purchases via small ads, the Internet, informal markets, pubs, homes, secondhand shops, and the like. Some 20 percent of laptops or other electronic equipment and 16 percent of bicycles were bought on the side. Whether the buyer knows it or not, many of these goods were probably stolen. Buying "on the side" is, however, a broader issue than stolen goods themselves.

Second-Class Goods

Interestingly, goods not stolen can help camouflage those that are. A modern society, with its tremendous production of goods, produces a vast array of second-class goods. These include:

- overstocked products,
- items no longer fashionable,

- slightly damaged goods,
- irregular items ("seconds"),
- legal imitations of popular items,
- sellouts from stores that went out of business, and
- used goods.

A small store selling legitimate but second-class items can easily mix in some questionable merchandise bought on the side. Secondhand shops and flea markets include legitimately used or old merchandise, with stolen stuff mixed in. It is no accident that a secondhand market in Europe was historically called a "thieves' market." Stolen goods can easily be dumped into this sea of legitimate second-class merchandise and sold within the secondary market. That's why the line between a fence and a legitimate merchant is often thin (see Cromwell, Olson, & Avary, 1991; Johns & Hayes, 2003; Klockars, 1974; Steffensmeier, 1986; Sutton, 1995; Tremblay et al., 1994).

INVITING PEOPLE TO STEAL MORE

Stunning research by James LeBeau and Robert Langworthy shows us how society can produce more crime (Langworthy, 1989; Langworthy & LeBeau, 1992; LeBeau & Langworthy, 1992). Police departments in various cities can set up "sting operations" in order to catch thieves. The method is simple: open up a fake storefront to buy stolen goods, then arrest the offenders. It's very easy because the offenders come to you. Fence stings tend to bring the police excellent publicity and meet with widespread public approval (G. Newman, 2007).

LeBeau and Langworthy are trained geographers, so they know clever ways to study crime locations. In a real city with a police sting to fence stolen auto parts, they mapped exactly where cars were attacked. They found compelling evidence that the police had increased auto theft around the sting storefront by making it easier for offenders to get rid of the loot. The police had inadvertently harmed the very public that was cheering them on. They should have realized that theft thrives on the opportunity to unload the loot. Providing a convenient fence is probably one of the worst ideas that law enforcement has ever come up with. To their credit, some police departments figured this out themselves and decided to stop.

IT'S EASIER TO SELL STOLEN GOODS TO THE POOR

Why do low-income areas have more crime, even when their residents are not especially criminally inclined? As Chapter 5 indicated, the answer lies in the tangible features of life for the disadvantaged. Nowhere is this more evident than in their interest in second-class goods.

More Frequent Temptations

Sutton's (1998) work found that those in low-income areas were about as likely as anybody else to turn down offers of stolen goods. But they were offered stolen goods more frequently. Respondents were divided into six areas by socioeconomic status; those living in the upper-class area were offered stolen goods only 7 percent of the time. Those in the lowest-class area were offered stolen goods 17 percent of the time. What they say about their neighbors may offer a better indicator. Only 9 percent of those living in the highest-status areas believe that "quite a few" or "a lot" of their neighbors have stolen goods in their homes. For the lowest socioeconomic group, 38 percent think that.

To interpret these data as proof that poor people are more "criminally inclined" completely misses the point. Poor people are clearly more inclined to favor used and secondary merchandise for economic reasons. Add this to the points made in several earlier chapters; you now have a much better understanding of why low-income areas can have higher crime rates without necessarily having extra crime inclination.

Poverty Areas Offer More Outlets for Second-Class Goods

The consequence is that poverty areas have more outlets for second-class goods. And second-class goods provide more chances to unload stolen goods. As you drive through the low-income swath of a city, you may notice stores selling used appliances, pawnshops, sidewalk merchants, and signs stating "discounts," "seconds," "reductions," "liquidation," or the equivalent words in other languages. A city provides additional outlets for used merchandise, parts, or commodities including scrap rubber dealers, auto parts shops, auto body shops, retread tires, scrap metal dealers, car wrecking services, used car lots, junk dealers, and plumbing fixtures. There may also be stores advertising "We buy gold and diamonds." Many low-income areas also have street merchants offering used goods to crowds on the street, selling every kind of used product, from an old fan to an old book or cheap, chipped plates. As a result, items are stolen there that would be passed over in the suburbs. All of these could be outlets for stolen goods or provide means for camouflaging these goods among other items. It does not really matter who knows the goods are stolen; the point still holds.

The car lots in the central city sell only used models. Older cars need more replacement parts, which then become more valuable. That makes the cars targets of car-part theft while giving their owners an incentive to steal parts or to purchase those stolen by someone else.

Even if some middle-class people would like the savings from buying second-class goods with their low markup, secondary stores cannot easily afford to move into a higher-rent district. Low-income areas solve the problem by offering low-rent storefronts. Exhibit 9.2 puts all this together, showing how a low-income area can pull in crime by providing both buyers of second-class goods and places to sell them.

The previous chapter explained crime multipliers in general. But such multipliers are important for understanding extra crime on the other side of the tracks. The Poverty-Area Crime Sequence helps explain how fencing opportunities can bring more than property crime to low-income urban areas:

- The poverty area provides customers and outlets for second-class goods.
- That encourages property offenders to be active in a poverty area.
- Proceeds from these property offenses assist drug purchases and drug sales there.
- More serious offenses follow and proliferate in the poverty area, derived from its stolen goods market.

Many features of poor neighborhoods increase crime opportunity there, as several other chapters indicate. The current chapter shows how markets for stolen goods can enhance those problems. You can see that middle-class people have made a major contribution to the "moral order of suburbs" by refusing to buy second-class things from a shabby store or car lot with no warranty offered. If the United States, like Japan, exported all used cars after three years, we would save ourselves a lot of crime.

Exhibit 9.2   Poverty Pulling in Crime

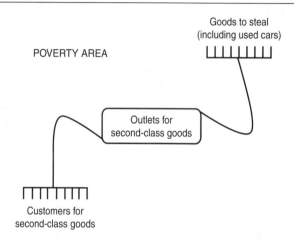

NEW AVENUES FOR STOLEN GOODS

As the routine activities of life change, so do the opportunities for buying and selling stolen goods. The Internet has changed the face of a lot of our everyday behavior, such as researching a half-forgotten fact or newspaper story, looking up a business in the Yellow Pages, and printing maps and directions to a friend's party. It has also affected stolen goods markets. Sites like eBay, Craigslist, and literally hundreds of others serve as the middleman for fencing stolen goods. The trend is so new that there is little criminological research about it, but some scholars have termed this phenomenon e-fencing (Spencer, 2011). Websites are used to advertise and sell personal and other used or new items with no questions asked and almost no personal interaction.

Many Internet sites sell products to the highest bidder, whereas others exchange goods, such as gold and jewelry, through the mail for cash. The anonymity of the Internet and the fact that thieves can often get 70 percent of the retail value of the product make this a very lucrative way to fence stolen goods (Sherman, 2009). The anonymity also attracts buyers who would not likely be offered stolen goods in the streets of low-income areas. Over the Internet, buyers are actively seeking "a good deal"—not knowing or even having to think about whether they are buying stolen property.

Thinking back to the crime triangle, in this situation, the Internet and these websites are the "places" where the process is initiated and the US Post Office or other mail delivery service completes the transaction. Regulating these practices is very difficult because the Internet has no clear structure or ownership and is ever-changing and growing. However, in recent years, several legislative bills have been introduced at the federal level in the United States to address these issues. One of these bills is called the E-Fencing Enforcement Act of 2009, H.R. 1166, sponsored by United States Congressman Bobby Scott (Democrat–VA; https://www.congress.gov/member/robert-scott/1037). The bill is summarized as follows:

> E-fencing Enforcement Act of 2009—Amends the federal criminal code to impose a duty on any online market provider to disclose the contact information (i.e., name, telephone number, and address for service of legal process) of any high-volume seller who has listed goods or items for sale on such provider's online marketplace that match the description of stolen goods listed in a signed report from a criminal law enforcement agency. Defines "high-volume seller" as any person who, through an online marketplace, sells or offers for sale in a single offering goods or items worth more than $5,000, or more than $12,000 in one or more offerings during the preceding 365 days.
>
> Requires an online market provider to: (1) retain contact information on high-volume sellers for three years; and (2) deny high-volume sellers access to the marketplace if such provider has good reason to believe that such sellers acquired their goods unlawfully. Allows high-volume sellers to bring a civil action to challenge the denial of access to an online marketplace.

Unfortunately, this bill seems to be bottled up or dying within a congressional committee.

CONCLUSION

The market for stolen goods is very important. It is difficult to control because it fits within a larger market for second-class goods. Recently, that market has expanded with the Internet. While electronic purchases have shrunk the opportunity for shoplifting, they have widened the opportunity for fencing stolen goods. You can see again that crime feeds on a larger system of activities. You are embedded within a system of temptations beyond stealing things yourself. The average citizen has an incentive to buy second-class goods for a good price and to avoid asking tough questions when someone offers a good deal. Even a person who does not directly participate in buying stolen goods may easily receive them by accident, or share their usage. Citizens in many walks of life are more intertwined with criminal behavior than they like to admit.

MAIN POINTS

1. Stolen goods markets are much more important than previously thought and could be the driving force for property crime.

2. The offender depends on the public to buy stolen goods—sometimes directly. Many people have been offered goods they knew or thought were stolen.

3. Used goods and second-class merchandise help camouflage stolen goods. Poor people are more likely to use secondhand stores and be offered stolen goods.

4. Police stings can backfire by creating the opportunity for easily selling the stolen goods.

5. The Internet has created an entirely new and expansive system for selling stolen goods.

PROJECTS AND CHALLENGES

Interview project. Interview someone from the wholesale or retail goods sector. Without talking about crime, find out how and why goods are rejected by or shipped away from first-line stores and where they end up.

Media project. Look for advertisements in the newspaper or on TV that could conceivably involve stolen goods. What makes you suspicious of some but not others?

Map project. Pick a part of a city. Map out an area containing several possible outlets for stolen goods, even if the buyers and sellers might not know they are stolen. Show where the outlets are on the map and discuss.

Photo project. Photograph six store signs that seem to invite thieves to unload stolen goods. Discuss.

Web project. On the Internet, find five websites that conceivably could be used to sell stolen goods. What about the way the websites work would make it easy to conduct this type of crime? Discuss.

10

SITUATIONAL CRIME PREVENTION

Great Britain's Home Office is roughly equivalent to the US Department of Justice. Within
this agency was a small research unit, located during
the 1970s at Romney House on Marsham Street, a
five-minute walk from Scotland Yard. There, in 1973, a
31-year-old research officer named Ron Clarke (pictured
here) had just completed a study of why youths abscond
from borstals (American translation: why juvenile
delinquents run away from a youth facility).

Clarke realized that the usual social science ideas did not successfully
explain why some boys ran away whereas others stayed put. Most boys ran
away on weekends when staffing and supervision were light. Because these
were not prisons and staff members were not guards, their influence was largely
informal. Adults by their mere presence could prevent a certain amount of trouble, including absconding. With these results, Clarke began to think of crime in
general as the result of human situations and opportunities (P. Mayhew, Clarke,
Sturman, & Hough, 1976). This chapter is based on his efforts to reduce crime
around the world using very fast, simple, and practical methods. He earned
the 2015 Stockholm Prize in Criminology for this body of work.

Ron Clarke is the father of *situational crime prevention*—a set of techniques for slicing away at crime. His work has been used around the world by
police, local agencies, armies, and private industries, all seeking to control illicit

behavior. His work has helped understand a wide range of problems, including shoplifting, barroom violence, terrorism, and child molestation. He has also worked closely with Herman Goldstein, the developer of "Problem-Oriented Policing," and with Mike Scott, the professor at University of Wisconsin Law School and former police chief, who developed the remarkable crime prevention website www.popcenter.org.

Clarke was appointed head of the Research and Planning Unit of the Home Office in London. These government offices usually put out boring reports or fund universities to do that for them. But Clarke was different. He developed his own version of practical crime research and theory. The question Clarke always would ask is, "Will it reduce crime?"

But the answer to that question is connected to a major problem: the displacement hypothesis, which argues that preventing specific crimes here will "simply drive them elsewhere." If the displacement hypothesis were correct, local policing and specific crime prevention efforts are hopeless tasks. According to the displacement hypothesis, such specific efforts are trivial, since they leave intact the underlying causes of crime. However, Clarke carried out and collected a good deal of research evidence indicating that the displacement hypothesis is largely false. This evidence means that it is possible for problem-oriented policing and situational crime prevention to reduce overall crime, not merely to push crime from here to there.

FOUR NATURAL EXPERIMENTS

One of Clarke's greatest talents is discovering "natural experiments" in crime reduction. Sometimes a new law, policy, or business decision produces a great change in crime rates. Clarke found several of these examples and told their scientific story. We begin this chapter by telling several of these stories.

The Motorcycle Helmet Story

Don't listen to the motorcyclists who keep complaining about laws that force them to wear helmets. Not only do helmets save lives, but (as Clarke discovered) *helmet laws lead to great declines in motorcycle thefts.* Many motorcycles are stolen on the spur of the moment for joyriding. A youth walks by a shiny motorcycle but has no motorcycle helmet with him at the time.

In the past he could steal it anyway. But after helmets are required, a motor-cyclist without a helmet is immediately suspected. Enacting and enforcing motorcycle helmet laws causes motorcycle thefts to go down and stay down. These reductions do not displace thefts to other vehicles (P. Mayhew, Clarke, & Eliot, 1989). After Texas enacted its universal helmet law, motorcycle thefts in 19 Texas cities decreased 44 percent in two years (Insurance Institute for Highway Safety, 2008). We see that something very simple and focused can bring down crime.

The Gas Suicide Story

British kitchens not too long ago cooked with coal gas. It was rather dirty and very toxic. That's why a common British suicide method was to turn on the "cooker" and stick your head in for a short time. But then the British and Norwegians discovered new energy in the North Sea, including relatively cleaner natural gas. Although the newer gas can blow up the whole neighbor-hood, it's not very efficient for killing oneself. After discovery of North Sea gas, British suicide rates went down markedly, with little substitution of other suicide methods.

In the United States, a common suicide method was to turn on the car and close the garage door, with death resulting from the toxic fumes. After auto-emission laws changed, toxic agents (including lead) were removed or reduced. This form of suicide then declined in relative numbers and was not substantially displaced to other forms of suicide (Clarke & Lester, 1987).

The Double-Deck Bus Story

The British have shifted away from traditional double-deck buses with conductors who collect the fare. In the old buses, a conductor would ascend the stairs to the upper deck to collect fares and thus serve as a guardian against the crime of vandalism. However, today's British buses are often single deck, and remaining double-deckers seldom have conductors to watch and make sure people follow the rules.

Clarke discovered another natural experiment—some companies had removed the conductor to save money, whereas other companies had not done so. Those buses still served by conductors had less vandalism, but they also had more assaults on conductors. This is an instance of how crime prevention can *sometimes* backfire, solving one crime but leading to another. But most often displacement does not occur, or is only partial (as illustrated later in this chapter with Exhibit 10.1). Denying opportunity not only helps reduce crime and suicide, but it even applies to rule-breaking in sports.

The Water Polo Story

One of my former students was an experienced water polo player and coach. People cheat a lot in this sport, since officials have trouble seeing and punishing underwater fouls. Common illegal techniques (*iSport*, 2014) include:

- *The grab-and-go.* Keeping your arms underwater, yank the defender behind you and use the momentum from the pull to get a head-start toward the goal.
- *Suit-grabbing.* Grab a defensive player's suit around the hips and use it to keep the opponent too low to do anything to stop your team.
- *Wrist-grabbing.* Grab to keep the opponent low to the water. So the referee won't see you, be careful to let go if the other player raises the hand above the water level.
- *Kicking.* Use your normal kick to disguise an illegal kick at the opponent, to keep him away from you.

Some years ago, swimming pool chemicals were primitive and water was murkier than today. Water polo violations included putting your hand into the opponent's bathing suit to grab him at a crucial moment in the game. However, chemicals have made pool water much more transparent. Water polo still involves cheating, but officials today have a better chance to spot it. Although this example derives from sports, it fits a larger pattern—that people with an incentive to break the rules can be stimulated or inhibited by features of daily life. Some of these features can be changed to make things better.

SITUATIONAL CRIME PREVENTION AND CRIME ANALYSIS

After studying examples such as those above, Clarke wanted to develop a systematic method for reducing crime under many circumstances, at low cost and with quick impact. The following lists summarize the strategy that he sorted out:

How to Think About Criminology

- Avoid grand theories.
- Focus on crime events and situations, not variations among individuals or social groups.
- Don't look for a general motivation for all crime; instead, find the specific motive for specific crimes.
- Don't expect displacement, unless you really see evidence that it happened.

How to Think About a Crime

- Focus on very specific crime types, such as "car theft to strip parts."
- Think like a thief. Find out what's on her mind, what she wants.
- Find out *exactly how* the offender does the crime.
- Learn what tools or "facilitators" offenders need, so you can deny these.

How to Gather Information About a Crime

- Describe crime patterns carefully, including time of day and day of week.
- Interview real offenders, and ask them exactly how they do it.
- Look for natural experiments (mentioned earlier in this chapter).
- Do preventive experiments to see what works.

How to Organize Your Information

- Build science step by step from small studies.
- But look for *big effects* in these small studies; forget the little differences.
- Use very simple statistics and charts.
- Make sure practitioners can use at least some of your information.

How to Act Against Crime

- Don't seek prevention "in the long run"; work on the short run.
- Prevent very specific crime types, such as "thefts from downtown parking areas."
- Use your knowledge about what the offender needs to keep him from doing the crime.
- Find cheap and simple crime reduction methods.

These ideas are neatly summed up in his free online booklet, *Crime Analysis for Problem Solvers in 60 Small Steps* (Clarke & Eck, 2005). It includes a famous chart that sums up 25 techniques for carrying out situational crime prevention. That chart is available at www.popcenter.org, and you should study it on your own. It is a source of many term papers and dissertations, as well as a normal tool for police and city planners. To oversimplify the chart, there are three basic methods to interfere with the offender. Make his efforts

1. more difficult,
2. more risky, and
3. less rewarding.

Hundreds of case studies, available at www.popcenter.org, illustrate how these principles are applied. Perhaps we could sum up his approach in two phrases: "Don't get fancy" and "Make it work!"

Three surprises have emerged from this process.

- *The surprising magnitude of crime reduction.* The first surprise is that situational crime prevention *reduces crime by such great magnitudes*, often from 30 to 100 percent.
- *The surprising diversity of applications.* The next surprise is that situational crime prevention and routine activity theory apply to *such diverse crime problems*, ranging from theft from porches to piracy at sea.
- *The scientific bonus.* Situational prevention was designed mainly to reduce crime, but it also gives us a scientific bonus. The extra practical knowledge about crime helps improve theory and accumulate *basic* knowledge about crime for future use.

The next sections talk about some of these surprises.

DIVERSE APPLICATIONS OF SITUATIONAL CRIME PREVENTION

Long before Ron Clarke systematized situational crime prevention, people were using it. The cliff-dwelling Indians in the American West built homes in cliffs for security. From cowboys in the past to today's ranchers, people were not completely at home on the range. I had a wonderful visit to the National Cowboy and Western Heritage Museum in Oklahoma City; after that, Professors Shawna Cleary and Rashi Shukla at the University of Central Oklahoma collected several examples of situational crime prevention in the Wild West (see Cleary, Shukla, & M. Felson, 2014). Ranchers branded cattle to discourage theft. The invention of barbed wire changed the West, keeping cattle from straying and then being stolen. Ranchers also used pens to keep their horses from fighting. They not only relied on watchdogs, but burros, bulls, and long-horn cattle discouraged intruders, ranging from coyotes to humans. Now I turn to some modern urban examples.

Refusing to Accept Subway Graffiti

For many years, the subway trains of New York City were covered inside and out with graffiti and surely were among the ugliest anywhere. The transit system was in chaos, ridership was dropping, and employee morale was low. Increased arrests failed to correct the problems.

Then the New York City Transit Authority figured out that youths who painted graffiti mainly wanted to have their work traveling all over town. By cleaning up each transit car's graffiti quickly, New York officials denied them any incentive to paint graffiti. The program was a dramatic success (see Sloan-Howitt & Kelling, 1997).

Other subway systems succeeded, too. The Washington, D.C., subway designed rough surfaces and a gap from the platform to interfere with painting. The Stockholm subway system installed their own art, including mosaics, textured paintings, engravings, and bas-reliefs. Their surfaces were graffiti resistant: some too smooth to absorb paint, others so rough that they absorbed most of the paint. Some surfaces were uneven or covered with grills, or were pre-painted with so many bright colors that graffiti was too difficult to add.

Correcting Cellphone Fraud

Clarke, Kemper, and Wyckoff (2001) documented more than $1.3 billion in cellphone fraud losses during 1995 and 1996. Six technical changes were designed to cut off fraud quickly:

1. Computer profiling to detect strange call patterns

2. Personal identification numbers (PINs)

3. Precall validation by computers

4. Operator checks

5. Radio wave checks

6. Encrypted checks of each phone

These adjustments resulted in a 97 percent cut in cellphone fraud.

Fixing Bad Central City Parking Lots

Car theft is a multifaceted problem with many layers of prevention opportunities. Ron Clarke first studied how Germany required steering wheel locks on all cars, which reduced its car theft rates significantly—without any evidence of displacement. Since that time car locks have become electronic, replacing the old buttons that were so easy to lift with a hanger. The dramatic declines in auto theft are not coincidental.

Given the heavy concentration of auto theft, it makes sense to focus crime reduction on the hot spots. Ron Clarke and Herman Goldstein (2003) noted that a limited number of downtown parking areas in Charlotte, North Carolina, were the worst places to park by far. Then they began working with the city and its downtown parking companies to reduce the problem. After studying 206 downtown parking areas, they learned that the surface lots were much riskier places to park than the decks. Then they found that the worst lots had bad fencing, poor lighting, and no attendants. They graded the lots A, B, C, and so on, but gave the owners time to improve fencing and lighting before posting the final grade in front of each lot. The net impact was a major reduction in auto theft in the downtown area.

Tackling Pirates

Somalia is a very weak state, with pirates operating from its shores unpunished. They get quite rich attacking one of the world's busiest and narrowest shipping lanes in the Gulf of Aden and the Indian Ocean, forcing the ship, cargo, and crew to the Somali coast, holding it all for ransom. It has succeeded. Police actions have not succeeded, although recently President Obama organized a rather successful military response, cooperating with other governments. Nonetheless, the number of ships and ease of attack are realities.

Most of the attacks occur at night and require 30 to 45 minutes to gain control of the ship (Rengelink, 2012). The pirates attack in fast-moving open skiffs, some of which had also been hijacked. After entering with hooks and ladders (like pirates in the old movies), they intimidate the crew with firearms and grenades then take the ship to their port.

A situational prevention method proved highly effective in reducing piracy to a much lower level. It's simple: The ship owner constructs a *well-reinforced safe room*, allowing the crew to shut the engine, disconnect the electricity, and send out distress signals uncontrolled by the pirates. A military response knows that anybody in view is a hostile target. The safe unit protects ship and crew while help is on the way—and it works quite well.

Reducing Shoplifting

Shoplifting is a huge problem for business, but it has more impact on larger society than many people realize. Many drug abusers fund their habits through shoplifting, and it is the entry crime for many long-term offenders (Clarke & Petrossian, 2012; B. Smith, 2013).

Interestingly, some of the most obvious control techniques do not work very well. This includes store detectives, increasing arrests, shaming first-timers, banning known shoplifters, and launching public information techniques. This is a very good example of why we have to stop focusing on police, guards, and confrontation. Perhaps the most effective methods for reducing shoplifting is (a) to improve store layout and displays, (b) use security technology, and (c) give employees better training in how to make these work. Store layout and displays must make it easier for staff to exercise effective surveillance, but also to check and balance one another to prevent thefts. Don't forget that employee theft exceeds shoplifting. Barry Masuda (1993, 1997) shows that employee theft also can be reduced by anti-shoplifting techniques. Among the small changes that reduce theft rates are these:

- Keeping goods away from entrances and exits
- Reducing the number of exits, blind corners, and recesses
- Creating clear sight lines in aisles and reducing the height of displays
- Eliminating clutter and obstructions
- Moving hot products into higher-security zones
- Speeding up checkout to reduce congestion and concealment

Security technology does not always have to be highly sophisticated. Ink tags work on a simple principle—they ruin the garment someone is trying to steal. The store keeps close watch on the tools that remove the tags, and homemade methods are not very efficient. The use of technology is important, but somebody has to attach the tags correctly, watch the right screens, and know what to do.

The human factor is always the most important. That's why some of the most important controls involve simple improvements in how packages are designed. Crime goes down when smaller but valuable items are packed in large and cumbersome materials that do not fit under a shirt or skirt. One of my favorite examples is the woman's dress shop that alternated the direction of hangers; any thief hoping to grab a bunch of garments would find them locking to the rack.

Making Lights Effective

Lights do not automatically reduce crime. This reminds us that crime is a human process and crime prevention must think about the people who act as offenders, place managers, and guardians.

- If neighbors cannot see your entries, lights can't do much good.
- For very low crime areas, lights can't do much good.
- For daytime crime, lights won't do much *direct* good.

Lights can even backfire, making crime get worse:

- Lights glaring into the eyes of onlookers interfere with guardianship.
- Lighting up an empty building helps a prowler find his way around.
- Lights can help drug dealers to do business outside after dark.

So don't use lights unless you have *a plan that applies to the problem at hand* (Clarke, 2008; Painter & Farrington, 1997; Painter & Tilley, 1999; Pease, 1999).

Lighting can definitely reduce crime. Painter and Farrington (1997) produced a rigorous study, with victim surveys showing a 41 percent reduction in crime in the lighting-enhanced area, compared to a 15 percent reduction in the control area. Clarke (2008) reviews studies in 11 cities in the United Kingdom and the United States.

Keeping Crowds Safe

Big crowds create big problems. This year (2014) police in Ferguson, Missouri, badly mishandled a political demonstration, producing a much worse threat and a national scandal. However, the worst crowd problems are usually non-political. In 1979, the British rock group The Who performed a concert where 11 people were trampled to death. Drunken crowds at a football stadium have beaten up fans and even killed people. Special holiday celebrations can get out of hand, producing major confrontations with police and sprees of violent attack.

Exhibit 10.1   Crime Impact of Improved Street Lighting, 11 Cities

Seven Cities Where Lighting Reduced Crime	
Atlanta, Georgia, USA	Crime reduction with no displacement
Bristol, UK	Crime reduction, displacement unknown
Dudley, UK	Crime reduction with no displacement
Fort Worth, Texas, USA	Crime reduction with possible displacement
Kansas City, Missouri, USA	Crime reduction with some displacement
Milwaukee, Wisconsin, USA	Crime reduction with some displacement
Stoke on Trent, UK	Crime reduction with no displacement
Four Cities Where Lighting Did Not Reduce Crime	
Harrisburg, Pennsylvania, USA	No crime reduction
New Orleans, Louisiana, USA	No crime reduction
Portland, Oregon, USA	No crime reduction
Indianapolis, Indiana, USA	No crime reduction

SOURCE: Clarke, R. V. (2008). *Improved street lighting to reduce crime in residential areas.* Problem Guide No. 8. Washington, DC: U.S. Department of Justice, Office of Community Oriented Policing Services. Accessed July 30, 2014.

It would seem that an unruly mob could only be stopped with brute force. But most of the time that's absolutely wrong.

Ron Clarke (1983) documented how to design less football violence by allowing only a few minutes to buy a bus ticket and no time to get drunk. British football today seldom has the volume of incidents observed before situational prevention was applied. Johannes Knutsson and colleagues studied holiday violence in Sweden, where on Midsummer's Holiday thousands of people have been known to get drunk and run wild. By organizing activities to channel the holiday spirit, the Swedish authorities were able to maintain reasonable control and problems declined greatly (Bjor, Knutsson, & Kuhlhorn, 1992).

The Los Angeles Dodgers know well that limiting alcohol sales is highly effective for crowd control, and the point is well recognized among facility managers of major baseball and football stadiums. Many sports teams encourage women to attend and welcome families, which is good for sales as well as security. Family-based crowds produce fewer problems than those dominated by young males—just what you would expect from what you learned in Chapters 4 and 6.

The most common forms of spectator aggression are

- aggressive words or gestures,
- vandalism,
- throwing things,
- physical attacks on individuals, and
- crowd swarming (as occurred in the concert discussed at the start of this section). (Knutsson, 2000; Madensen & Eck, 2008; Madensen & Knutsson, 2011)

These problems respond to better design, including barriers to keep rival teams apart or to separate fans from players. Every professional athlete knows which stadium makes it easier to throw missiles at them and hit the target.

Crowds are not automatically wild. William Sousa and Tamara Madensen (2011) studied how the Las Vegas Police Department carries out crowd control. Las Vegas has the second largest New Year's celebration in America and has had some very bad problems. The police introduced new moveable barricades on Las Vegas Boulevard, and changed the barricade position as the night wore on.

6:00 p.m. Street closed, pedestrians on sidewalks, police are scattered in the middle section of the street itself.

7:00 p.m. Crowd growing. Police move barricades to widen pedestrian area and relieve crowding, while giving themselves less street space.

8:00 p.m. Crowd even larger. Police move barricades to give pedestrians even more space, but stay within the middle in a smaller lane.

Thus, the conflicts within the crowd and between the crowd and police were minimized.

Protecting Women's Purses in Public

Clarke and Newman (2005) collected an entire volume of evidence on how product design and development can reduce crime. Three universities have become involved in this process:

- University College London (http://www.ucl.ac.uk/scs/)
- University of the Arts, London (http://www.designagainstcrime.com/)
- University of Technology and Science in Sydney, Australia (http://www .designingoutcrime.com/)

Among the product designs are more secure pocketbooks and purses that are easier to clutch, with straps harder to cut. Also bar or restaurant clips help place women's purses where they are less easily taken and hook them to thwart the thief. Designers have produced chairs with grooves built in to hold pocketbooks in front. The product design field ranges from automobiles harder to steal to metro trash bins inhospitable to concealed bombs. Keep on the lookout for new developments in this area.

Improving Teenage Hangouts

Teenage convergence settings are a widespread problem. Vandalism, fights, and other problems often occur at or near teen hangouts, partly because co-offending is so important in early and mid-adolescence (Andresen & M. Felson, 2010). Disorderly youths in public places were addressed in detail by Scott (2001), who noted how much they irritate residents and merchants. Motorized versions of the youth hangout involve cruising around in cars, also irritating other drivers in addition to residents and merchants (Glensor & Peak, 2004). Their speed is either too fast or too slow, but usually not in sync with the other drivers. This is a classic case of conflicting activities and uses of public space.

Suppression of teenagers is the traditional approach to this problem, and it doesn't work very well. Situational prevention offers a better alternative. Two general strategies emerge:

Strategy A. Set aside an area for teenagers to hang out or cruise, trying to minimize damage and conflict with other segments of the population.

Strategy B. Try to swamp teenage areas with non-teenagers, not necessarily driving them out but certainly lowering their dominance.

I prefer Strategy A. In 1992, a city councilman in Arlington, Texas, figured out how to minimize the problems caused by cruising teenagers by arranging with the University of Texas at Arlington a cruising area in one of its large parking lots. He talked to teenagers and learned that they actually wanted some police nearby—but not too many and not too near. They also wanted bathrooms, which the city provided. Earlier problems with crime and traffic congestion were largely averted and everybody was reasonably happy (Bell & Burke, 1992).

As we learned in Chapter 8, one problem may be related to another; solve the other problem, and the crime problem takes care of itself. In this case, the problem was to provide youths with a safer outlet for a social need in the context of the local situation. When this was done, the related crime problems dissipated.

An interesting innovation is "teenage hangout furniture" manufactured for placement in public parks. These steel shelters provide a social configuration for six to 10 youths, often including a right angle. Designs offer a touch of privacy but no more. We have no evaluation of success, but I believe teen hangout furniture will succeed best if located in moderate public view. If too isolated, it will produce drunken behavior. If it gives them no group sense at all, they won't go.

Making Barrooms Safer

On any given weekend night, more than 6,000 people from the surrounding towns and suburbs would go into Geelong, Australia, to socialize and drink alcohol. Some groups, drunk on the streets, would commit thefts or get into fights with one another. A typical pattern was this:

1. Drive to a packaged liquor outlet to purchase beer.
2. Drink beer in the car for an initial effect.
3. Go to the nearest bar for special prices.
4. Move to the next bar for its specials.
5. Go back to the car and drink more.

At this point, some people would use empty bottles as missiles to throw at people or property. The bars not only involved males in these efforts but also gave free drinks to young females to attract males. As the situation got worse, there were attacks on pub personnel and more fights between customers, sometimes on the street outside. (Look back to Chapter 4, where I discussed how bars influence violent escalations.)

Fortunately, bars worried about the money they lost by offering so many specials. That gave police a handle on the situation—along with their power to close bars if they break the law.

The police decided to do something and got the bar owners or managers together with the liquor board. They formulated "The Accord," a set of policies to discourage bar hopping and other alcohol-related problems. It had more than a dozen provisions, but the most important were these:

- Cover charges to enter bars after 11:00 p.m.
- Denial of free re-entry after someone exits
- No free drinks or promotions
- No extended happy hours

- A narrower drink price range
- Enforcement against open containers on the street

The Accord was a success in removing most of the street drinking and pub hopping, while reducing the violence and other crime problems in the central city (M. Felson, Berends, Richardson, & Veno, 1997). I merely did one assessment, but the idea was really invented by a team of clever criminologists and police, including professor Ross Homel at Griffiths University, not far from the Great Barrier Reef (see Graham & Homel, 2008; Homel, Hauritz, McIlwain, Wortley, & Carvolth, 1997). They studied drunkenness and violence around nightclubs in Surfer's Paradise, an Australian tourist resort. Tourists generate a lot of crime victimization and offending alike. The problems and policies that Homel's group discussed, however, can apply to any entertainment district. Among the alcohol policy features considered were:

- No more happy hours or binge-drinking incentives.
- Lower prices for non-alcohol or low-alcohol drinks.
- No more admission of those already drunk.
- Food and snacks for longer hours.
- Smaller glasses of alcohol, and less alcohol per drink.
- Better staff training.

The result was a substantial reduction in drunkenness and violence around the nightclubs. Sadly, some of these innovations were forgotten in subsequent years. Crime prevention is not permanent any more than cleaning the house. You have to keep doing it. But it's better to run a good bar than to run a bad bar and then try to arrest people.

Preventing Drunk Driving

Liquor policies influence not only intentional violence but also drunk driving and any accidental damage to property or people. H. Laurence Ross (1992) gave a brilliant analysis of how liquor policies and abuses are linked to drunk driving and subsequent deaths in his book *Confronting Drunk Driving: Social Policy for Saving Lives*. Ross offered many surprising facts:

- Most drunk drivers involved in accidents or fatalities have never been arrested before for drunk driving. That means that "getting tough" on drunk drivers has its limits for preventing deaths.

- Upping the punishment levels has not accomplished anything in the past and probably will not accomplish anything in the future.
- Modern American society is organized so that it is natural to take cars to the bar and back, hence to drive with a blood alcohol level over the legal limit.

We can prevent drunk-driving deaths and injuries only with more focused policies. These include making roads and cars safer to prevent accidents or reduce the injury from them, or to use the regulatory system to get bars to stop serving people who are already drunk.

Australian and Scandinavian efforts include random breath tests on highways (see Graham & Homel, 2008). In New South Wales, they have learned to give dramatic publicity to their breath testing, not only with media coverage but also by placing at the side of the road a large testing vehicle with a big sign reading "Booze Bus." Even the license plates have these words, helping to get people talking and reminding one another not to mix drinking and driving. The public responds quite well to these efforts and tends to reduce its drunk driving, without many arrests and with no draconian punishment.

American efforts to raise drinking ages and make them consistent among states also have produced a major decline in drunk driving and related injuries and deaths. American society has long had in place rules or laws against drinking in the streets and serving alcohol to those already drunk, and limiting the size and conditions of bars. In addition, a number of civil laws permit sanctions against bar owners and managers, without requiring criminal cases. (For a concise summary of literature and evaluation of strategies for drunk driving, see Scott, Emerson, Antonacci, & Plant, 2006. For a review of how civil law can be used, see Mazzarole & Roehl, 1998; Plant & Scott, 2009.)

Preventing Public Corruption

Public corruption can often be controlled by redesigning procedures, setting up checks and balances, and extending auditing. Sometimes it can even be reduced through access controls. A new area is developing on this very topic, involving researchers in several nations, as well as various international agencies (see Graycar & Sidebottom, 2012).

We know from past research that tightening rules can greatly reduce abuses against both public and private organizations (Knutsson & Kuhlhorn, 1997; Tremblay, 1986). Kuhlhorn (1997) studied how people cheat the government by filling in conflicting information on different forms. Computer comparisons enabled different government agencies to reveal fraud, and the public was told about this to discourage cheating.

Well-designed auditing and accounting systems make it harder for one person to steal money from an organization (see Chapter 12, on specialized-access crimes). For example, when more than one person signs each large check and when independent auditors go over the books, less fraud occurs. Some people still conspire to commit fraud, but the whole idea of designing out fraud is to *require* conspirators for crime to be committed and hope one of them will lose his or her nerve.

Cybercrimes and Abuses

A whole new area for crime has opened up in the past decade or so— Internet fraud and abuse. At the outset some people said that such crimes were unrelated to routine activity theory or to situational crime prevention. That proved false. Internet crime victimizations are very highly concentrated and follow opportunity patterns. Information technology employees have specialized access to passwords and other information (see Chapter 12). Other participants are people who can steal manuals and codes through physical access. However, a good deal of cybercrime depends on traversing cyber obstacles—again with routine activity and opportunity features.

Research repeatedly shows that cyber routines are closely related to cyber victimization. In addition, situational prevention measures work very well in reducing problems. Unfortunately, this topic goes beyond my expertise, so I have to refer you to a dozen studies by others (see Farrell, Clark, Ellingworth, & Pease, 2005; Grabosky, 2001; Holt & Bossler, 2009a, 2009b; Hutchings & Hayes, 2009; Llinares, 2011; Maimon, Kamerdze, Cuiker, & Sobesto, 2013; Marcum, Ricketts, & Higgins, 2010; Navarro & Jasinski, 2012; Pratt, Holtfreter, & Reisig, 2010; Reyns, Henson, & Fisher, 2011; Sampson, Eck, & Dunham, 2010; Yar, 2005).

The vast improvements in software have helped reduce computer viruses and phishing. Internet service providers increasingly screen out scams before they arrive. Software is now designed to help keep passwords more private and to warn people as they open fraudulent e-mails or web pages. Some credit card issuers offer "substitute" or "single-use" credit card numbers—these allow you to use your credit card without putting your real account number online. Entire companies have been created whose main function is to constantly monitor people's credit scores to help protect individuals from serious identity theft (see G. Newman, 2003, 2004; G. Newman & Clarke, 2003).

Thwarting Terror

There are eight elements, which can be remembered with the acronym "Evil-Done," that explain how terrorists pick their targets. They look for targets that are *exposed, vital, iconic, legitimate, destructible, occupied, near, and easy* (Clarke & Newman, 2006). For example, the Twin Towers in New York were highly exposed, the tallest buildings in the area. They were vital for the region and iconic because of their symbolic status. It was legitimate among the terrorists' supporters to attack it. The towers were destructible, but still big enough to be a worthy target. They were occupied, allowing the terrorists to kill a lot of people. More frequently than the Twin Towers, targets of terror are near where terrorists are located and are easy for them to attack.

After an act of terror occurs, there's a tendency to glorify the terrorists' organization and sophistication—the ingenuity fallacy discussed in Chapter 1. But most acts of terror are more ordinary and require rather less expertise than meets the eye. The Twin Towers attackers did not even know how to take off in or land a plane, only how to aim and crash it. For air safety, the reinforcement of cockpits and rules about protecting pilots have been highly effective, along with screening procedures, in reducing hijackings.

Wildlife Crime

Animals don't vote. But they share the environment with humans, and animals often get the worst of it. Laws have been enacted to protect wildlife, perhaps in recognition that they are part of our natural heritage.

Ron Clarke started a new field studying wildlife crime, and he began to apply situational crime prevention to it. The conflict between the human species and the rest of the environment continues to grow with the human population. That includes human-animal conflict. Poaching elephants, killing rare rhinos, taking rare parrots or cactus home—all of these exemplify wildlife crime. Wildlife crime is not at all random. Its location in remote areas makes its control difficult, but not impossible.

Illegal Fishing. Petrossian and Clarke (2014) compared 58 illegally caught fish species with 58 controls. Illegal catches are closer to ports of convenience, more abundant and accessible to nations known for illegal fishing, and are more likely to be included in popular fish recipes. The research recommended more focus on ports of convenience and long-line fishing vessels, and warning consumers which species to avoid.

Parrot Poaching. Ron Clarke (along with Steve Pires and Will Moreto) studied parrot poaching in Bolivia and Mexico. They found that most parrots were gathered from nearby and resold in city markets to relatively local people, not shipped abroad. This means that local application of a market reduction strategy could replenish the parrot species (Clarke & de By, 2013; Pires, 2012; Pires & Clarke, 2011, 2012; Pires & Moreto, 2011). Poaching research demonstrates that crime can be highly symbiotic and interdependent (see M. Felson, 2006). For example, farmers forage for parrots to re-sell, itinerant buyers forage among farmers to find parrots for town markets, and in those markets others shop for illegal parrots in the local marketplace.

Lion and Elephant Poaching. Andrew Lemieux is a researcher at the Netherlands Institute for the Study of Crime and Law Enforcement (NSCR). He spends much of the year in Uganda working with a dedicated but small group of game wardens to protect elephants from ivory hunters carrying machine guns. His Wild Leo Project uses modern computer mapping to track down poachers, using digital cameras with GPS inside to locate poachers' snares and animal carcasses (Main, 2013). The rangers are already skilled trackers, but the statistical maps augment those skills. Elephant poaching is concentrated near roads and amenable to modern crime analysis and situational prevention, as well as law enforcement. In addition, poachers will be photographed at the hunting site and the photograph, which shows the latitude and longitude where it was taken, will be used in court to prove the hunting occurred inside a protected area. The goals of the project are twofold: (1) increase poacher apprehension using crime mapping and analysis techniques and (2) increase poacher conviction rates using better courtroom evidence. Lemieux (2014) has edited a volume on the situational prevention of poaching, including papers on how to protect tigers and other species.

These projects have demonstrated that rural crime is often just as amenable to scientific analysis and situational intervention as urban crime (see Ceccato, 2013).

CONCLUSION

Situational crime prevention offers a broad repertoire for preventing crime here and now, rather than there and eventually. It is verifiable, clear, simple, and cheap. It is available to people of all income groups, seldom treading on civil liberties (see M. Felson & Clarke, 1997). Situational crime prevention bypasses the hardliners and softheads. It is not utopian, but it offers a practical idealism. Situational crime prevention (broadly speaking) offers us our best chance to minimize crime, without interfering substantially or negatively with people's lives. As the repertoire of prevention methods continues to grow, we have a means for slicing away at crime.

MAIN POINTS

1. Situational crime prevention seeks inexpensive means to reduce crime by designing safe settings, effective procedures, and secure products.

2. The idea is to make crime less seductive (i.e., less rewarding), with greater risks and efforts required.

3. Situational crime prevention generally does not displace crime elsewhere. Indeed, crime prevention often leads to a "diffusion of benefits," reducing crime even beyond the immediate setting.

4. Very diverse successes have been demonstrated, from shoplifting to terrorism.

5. Traditional strategies, such as lighting and fences, must be implemented in thoughtful, constructive ways.

6. Crime analysis and prevention works best when highly focused.

7. Many of the old strategies apply to new crime types.

PROJECTS AND CHALLENGES

Interview projects. (a) At the end of Chapter 4, I asked you to interview a bartender, owner, or server about conflicts and escalations. Find another bartender to interview, but this time ask about different bars where he or she has worked and how their design and management affects security. (b) Talk to a retail security person about their crime controls. Ask specific questions about each type of situational crime prevention. What does he or she prefer, use, or ignore?

Media projects. (a) Check out the magazines in the security field. What products are advertised there, and what situational crime prevention methods are left out? (b) Find out whether any car manufacturer has made major efforts to reduce a certain model's vulnerability to theft. Then use the Highway Loss Data Institute pamphlets to see whether its theft rates really declined relative to other models.

Map project. Map out a shopping mall or mini-mall. Where are its weak spots and strong spots from a situational crime prevention viewpoint?

Photo project. Devise a low-cost situational crime prevention method to make a college dormitory more secure from crime. Cover as many types of situational crime prevention as you can, using photos to strengthen your argument.

Web project. Go to www.popcenter.org and read one of the problem guides. Using the response table at the end of a guide, think about which responses are shown to be most effective and which are based on situational crime prevention. Do they overlap?

⊰ 11 ⊱

LOCAL DESIGN AGAINST CRIME

——•◦•——

Local security is founded on two principles:

1. People must be able to supervise very local space.
2. That ability must be assisted by physical design.

Blocking the view interferes with human processes of self-protection and protecting neighbors. It is important to locate buildings, streets, trees, and bushes carefully, since these can obstruct the view and make security worse.

We can elaborate this one step further (see summary in Exhibit 11.1). To supervise a place or space effectively, people must be

a. positioned in close proximity to that location,
b. with direct view of what is happening there, and
c. have a defined responsibility for looking after it.

Thus, effective supervision requires people to be near, to see, and to know or sense their specific duty (see Peel, Reynald, van Bavel, Elffers, & Welsh, 2011; Reynald, 2010a, 2010b, 2010c, 2014).

Unfortunately, there's a lot of wishful thinking on the "secure community" topic. One wishes that everybody in the area would help prevent crime. One wishes that good citizenship would extend to all of the human race. One wishes that everyone will risk their lives to protect a total stranger, or to look after neighbors whose names you do not know. All of that happens sometimes. But you can't depend on it.

Exhibit 11.1   Routine Local Supervision Has Three Components

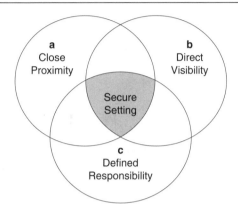

Of course, lots of people will call the police if they see something wrong. But police take a while to arrive. Those who call the police might *feel* like they are good citizens, but they might be shifting the major risks to somebody else.

The words "community," "neighborhood," and "local" exaggerate the extent to which people really can help each other when danger arises. A named community in today's world includes many people who do not know one another, cannot see each other's homes, and have unclear responsibility for doing so. That's not good enough for security.

REMARKABLE RESEARCH ON LOCAL SUPERVISION

Danielle Reynald is a faculty member at Griffith University in Australia. While still a doctoral student in the Netherlands, she developed a remarkable method for studying local risk of crime. It's so simple. She visited each home address, walked up to each door, and checked whether she could see anybody around. If yes, she checked whether they could see her. If yes, she noted whether they *said* anything to her, such as, "What the hell are you doing here?" And then she noted whether they called the police on her (Reynald, 2010c, 2011a, 2011b).

These simple measures of guardianship predicted residential crime. *Seeing nobody there is the best predictor of local crime.* If you see somebody, but they don't see you, that's the second best predictor. If they see you but say nothing, that's the third best. Whether or not they call the police is the least important of the four variables. This helps explain why local design of environments is so important, since building and street design make it easier or harder for people to see what's happening in the very local area. Reynald's method has been replicated in an American city (Hollis-Peel, Welsh, & Reynald, 2012).

These findings are not only intellectually interesting, but also important for policy.

If we design local environments correctly, an intruder is more likely to see people and depart, or else somebody will see the intruder and perhaps say something. So long as somebody is clearly around and appears to be looking, the local risk declines considerably.

Reynald's work also has some very negative implications. It suggests that the vast array of research on "community spirit" is misplaced. No matter how strongly you love your community, you cannot really protect it if you are gone when offenders show up.

Recently Professor Reynald launched another fascinating study, *asking residents in detail how often they look out the window*. Think about how important that is from a crime prevention viewpoint. If nobody looks at the street, local security can only decline. If residents close up their curtains and shutters most of the time, offenders have little to worry about.

Researchers have long known that ugly environments tend to have more crime. Is it possible that an ugly street causes people to close the curtains and avoid looking outside? Maybe that's a central factor in crime prevention: And maybe we can design environments, windows, and streets to maximize visibility and to get people to look.

Do not assume that beauty alone produces lower crime rates. High bushes or trees with low branches may be pretty, but landscaping can *increase* crime by blocking the view of the street, sightlines within the park, or the areas between homes. Students of crime prevention have learned that it is safer to avoid evergreen trees with low branches, and to trim the bushes so burglars cannot conceal an illegal entry. They have learned where to place big trees to avoid assisting attacks. Secure design must always balance aesthetics with practicality. In philosophical terms, we cannot assume that good always leads to good, since beautiful trees can sometimes harm the security of those who plant them.

We can see that security is not a simple matter. If nobody is near enough to watch, that creates crime opportunity. If people are near but cannot see what's going on, that still creates crime opportunity. Even if people are close and can see what's going on, that may not be enough. Even if people like the neighbors and neighborhood, that does not mean they feel definite responsibility to check out every inch of it every day, or that they will see a crime while it is in process. The key to security is to think about the *immediate* environment. *The safest places have people very near most of the time, able to see what's happening, and with a definite responsibility to act against crime.* Human supervision is also very time dependent: your very friendly neighbors cannot help you if your burglar entered early, but they came home late.

OSCAR NEWMAN'S FOUR TYPES OF SPACE

You recall from Chapter 2 that Oscar Newman (1972) divided local space into four categories: *private, semiprivate, semipublic*, and *public*. These are defined in terms of access, not official ownership. Thus a rental apartment is still private space. At the other extreme, a park is public space because it has public access. But a privately owned shopping mall is also public space because the general public has access to it.

Someone has specific responsibility to look after private space, but public space usually has nobody on hand with such responsibility. Police cannot be everywhere or have direct visibility of most public space most of the time. Indeed, it is a mistake to think that "public access" guarantees "public enjoyment," for there are occasions and locations where the toughest guys take over public space for their own purposes. We need all four types of space in our community, but we also need to figure out how to locate them and make them work as they are supposed to.

That's why environmental design is so important (see Zahm, 2007). Newman realized that designs with more private and semiprivate space were also more secure. Designing townhouses with outdoor private gardens creates semi-private space in front; that's much more secure than letting the area be open and unassigned. Designing buildings with only three or four apartments per entry makes each entry a semi-private space. Somebody takes responsibility for locking the door and keeping an eye on it. But when 100 apartments use a single entry door, it becomes much more accessible to the general public. Nobody watches or locks it. Few people can even see it, and offenders figure that out.

It's fascinating that these same design principles apply in both public housing and very wealthy suburbs (Rengert & Wasilchick, 2000). The underlying point is that human supervision, with physical design to support it, makes a local area fundamentally more secure. Such supervision and design is sometimes associated with our idyllic image of village life.

VERSIONS OF A VILLAGE

You recall from Chapter 5 my discussion of the urban village—a small section of an old city where pedestrians are comfortable walking around and city life is vibrant. The urban village is known for relatively low risk of crime. The next section examines the urban village, and later I consider some of its mimics.

The Urban Village: It *Acts* Like a Village

The urban village is not a real village, but it acts like one. It was common in old American cities before 1950, when urban renewal and automotive dominance began to undermine the insular neighborhood. So the urban village is largely a thing of the past—although there are some remnants and imitations today. Its houses were mostly two or three stories high, so residents were physically closer to the street, and could see it. Often an urban village housed people of the same ethnic background, reinforcing local responsibility. Usually very few apartments would share the same entry, so responsibility was not diffused. In historic urban villages,

- women were housewives, staying near home;
- people lacked cars, and traveled on foot;
- people resided many years in the same place; and
- friends and family lived nearby.

If you re-read the list above, you will see why urban villages reinforce human supervision. People in the neighborhood were very near, had clear visibility, and their local responsibility was rather well defined. Now you see why Jane Jacobs (1961) argued against bulldozing old neighborhoods (as I explained in Chapter 5). She pointed out the importance of "eyes on the street," an idea reflected in the points I made in starting this chapter. Unlike the low-rise urban past, high-rise buildings and modern automotive travel locate human eyes farther away from the street and unable to watch it. Yet there are some efforts to bring a village feel, even today.

New Urbanism: It *Looks* Like a Village

New Urbanism is a movement among urban planners and architects to mimic the urban village in a modern context. New Urbanists design houses with porches in front, build a village square, install shops, connect all the streets neatly, and include many foot paths. Examples of New Urbanism developments are Celebration, Florida, and the Cotton District in Starkville, Mississippi. A new urbanism town, Plum Creek, is located in Kyle, Texas, not far from where Mary and I live in Austin (see http://www.terrain.org/unsprawl/23/, accessed October 19, 2014). The movement goes well beyond the United States, and examples are found in the UK, Sweden, France, and elsewhere.

New Urbanism makes a place *look* and *feel* like traditional villages. *Yet its security is not really as good as the urban village or the rural village of the past.* New Urbanists cannot reverse all of history for people living in their developments:

- Their residents still rely on cars and still carry out most activities away from the neighborhood.
- Their female residents still tend to commute to work somewhere else.
- Their front porches don't make people go outside in an air-conditioned world.
- Footpaths between homes assist burglars on foot.
- Interconnected streets help burglars who arrive by car.

Thus, New Urbanism is oversold by the developers and theorists alike. But I have seen some of these towns and would be happy to live there.

Social Cohesion: It *Sounds* Like a Village

In the 1920s and 1930s, the Chicago School of Sociology developed, using Chicago as an urban laboratory. These diverse scholars did not have a single opinion, or even work in the same building or department. But they all used Chicago as an urban laboratory.

In a real laboratory you can add one chemical at a time to the test tubes and see what happens. Unfortunately, a social laboratory has a lot of things going on at once, producing confusion. That confusion goes beyond the capacity of theory or statistical analysis to sort everything out neatly.

One hypothesis that came out of this research (and its followers) is the hypothesis that "social cohesion" drives down neighborhood crime. Unfortunately, both the definition and measurement of "social cohesion" are confusing to all concerned, even the researchers (see review in Hipp & Perrin, 2006).

But they still produce social cohesion scales from responses to such questions as these:

Do you like this neighborhood?

Do you feel attached to this neighborhood?

Do you consider your neighbors to be your friends?

Is this a close-knit neighborhood?

Do people here share the same values?

Can people in this neighborhood be trusted?

Negative answers to such questions "predict" high neighborhood crime, according to these researchers. But which is the cause and which the effect? If you live in a high-crime area, won't you also say that you can't trust your neighbors?

It *sounds* like a cohesive urban village when people say yes to questions such as these. But neighbors in today's world are often *too mobile to deliver local supervision*, even if they feel like doing so. Ask three simple questions:

- Do your friendly neighbors spend most of the weekday away from the immediate area?
- Do your friendly neighbors lack a direct sight line to your windows or doors?
- Do your friendly neighbors really recognize everybody, and are they sure who is an outsider?

The answers depend on how much area is included in the word "neighborhood." If you just mean the houses next door and across the street, you have a good chance for security. But if a neighborhood consists of the nearest thousand people, that's a different matter entirely. Someone who knows a dozen people in the area remains unfamiliar with 988.

For a safe place to live, look for a block with three important human categories:

- retired persons, who spend most of their time nearby;
- homeowners, who have an incentive to protect their investment; and
- long-term residents, who have more stake in the community and recognize more people. (Look back to Exhibit 5.1.)

Sometimes the trendiest part of town is also the least stable, making it very vulnerable to crime. Often the oldest part of town is safer. That's why I've always chosen to live near retired people and long-term residents.

The Village Image and Reality

To sum up the sections above, the urban village is indeed a low-crime solution, but it is not easily applied in a modern society. As modern people leave their neighborhoods in the course of their daily routines, they open themselves up to crime. Thus the village "imagery" can give us a misleading sense of security. Looking and feeling like an urban village does not suffice to produce low crime rates. More generally,

- human supervision is central for security;
- a neighborhood's physical features affect human supervision;
- supervision should be very direct, with defined responsibility;
- retired people, homeowners, and long-term residents have a central role; and
- design is very important for enhancing local control.

For a local area to be secure, it must have people around who can see what's going on. That's why we need to pay close attention to how potential offenders, targets, and guardians move around in the course of a day. The next section focuses on offender movements.

THE OFFENDER-TARGET CONVERGENCE PROCESS

In everyday life, *offenders travel about like anybody else*. Fundamental work by Patricia J. and Paul L. Brantingham (1984, 1998; P. L. Brantingham & Brantingham, 1981, 1999) explained this process. They have a daily awareness space based on where they live, work or go to school, shop, or find entertainment. That awareness space includes the routes they take among those places. Exhibit 11.2 depicts the offender awareness space, and helps organize what we know about offender movements and how they discover crime targets. Offenders find their crime targets near home, near work, near school, near shopping, and near entertainment—as well as along the routes between.

The offender is unlikely to know about or attack crime targets outside that awareness space, even if those are good targets. You can see in Exhibit 11.2 that the set of targets on the left is vulnerable to this offender, while the targets

Exhibit 11.2   The Offender's Awareness Space

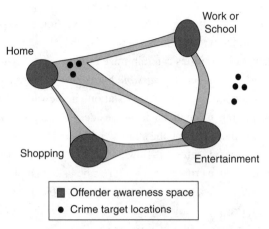

SOURCE: Adapted from a well-known model designed by Patricia L. and Paul J. Brantingham (1993, 1999).

on the right are outside his awareness space. This gives us a simple but general idea to help design places and spaces to lessen crime. Planners, builders, architects, school officials, and university administrators who design places and spaces can help reduce crime while they are doing so. Planners need to pay very close attention to how they locate the best crime targets and the riskiest activities, and where they place the paths people use to get around.

Interestingly, serial killers and sex offenders have patterns. Each has an awareness space and finds targets within it (Beauregard, Proulx, & Rossmo, 2007). Indeed, these offenders in repeating provide us with a map to work backwards and then to find out whom they are.

Risky Mixes

One of the simplest design principles is stated by Crowe and Zahm (1994). Their "mixing principle" tells us to

- place safe activities in unsafe locations, and
- place unsafe activities in safe locations.

Consider the unsafe activity of drawing cash. A bank designer should not place automated teller machines in dangerous spots with little natural surveillance, or where it is easy to jump somebody. On the other hand, it might make sense to put the garbage cans in an alley, since nobody really wants to steal garbage. Similarly, it's a bad idea to put a heavy-drinking bar next to a store where shoplifting is easily carried out. The next section says more about the wrong activities in the wrong places.

Fortunately, safe locations can minimize crime from otherwise dangerous activities. Indeed, it is *sometimes possible to overwhelm unsafe activities with safe ones.* My team studied the subway stations in Newark, New Jersey, and recommended putting a small business beside each of the riskier subway stations to provide more eyes on the street (M. Felson et al., 1990). Urban park managers have located cafes or flower vendors strategically to increase guardianship and reduce crime. Next I offer some bad examples.

We have learned a lot since C. Ray Jeffery (1971) invented the term CPTED—Crime Prevention through Environmental Design. In particular, we have learned that certain land uses mix very badly.

- Do not open a gay bar next to a bikers' bar.
- Do not put a teenage center next to a senior citizen center.
- Do not put a homeless shelter next to a nighttime entertainment district.
- Do not put a high school next to a shopping mall.

The last example is malignant both for the high school and the mall. It's harder to keep teenagers from skipping school when they can easily walk over to the mall. And the mall suffers more shoplifting and problems with teens hanging out.

Today we have much larger crime data files and much more ability to map crimes and land uses. Accordingly, we are learning more each day about risky mixes. Dr. Andrew Newton at the University of Huddersfield is considering the circumstances in which alcohol outlets produce crime. Some drinking establishments and liquor stores do little damage to their communities, but others do a whole lot of damage. The important question to ask is whether an alcohol outlet is dangerously located near other activities, producing disproportionate crime (Newton, 2014).

Risky Fences

Exclusion is a visceral approach to security. It includes building tall and solid walls to exclude outsiders. Exclusion might reflect fear of strangers (xenophobia) and racial profiling. It can even produce a "fortress society" in which fear and exclusion are the central organizing feature of daily life. Perhaps the most important problem with exclusion is that stereotypes are so inefficient. Most of the local crime is done by the local boys or those just over the hill, not those from far away.

Robert Frost wrote that "Good fences make good neighbors." So what are good fences? To answer that question, consider that fences can be

- solid—difficult to scale and impossible to see through;
- transparent—difficult to scale but easy to see through; or
- symbolic—easy to scale but conveying to others that an area is private or assigned.

Each type of fence has its place. However, walls can backfire and make things worse if constructed without thinking about why. Many youths can climb over a wall; after entering the perimeter, the wall blocks anyone outside from viewing their final entry into the home.

We learn from Oscar Newman that symbolic fences can send a simple signal that this is your yard, thus reducing crime on the street for most purposes. Indeed, a symbolic fence is low enough to allow easy visibility of the street. In contrast, a solid wall creates a cavernous street and enhances the crime risk when residents go outside. A transparent fence, such as one made of chain link or iron grill, can greatly enhance security while neighbors maintain visibility. This process of "territorial reinforcement" is kinder and gentler than a walled city, but it still makes the point that you don't just walk into someone else's space without asking.

The same wall that keeps others out keeps you walled in. The same wall that makes the inside safer makes the street in front of your house worse. Thus, exclusion often backfires. Yet good fences in the right place can produce more private and semiprivate space, making our local environments more secure for everybody.

Risky Housing

If you like living dangerously, pick a home where cars are parked out of your sight and easily stolen. Pick a home where neighbors cannot see each other's windows or doors, hence cannot notice intrusions. Creative, modern street layouts often make it harder to supervise the street and for neighbors to protect one another.

Designers have better choices. The human race has never discovered a better urban orientation than square or rectangular houses lined up on a street and opening to the front.

Exhibit 11.3   Traditional Layout: Houses on Street With Good Sight Lines

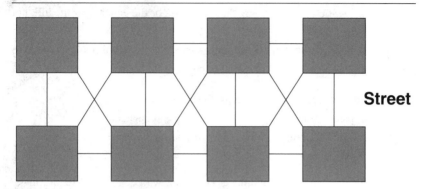

SOURCE: Adapted from Poyner, B., & Webb, B. (1991). *Crime free housing*. Oxford, UK: Butterworth, p. 99.

Exhibit 11.3 shows what it looks like, and how good the sight lines really can be. That's why good design makes sure that

- front windows face those across the street;
- side and back gardens or yards are modestly fenced;
- street parking is in the front;
- garages, if present, are on the side near the front entrance, and open carports up front (Poyner, 1998; Poyner & Fawcett, 1995; Poyner & Webb, 1991); and
- bushes do not hide entries, so break-ins are visible.

Poyner helped start a movement that lasted after his death—a fitting memorial. The *Secured by Design* movement in Britain (www.securedbydesign.com) advises architects, licenses and grades housing developments, and sets standards to make housing more secure. Armitage and Monchuk (2009) evaluated 16 approved housing estates in great detail over time. Using crime measures they found dramatic reductions in crime compared to other estates. This is proof that design makes a difference.

SEVEN STUDIES IN REDUCING LOCAL CRIME

To illustrate the diversity of designing out crime, I offer seven case studies. Do not worry about the order these are presented. Just use them to broaden how you think about crime and its reduction.

Alleygating in London

Alleygating refers to installing security gates and fences to block foot-paths and alleys along or behind buildings. The purpose is to reduce the opportunity to burgle or steal, usually in a residential area. Alleygates reduce access to target areas or windows leading into them. Once alleys are gated, keys to unlock them are provided only to residents (Johnson & Loxley, 2001).

Alleygates have become widespread across Britain and are serving to reduce crime in several cities and thousands of homes. Bowers, Johnson, and Hirschfield (2004) found a 30 percent drop in burglary after alleygates were installed behind residences and apartment buildings.

Designing Out Drive-By Shootings

Some years ago, Los Angeles experimented with creating some cul-de-sacs in a very dangerous local area with lots of drive-by shootings. When streets were blocked off without much thought, they achieved relatively little. When some streets were closed to cars on a strategic basis—calming traffic but still allowing a natural flow—drive-by shootings declined noticeably (Lasley, 1998). This points to a general lesson of designing out crime: be attuned to local facts and realities.

Critics of closing streets often say this is a method for excluding people, but to reduce crime, street redesign does not have to exclude people at all. There are simple ways to slow down traffic and reduce residential crime risk without closing off streets. Traffic engineers call these techniques "traffic calming." People often have vast differences of opinion about traffic calming. Younger people who have no children are on the go and usually do not want to slow down. Older people who have young children like the idea, especially because the slower traffic is less likely to run over or scare their children. This alerts us to the complexity of crime prevention in practice and the many choices we must make. It also reveals the importance of many alternatives, just in case one solution leads to another problem that's worse.

Whatever your opinion, traffic calming techniques have been shown by research to be particularly effective in reducing speeding in residential areas (Scott, 2001) and are a way to reduce some types of crime at very little monetary cost. Common methods that affect the psychology of speeding include narrowing roads, adding markers that make a road feel narrower, and planting trees along roadsides.

Disney World Security

Disney World organizes visits in great detail. From parking lot to train to monorail to park and back, activities are planned to minimize risk of accident or crime. Disney World embeds its control processes in other processes, so they are barely noticed. For example, entry into most exhibits occurs only within a vehicle controlled by Disney personnel. The Disney people may have been the first to use rails to wrap their lines back and forth. That encourages people waiting in line to engage in conversations, creates more adult monitoring of teenagers, and reduces rowdiness (Shearing & Stenning, 1997). In more recent years, Disney allowed each group of visitors to register their place electronically and then do something else while waiting their turn. This is an interesting use of technology to enhance security.

The most important lesson of Disney planning is that almost all visitors to Disney World are quite contented with the way their visit is managed and comply voluntarily. We learn that crime prevention can be most effective when it is incidental. Of course, people are not spending the rest of their lives in Disney World, so there's not much reason to rebel.

Secure Convenience Stores

Small stores with late hours are very vulnerable to robbery, especially when located near freeways. In some cases, employees or customers have been injured or murdered in the process. One large convenience store chain, 7-Eleven, hired convicted robbers to help redesign stores and reduce holdups. The statistical results indicated definite success (see Duffala, 1976; see also Altizio & York, 2007; Matthews, 2002; C. Mayhew, 2000). The key measures included:

- channeling all customers through one front door;
- removing advertising from windows for street visibility into the store;
- moving cash registers to the front for street visibility; and
- installing timed-access drop safes so robbers can't get more than a few dollars.

The result was a substantial reduction in robberies.

A Safer Subway System

Nancy LaVigne (1996, 1997) offers a remarkable account of the design of the Washington, D.C., subway system. That system is almost the opposite of the old systems in America. Its stations are voluminous and have excellent "sight lines." In other words, it is difficult for an offender to act or escape unseen. Entries are visible, and pedestrians are funneled into spaces where they can provide mutual informal protection. The net effect is a remarkably low crime rate, even though the subway is located within a high-crime city. The main crime problems are in the parking lots outside the suburban stations, where cars are targets of crime.

The World's Largest Bus Terminal

New York City got rid of 70 percent of the crime inside the Port Authority Bus Terminal (M. Felson et al., 1996). There were already more than 100 police officers assigned to the building, and they could not hope to control the place. Homeless people lived there. Elderly people hung out there. People with psychiatric problems came in and out. Rapes occurred there. Drugs were sold and heroin used there. People had sex in the parking garage and elsewhere.

The Port Authority created Operation Alternative, which offered transient people a good variety of social services. They began to put safe activities in unsafe locations, locating flower venders to interfere with drug sale locations. They put unsafe activities into safe locations, concentrating ticket purchases in an uncluttered area, so people taking out their wallets to pay would not have them snatched.

The bus terminal

- removed niches and corners, by filling empty spaces and blocking columns;
- blocked off areas where misbehaviors occurred most often;
- reduced the seating to discourage hanging out;
- replaced the worst stores with known stores that commuters would like;
- designed away sex pickup sites within the building; and
- renovated washrooms so they were no longer used for illegal liaisons.

These changes in design and management restored the Port Authority Bus Terminal and helped transform the Times Square area.

Making University Parking Areas Safe

American university campuses can create a lot of crime. Cars, their contents, or accessories are stolen. Wallets are removed from offices, libraries, and dorms. Electronic equipment is taken. Sometimes, personal attacks occur. Important research on college campus victimization by Bonnie Fisher and her colleagues at the University of Cincinnati (Fisher, Daigle, & Cullen, 2003,

2007) helps confirm the routine activity aspects of student and staff victimization. Fortunately, it is possible to design safer campus.

Take the example of campus parking. These 10 design features can have a dramatic effect on the safety of students and staff:

- Arrange nighttime parking closer to classrooms.
- Close off unneeded parking areas after dark (to concentrate cars and people).
- Require assigned parking stickers, even when parking is free.
- Get visitors in cars to sign in and give them time limits.
- Eliminate nooks and corners in parking structures.
- Build parking structures on slopes for clear sight lines.
- Use glass for stairwells so one can see inside.
- Avoid thick foliage nearby.
- Orient buildings to face parking areas.
- Post signs and organize traffic so neither cars nor pedestrians get lost.

You can see from this list that designing out crime requires you to think big and to think small. I began this chapter with two big principles. But applying those principles requires attention to detail. The payoff is that fewer people fall victim to crime, and fewer get into trouble as offenders.

CONCLUSION

Solid principles guide us in designing out crime in local places. Such principles lead to specific advice and ideas that are accessible to people in every walk of life. With these principles, crime can be sliced away. Evaluations of various crime prevention methods continue to demonstrate that well-focused methods are much more effective than those lacking a clear focus (Clarke & Eck, 2007; Eck, 1997; Weisburd, Telep, Hinkle, & Eck, 2008; Weisburd et al., 2006).

A central theme of crime prevention in this chapter and throughout this book is that crime prevention works more naturally when human activities are divided into smaller and more manageable chunks. Responsibility depends on people in the immediate area, people who are present. Security is not provided by warm feelings alone.

MAIN POINTS

1. Human supervision of very local spaces and places is essential for security.

2. Such supervision depends on close proximity, direct visibility, and defined responsibility.

3. By opening or closing up sight lines, planners and architects have a great deal of impact on crime.

4. Urban villages have low crime rates, but they are not easily replicated in the modern world.

5. Strong community cohesion does not automatically deliver security if friendly neighbors are absent while offenders are present.

6. Offenders operate within their normal awareness space, usually not attacking targets outside it.

PROJECTS AND CHALLENGES

Interview project. Talk to an architect or planner about whether or not crime enters into decisions and designs.

Media project. Find an article about crime in a commercial or downtown area. Does it discuss the physical environment and its effect on the crime? Why or why not?

Map project. Map a park where some people seem to have driven out or scared off others. Who hangs out where and when? Examine how the park relates to the area surrounding it. How are the bushes and trees located and trimmed? What suggestions would you make for redesigning the park for wider and safer use?

Photo project. Take photos of four residential buildings to compare how some invite burglaries more than others. Be sure to take photos of the features you will focus on in your discussion.

Web project. Find a design for a future project (e.g., residential area, high school, city building, commercial complex). Do you think this project will generate more crime or less? Do not be taken in by the pretty picture.

"WHITE-COLLAR" CRIME

———•◦•———

I t makes no sense to classify crimes as "Catholic crime," "Protestant crime," "Black person crime," or "Hispanic crime." So why should we have a special category of "white-collar crime"? We should never define a type of crime by the people who might do more of it, least of all the color of their collars or skin. Instead, check the specifics of what the offenders actually do. Then figure out what these specific illegal actions have in common.

When Edwin Sutherland (1939) coined that term, only a small percentage of the public had white-collar jobs. Sutherland made a good point: middle-class and upper-class people also commit crimes, and sometimes steal or cheat vast amounts. However, white-collar workers are now a majority of the labor force, not elites. Moreover, the finagling we associate in our minds with white-collar crime is not really that different from tricks by blue-collar workers, such as those auto mechanics who charge for services not rendered, industrial work-ers who pilfer at the plant, or restaurant workers who scam the customers or owners (Benson & Simpson, 2009; Crofts, 2003; Greenberg, 2002; Kidwell & Martin, 2005; Locker & Godfrey, 2006; Payne & Gainey, 2004; Rickman & Witt, 2003).

White-collar crime implies elite crime by skilled offenders, involving vast amounts of money. However, this longstanding impression was debunked by Professors David Weisburd, Elin Waring, and Ellen Chayet (2001). Their study showed that most white-collar crime cases involve a few thousand dollars, not millions. Most cases involve small companies or employees, using rather simple methods. Although high-level white-collar offenses can do dramatic damage, those are the exceptions rather than the rule. Most organizational and occupational crimes are "relatively mundane, unskilled, easily accomplished, and modest in economic return" (Wright & Cullen, 2000, p. 863). Such offenders are not really that clever. They commit ordinary thefts or abuses while nobody is looking (Benson & Simpson, 2009; Weisburd et al., 2001). Is it really so fancy to pilfer accounts, make off with equipment, shortchange customers, write yourself a check, or to pressure an employee for sex? What irritates me most about the traditional treatment of white-collar crime is the implication that it is fancy and advanced, rather than something simple and crass.

To be sure, many white-collar offenses do involve very large losses, well documented by Terry Leap (2007, 2011). This includes a vast array of medical insurance fraud by doctors and other health professionals, and numerous varieties of scams and false billings. However, the tactics used by the offenders, and the offenders themselves, are extremely diverse. It makes no sense to continue using "white collar" as the defining feature. Indeed, white-collar crime experts themselves have long complained about their own term and the confusion it produces (Friedrichs, 2006; Geis & Meier, 1977; Wheeler, 1983). In this chapter I seek to gain clarity by taking a different approach.

Exhibit 12.1   How Offenders Get to Their Targets

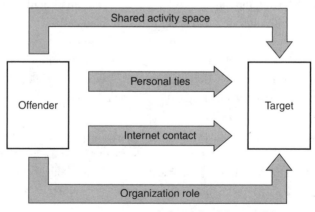

* *Specialized-Access Crimes*

HOW OFFENDERS GET TO THEIR TARGETS

Two principles guide this chapter. First, white-collar crime fits *within* the larger system of criminal behavior. Second, that system is structured by *how the offender gets to the target of crime.* This can happen in four ways, depicted in Exhibit 12.1.

> *Shared activity space.* Many offenders carry out their own routine activities in the same places as their victims. This overlap helps the offender to find access. For example, boys in the neighborhood pass by when nobody is home, quickly realizing they can break into a house.
>
> *Personal ties.* Offenders learn about crime targets through their personal networks. For example, a burglar learns from common acquaintances who is leaving on vacation, using that information to pick a time for the burglary.
>
> *Internet or other communications.* Some offenders set up meetings via the Internet and take advantage of those they contact, or call to see who's home before breaking into a house.
>
> *Organizational roles.* Some offenders abuse their specialized organizational roles to gain information or other access to victims. For example, a postal worker may learn whose mail is held during a vacation, then share that information with a burglar.

The asterisk on the diagram alerts you to the fact that, for specialized-access crimes, offenders abuse their occupational roles to get to the targets. More examples follow: An attorney pilfers the money in a trust fund he administers for an elderly widow. An unethical psychologist talks his client into having sex with him. A contractor fakes an insurance claim. A building inspector shakes down owners in return for building permits. An auto mechanic lies about how much work he did on your car. A cashier shortchanges a customer. A meter reader notes which residents are away and when. A corporate executive misleads his shareholders about the value of their stock. A vast variety of such violations have been documented (Friedrichs, 2006; Leap, 2007, 2011).

In each example, somebody uses an occupational or professional role to gain specialized access to the victim, and then commits a crime. An information technology employee has access to passwords and then breaks into accounts. A stockroom job brings a chance to pilfer. Responsibility for control of checks gives a chance to misuse them. The city building inspector can solicit bribes. Work roles and positions in organizations explain all these crimes and more. This generalization covers such diverse offenses as fixing prices, shortchanging customers, cheating pension funds, faking insurance claims, fiddling expense accounts, dumping toxic wastes, abusing prisoners, mistreating patients, manipulating stocks, and enticing bribes (Friedrichs, 2006; Gill, 2000b; Leap, 2007, 2011). In each case the offender abuses a particular work role, profession, or organizational position.

CRIMES OF SPECIALIZED ACCESS

To reduce confusion I propose a new term: *crimes of specialized access.* Such criminal acts are defined by one key requirement: abusing one's job or profession to gain specific access to a crime target.

I have long argued that routine *legal* activities set the stage for *illegal* activities. That principle applies to these crimes, too. Legitimate features of the work role provide a chance to do misdeeds. However, the fourth path to the crime target is more specialized than the other three. Many neighbors or visitors may share your activity space, passing your house or car. Many people have indirect network ties helping them to find out something about you. Internet access is widespread. *But only one or two attorneys have access to your escrow account.* That's why I use the word "specialized." That also tells you how these crimes differ from the other varieties of illegal action.

Crimes of specialized access include a variety of crimes commonly called white-collar crimes, as well as many crimes by blue-collar workers. The term includes offenses by those higher and lower in the organizational hierarchy, so long as they use a specialized work role to carry it out.

ORGANIZATIONAL RANK

Most of us feel intuitively that those higher on the totem pole would have relatively more criminal access than those lower. But that's not always so. Some lower- or middle-tier jobs offer excellent criminal access, including:

- a janitor who uses his keys to steal equipment;
- a hotel desk clerk whose inside knowledge helps him rape a guest;

- a police officer on the beat who solicits bribes for looking the other way; or
- an ordinary purchasing agent with easy access to kickbacks.

However, we have to think very closely about how powerful positions relate to crimes of specialized access. Remember that most jobs are not at the top. Because middle- and low-level positions are so numerous, together we can expect many more offenders abusing these positions and far fewer offenders at the top of the heap. On the other hand, the highest-ranking offenders are more likely to do the most dramatic damage in sheer financial terms. Yet there is ample evidence that most of these offenses and the damage they produce never appears on television. That's why Weisburd and colleagues (2001) studied the statistics on more ordinary cases.

A good research agenda would examine how each work role sets up crime opportunities. Those opportunities will vary between and within ranks. As I regularly note, crime opportunities require guardianship to be absent or remote. Thus, abuse of position is more likely when job duties occur in late shifts or remote settings, when offenders are not closely supervised, when interactions with outside clients and customers is part of the job, and when potential victims are in a weak position relative to the jobholder.

Empirical research is needed to teach us how each occupation provides access to crime opportunities. Which positions handle money? How much and in what form? Exactly what jobs have access to computer accounts, files, keys, passwords, or confidential information? Which positions control or disperse valuable resources to others? Which employees or managers make decisions impinging on the health or welfare of others? Which jobs can deliver favors that might draw bribes? To make progress in studying these crimes, we need to follow the same principles we use for other offenses: learn the specifics, find out the modus operandi of the offenders, search for the practical features of the criminal acts, and find out what the offenders want. Research needs to answer four basic questions:

1. Exactly what did the specialized-access offender do?

2. Were there co-offenders?

3. Who were the victims?

4. How did specialized access make the crime possible?

It is premature to classify all of these crimes, but at least I can offer a tentative approach for organizing information about them.

THE SPECIALIZED-ACCESS CRIME GRID

Exhibit 12.2 helps organize specialized-access crimes, and I hope it will give you
an idea how diverse they are. The types of harm include illicit transfers (such as
stealing your money from an account). But other types are misinforming, manipulating, and endangering people. The victims are also diverse. Sometimes the
victim is the employee. Sometimes the victim is a customer, client, or patient.

Very often the harm is done to one's own organization or another organization. But we also have to consider harm to the general public. Thus a shipping company that dumps its garbage in the bay is harming the general public,
but probably nobody in particular. These extremely diverse offenses, covering
20 categories, have one common denominator: each offender abuses his
specialized role to carry out the offense.

Exhibit 12.2   The Specialized-Access Crime Grid

	How to Abuse Your Position and Harm Others			
The Victims	*Transfer*	*Misinform*	*Manipulate*	*Endanger*
Employees	Cheat overtime Raid tip jar	Distort worker rights Conceal evaluations	Rig promotions Pressure for sex	Misuse child labor Coerce long hours
Customers, clients, patients	Resell stolen goods Cheat at register	Overbill services Mislabel products	Fix customer prices Refer for kickback	Sell risky product Abuse sexually
Public	Receive stolen goods Cheat on dividends	Falsify stock reports Twist research	Fix market prices Bribe public officials	Spoil environment Imprison unjustly
Own organization	Fudge timecards Steal equipment	Pad expenses Double-cross partner	Take kickbacks Promote for sex	Sabotage project Neglect machinery
Other organizations	Steal secrets Evade taxes	Falsify deliveries Declare bogus bankruptcy	Pay kickbacks Delude inspectors	Sabotage competitor Understate danger

CONCLUSION

Crimes of specialized access, whether in office suites or shops, can be defined and studied as a part of ongoing life. As with other offenses, access to crime targets is essential. To understand crimes of specialized access, we must pay close attention to their very specific modus operandi. As with other types of crime, these illegal acts occur *within a larger system of legal activities*. Indeed, a specific work role can put someone in just the right position to do the wrong thing.

MAIN POINTS

1. "White-collar crime" is poorly named, because any work, any professional or occupational role, can get involved in crime. These offenses are usually not dramatic or ingenious.

2. These are better called "crimes of specialized access." These crimes depend on individuals being in a position to do a particular harm.

3. It is a myth that race or economic standing predicts whether individuals will commit violent crimes or crimes of specialized access.

4. Offenders of these crimes range from low-level employees with crime opportunities on the job to corporate executives and high-level government officials.

5. White-collar offenders have found a particular solution to the offender's general problem of gaining access to crime targets. Of the four general methods that are available to offenders—overlapping activity spaces, personal ties, the Internet, and specialized access—white-collar offenders use the last.

6. Some offenses can be carried out only through specialized access (or, at least, usually so). These offenses help us delineate a fairly distinct class of crimes, also fitting fairly well the traditional list of "white-collar" offenses.

7. These offenses might harm employees, one's clients, the public, one's own organization, or other organizations.

8. These offenses fall into four categories: offenders can make illicit transfers of money, goods, or other resources to the detriment of others; they can abuse their access to misinform others; they can apply their specialized roles to manipulate others; or they can endanger the health and safety of others.

PROJECTS AND CHALLENGES

Interview projects. (a) Interview any person in any occupation about minor crime at the workplace. Ask only about general awareness to avoid incriminating anyone. (b) Pick any offense in Exhibit 12.2 and interview somebody about how this would be done. Does this offense belong in its current location in the exhibit? Where else might it be placed?

Media project. Compare news media coverage of "white-collar crime" cases to the empirical work in Weisburd et al. (2001).

Map project. Map a business or plant where you have worked. Figure out the different types of crimes of specialized access that can occur within it, or, using its location, note how the physical layout of the place contributes to crime opportunities.

Photo project. Get permission to photograph some local business or professional offices, avoiding the names or signs. Imagine what crimes of specialized access could conceivably occur at each.

Web project. Identify a website and think about how it could be used to make illicit transfers of money, goods, or other resources; misinform people; manipulate people; and/or endanger the health and safety of people.

⊰ 13 ⊱

CRIME AND SOCIAL CHANGE

—·•·—

This book has covered a lot of ground—from simple local theft to crimes of specialized access to piracy. Underlying these fragments is a single and general approach that helps you think about how social change can influence crime. That approach is based on changes in technology.

TECHNOLOGY, RIGHTLY UNDERSTOOD

But let's be clear about what technology implies. First, do not think of technology (or inventions) only in terms of gadgets. Technology includes how *people* use machines. Inventions include innovations in business types, job responsibilities, software, ways to train people, credit card rules, methods for managing barrooms, money-machine protocols, or environmental designs. Each of these could bring along new crime opportunities or render an old crime obsolete. Even those crimes that persist can be managed and contained as a result of these innovations.

Second, technology (and criminal use of it) depends on the human touch. The impact of new technology on crime still operates through simple human processes:

- slipping into an office to abscond with a computer password;
- the former employee taking the company computer manuals home;
- stealing web-ordered packages at the doorstep;

- hiding illegal pills inside a pocket; or
- changing a number on the computer screen at work.

Third, people don't seem to change, even as machines, organizations, and locations are completely transformed (see Ekblom, 2002, 2005a, 2005b; Pease, Rogerson, & Ellingworth, 2008). They may find new ways to do the crime, but fraud is still fraud, bullying is still bullying, and sexual abuse is still abuse.

Fourth, not all inventions have an important impact—only those inventions that alter the daily routines and affect who does what, when, where, and how, or inventions that change how people can carry out criminal acts. The LED watch was a neat invention, but it worked no better than its predecessors and did little to change society or crime.

Fifth, the most important technology is often quite simple. Small inventions have big consequences. This book has demonstrated that point with respect to crime and crime prevention. But it applies to non-crime topics, too.

THE CLEAN WATER EXAMPLE

To understand the historical importance of inventions and technology, consider the following:

- Cleaning up the water supply in the United States in the early 20th century led to a reduction of 75 percent of infant mortality (Cutler & Miller, 2005).
- Good water quality is largely accomplished with simple inventions that keep sewage out of the water supply, leading to a major reduction in mortality (Jorgenson, 2004).
- A simple "invention"—getting new mothers who wash their hands with soap and clean water before touching the baby—reduced neonatal deaths by 60 percent (Rhee et al., 2008).

Now consider some of the steps leading to clean water (Environmental Protection Agency, 2000). In 1804, the first municipal water filtration works opened in Scotland. Thirty-one years later, chlorine was used to reduce odor in drinking water. The cholera epidemic of the 1840s killed at least a half million people, including 100,000 in France and 8,000 in New York City.

A solution came. In 1854, Dr. John Snow discovered that London cholera victims all drank from the same polluted well. That led to a situational prevention strategy that stopped the epidemic in London. In 1880, Louis Pasteur developed germ theory, two years later London started to filter drinking water, and in the 1890s chlorine was proven an effective disinfectant of drinking water. Note the dramatic historical importance of simple inventions for saving lives. But also note that learning what to do is a process of trial and error. Despite that process, epidemiologists and public health experts have developed a general perspective on how to approach a public health problem. Can we do so for the crime problem?

A GENERAL APPROACH: SUMMING UP THIS BOOK

I have long been influenced by reading the work of William F. Ogburn (1886–1959), a forgotten member of the "Chicago School of Sociology." Ogburn (1922, 1964) emphasized how technology drives history and society. I was also influenced by reading S. Colum Gilfillan (1910–1978), a rather odd but interesting chap. Gilfillan (1935) cautioned that inventions are not usually momentous. No single person invented the ship. Instead, it developed incrementally as people kept improving on what others had done before them.

Borrowing from Gilfillan, small inventions drive forward the level of everyday technology. Borrowing from Ogburn, everyday technology drives daily life, including our routine activities. Adding my own contribution, everyday routines drive the opportunity for crime. All this is put together in Exhibit 13.1. *In the short run*, A and B are most important. On the other hand, we live in a fast-changing society, so we might see the crime impact of inventions, D, even in a couple of years. *In the longer term*, inventions can transform daily life. I offer two examples that apply Exhibit 13.1.

Exhibit 13.1 How Crime Changes Within a Larger System

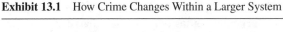

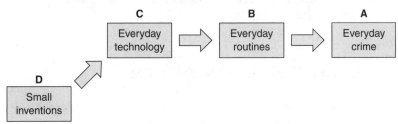

Example A: Brakes, Trains, and Dispersals

George Westinghouse invented the railway air brake in 1869. It depended on prior technology and needed improvement over the years. Over time this made possible the modern metro, whose underground trains had to be sure they could stop. Other technological developments were needed to perfect this process, and Westinghouse was smart enough to keep improving upon his earlier innovations, and then to put the technology into daily use. The development of extensive modern cities depended on these systems. This greatly widened the span of daily travel to work, and also made possible an urban night economy outside one's own neighborhood. Thus, offenders and victims widened their range of daily activity. But all this took time. Inventions are the mother of change, but the progeny take time to grow up.

Example B: Plastics, Transistors, and Products

The crime wave of the 1960s and 1970s was influenced by these converging developments:

- In 1956, George Bardeen invented the transistor—which ultimately made possible the electronic revolution. But it had to be perfected, developed, and applied incrementally over many decades, involving many people.
- Crude plastics have been around for thousands of years, but only after World War I was chemistry good enough to improve them, and only in the 1940s and 1950s was mass production of plastics feasible.

In time plastics and transistors combined to make possible very valuable but lightweight goods, ideal for a thief. Incrementally, plastics and transistor technology altered daily life in many positive ways, but also contributed to everyday crime. Of course, not all changes go in a single direction. The same transistors that made products easy to steal were later embedded within goods to *reduce* theft of auto parts and counterfeiting of goods (see Clarke & Newman, 2005; Davis & Pease, 2000; M. Felson, 1998).

HOW TO THINK ABOUT CHANGING CRIME

I am not impressed with the argument that technology changes people in a fundamental way. Rather, I think technological change brings out existing human traits. That implies that immediate environmental experiences should be the focus of crime reduction. The next section briefly puts that point into perspective.

Immediate Crime Reduction

We have six basic crime reduction choices:

1. Try to influence human character.
2. **Design secure environments**.
3. **Remove crime situations.**
4. Arrest and process offenders.
5. Try and convict them.
6. Punish and rehabilitate them.

The second and third on the list are in boldface to emphasize that they have the greatest chance to succeed quickly at the least cost. Trying to change people before or after the crime is expensive, inefficient, and doubtful. We don't really know how to do it—although we can give plenty of empty advice that people don't have to follow. That's why I emphasize design and situational options.

Looking back to Exhibit 13.1, we cannot always alter everyday technology quickly and easily. But we can change certain daily routines by locating youth centers, improving retail design and management, arranging public parks, and enforcing regulations in local pubs. These changes require specific knowledge about crime events. We have to learn exactly how, when, and where offenders act; their specific motives; how noncriminal realities give rise to criminal events; and the step-by-step sequences that crime follows in daily life. In so doing, we can find ways to reduce crime without waiting around. But we still want to know intellectually, or at least to speculate, how all this fits into the broad sweep of history.

Interpreting the Long Run

In Chapter 5, I referred to four historical stages in the history of crime. To cover an even broader sweep of history, permit me to expand this to nine stages (see M. Felson, 2012). In formulating these nine stages, I was guided by the approach depicted in Exhibit 13.1. The stages that enhanced crime are preceded by an up arrow, and those that decreased crime have a down arrow. The historical stages of crime occur in this rough order:

1. ↑ increased use of horse transportation;
2. ↓ the move to the relative safety of towns;
3. ↑ the growth of cities;
4. ↑ increased urban access to rural whiskey;
5. ↓ urban villages;
6. ↓ suburban sanctuaries;
7. ↑ expansion of lightweight products;
8. ↑ the spread of formal organization; and
9. ↑↓ the digital transformation of the 21st century.

The increased use of horses (1) allowed offenders to find targets over a wider area, while making horses themselves very worthwhile targets of theft. The move to the relative safety of towns (2) was partly a response to the problems from the first era, reducing risks. The increased commerce produced a growth of cities (3), which grew large enough to assemble likely offenders with targets of crime. The expansion of roads and commerce (4) also brought rural whiskey to urban centers, and rum from the West Indies to London, creating a new set of problems. For sanctuary from crime, people devised urban villages (5) for more security within cities; then they sought refuge in suburbanization (6), which temporarily reduced their vulnerability. This was offset by (7) the transformation of everyday products, with the production of lightweight but valuable products. The expansion of formal organizations (8) brought more jobs for women, exposing them and their property to attack and creating an array of specialized-access crimes.

The digital age (9) then brought new crime opportunities, while removing many of the old risks. This new era forces offenders to find special niches in the interstices of daily life. That's why I inserted a double arrow before it. I believe that we are entering a new age of fluctuating crime rates with shifting crime types. The arms race between offenders and defenders (Ekblom, 2002, 2008) should be especially acute in years to come. The recent declines in street crime mask a plethora of new illicit acts that will test the creativity and determination of the next generation. I hope I have provided you some of the tools you will need.

In all ages, the offender must complete a set of tasks. Society sometimes makes those tasks easy and other times difficult. There lies the secret of how crime varies, how it changes, and how it can be prevented. Inventions are what determine daily tasks and hence are the driving force in the history of crime. Students of crime analysis should stop wasting their efforts looking deep into social structure or the human soul or treating crime as melodramatic. Crime is ordinary behavior reflecting basic human selfishness, everyday temptations, and environmental cues. The key to crime reduction is hidden in plain sight.

REFERENCES

Alarid, L. F., & Cromwell, P. (Eds.). (2006). *In her own words: Female offender's views on crime and victimization.* New York: Oxford University Press.

Altizio, A., & York, D. (2007). *Robbery of convenience stores* (Guide No. 49). Retrieved September 25, 2009, from http://www.popcenter.org/problems/robbery_convenience/

Andresen, M. A. (2011). The ambient population and crime analysis. *Professional Geographer, 63*(2), 193–212. http://dx.doi.org/10.1080/00330124.2010.547151

Andresen, M. A., & Felson, M. (2010). The impact of co-offending. *British Journal of Criminology, 50*(1), 66–81.

Andresen, M. A., Frank, R., & Felson, M. (2014). Age and the distance to crime. *Criminology and Criminal Justice, 14*(3), 314–333.

Andresen, M. A., & Jenion, G. W. (2010). Ambient populations and the calculation of crime rates and risk. *Security Journal, 23*(2), 114–133. http://dx.doi.org/10.1057/sj.2008.1

Apel, R., Bushway, S., & Brame, R. (2007). Unpacking the relationship between adolescent employment and antisocial behavior: A matched samples comparison. *Criminology, 45*(1), 67–97.

Archer, J., & Coyne, S. M. (2005). An integrated review of indirect, relational, and social aggression. *Personality & Social Psychology Review* (Lawrence Erlbaum Associates), *9*(3), 212–230.

Armitage, R., & Monchuk, L. (2009). *Re-evaluating secured by design (SBD) housing in West Yorkshire.* Queensgate, UK: University of Huddersfield. Retrieved July 24, 2014, from http://www.securedbydesign.com/pdfs/Re-evaluating-SBD-Housing-in-West-Yorks.pdf

Barker, R. (1963). *The stream of behavior.* New York: Appleton-Century-Crofts.

Barker, R. G. (1968). *Ecological psychology: Concepts and methods for studying the environment of human behavior.* Stanford, CA: Stanford University Press.

Barker, R. G., & Wright, H. F. (1951). *One boy's day. A specimen record of behavior.* New York: Harper & Row.

Barker, R. G., & Wright, H. F. (1954). *Midwest and its children: The psychological ecology of an American town.* Evanston, IL: Row, Peterson.

Baumeister, R. F., Heatherton, T. F., & Tice, D. M. (1994). *Losing control: How and why people fail at self-regulation.* San Diego, CA: Academic Press.

Beauregard, E., Proulx, J., & Rossmo, K. (2007). Script analysis of the hunting process of serial sex offenders. *Criminal Justice and Behavior, 34*(8), 1069–1084.

Beckett, K., & Sasson, T. (2004). *The politics of injustice: Crime and punishment in America* (2nd ed.). Thousand Oaks, CA: Sage.

Bell, J., & Burke, B. (1992). *Cruising Cooper Street.* In R. V. Clarke (Ed.), *Situational crime prevention: Successful case studies* (pp. 108–112). New York: Harrow & Heston.

Benson, M. L., & Simpson, S. (2009). *White collar crime: An opportunity perspective.* New York: Taylor & Francis.

Bentham, J. (1907). *An introduction to the principles of morals and legislation.* Oxford, UK: Clarendon. (Original work published 1789)

Bernasco, W. S., Ruiter, S., Bruinsma, G. J. N., Pauwels, L. J. R., & Weerman, F. M. (2013). Situational causes of offending: A fixed-effects analysis of space–time budget data. *Criminology, 51*(4), 895–926.

Best, J. (1999). *Random violence: How we talk about new crimes and new victims.* Berkeley: University of California Press.

Bichler, G. (2010). Magnetic facilities: Identifying the convergence settings of juvenile delinquents. *Crime and Delinquency.* doi:10.1177/0011128710382349

Bichler, G., Christie, J., & Sechrest, D. (2011). Examining juvenile delinquency within activity space: Building a context for offender travel patterns. *Journal of Research in Crime and Delinquency, 48*(3), 472–506.

Bichler, G., Malm, A., & Enriquez, J. (2014). Magnetic facilities: Identifying convergence settings of juvenile delinquents. *Crime and Delinquency.* Available: http://cad.sagepub.com/content/60/7/971.abstract

Bjor, J., Knutsson, J., & Kuhlhorn, E. (1992). The celebration of Midsummer Eve in Sweden—A study in the art of preventing collective disorder. *Security Journal, 3*(3), 169–174.

Block, R. L., & Block, C. R. (2000). The Bronx and Chicago: Street robbery in the environs of rapid transit stations. In V. Goldsmith, P. G. McGuire, & J. H. Mollenkopf (Eds.), *Analyzing crime patterns: Frontiers of practice* (pp. 137–152). Thousand Oaks, CA: Sage.

Boba, R. (2008). *Crime analysis with crime mapping.* Thousand Oaks, CA: Sage.

Boba, R., & Santos, R. (2008). A review of the research, practice, and evaluation of construction site theft occurrence and prevention: Directions for future research. *Security Journal, 21*(4), 246–263.

Boggs, S. L. (1965). Urban crime patterns. *American Sociological Review, 30,* 899–908.

Boivin, R. (2013). On the use of crime rates. *Canadian Journal of Criminology & Criminal Justice, 55*(2), 263–277.

Boivin, R., Geoffrion, S., Ouellet, F., & Felson, M. (2014). Nightly variation of disorder in a Canadian nightclub. *Journal of Substance Abuse, 19*(1–2), 188–193.

Bouffard, J., Exum, M. L., & Paternoster, R. (2000). Whither the beast? The role of emotions in a rational choice theory of crime. In S. S. Simpson (Ed.), *Of crime and criminality: The use of theory in everyday life* (pp. 159–178). Thousand Oaks, CA: Pine Forge.

Bowers, K., Johnson, S., & Hirschfield, A. (2004). Closing off opportunities for crime: An evaluation of alley-gating. *European Journal on Criminal Policy and Research, 10*(4), 285–308.

Braga, A., & Weisburd, D. (2010). *Policing problem places: Crime hot spots and effective prevention.* Oxford: Oxford University Press.

Brame, R., Bushway, S. D., Paternoster, R., & Apel, R. (2004). Assessing the effect of adolescent employment on involvement in criminal activity. *Journal of Contemporary Criminal Justice, 20*(3), 236–256.

Brantingham, P. J., & Brantingham, P. L. (1984). *Patterns in crime.* New York: Macmillan.

Brantingham, P. J., & Brantingham, P. L. (1998). Environmental criminology: From theory to urban planning practice. *Studies on Crime and Crime Prevention, 7*(1), 31–60.

Brantingham, P. L., & Brantingham, P. J. (1981). Notes on the geometry of crime. In P. J. Brantingham & P. L. Brantingham (Eds.), *Environmental criminology* (pp. 27–54). Beverly Hills, CA: Sage.

Brantingham, P. L., & Brantingham, P. J. (1993). Nodes, paths and edges: Considerations on the complexity of crime and the physical environment. *Journal of Environmental Psychology, 13*(1), 3–28.

Brantingham, P. L., & Brantingham, P. J. (1999). A theoretical model of crime hot spot generation. *Studies on Crime and Crime Prevention, 8*(1), 7–26.

Britt, C. L., & Gottfredson, M. R. (Eds.). (2003). *Control theories of crime and delinquency.* New Brunswick, NJ: Transaction.

Bruggeman, E. L., & Hart, K. J. (1996). Cheating, lying, and moral reasoning by religious and secular high school students. *Journal of Educational Research, 89*(6), 340–344.

Bureau of Justice Statistics. (2006). *Crime victimization in the United States, 2005.* Retrieved October 14, 2014, from http://www.ojp.usdoj.gov/bjs/

Burgess, E. W. (1916). Juvenile delinquency in a small city. *Journal of the American Institute of Criminal Law and Criminology, 6,* 724–728.

Byers, S., Purdon, C., & Clark, D. A. (1998, November). Sexual intrusive thoughts of college students. *Journal of Sex Research, 35*(4), 359–369.

Ceccato, V. (2013, January). Crime prevention in rural Sweden. *European Journal of Criminology, 10*(1), 89–112.

Center for Problem-Oriented Policing. (2014). Retrieved July 27, 2014, from http://www.popcenter.org

Chainey, S. P., & Ratcliffe, J. H. (2005). *GIS and crime mapping.* London: Wiley.

Clarke, R. V. (1983). Situational crime prevention: Its theoretical basis and practical scope. In M. Tonry & N. Morris (Eds.), *Crime and justice: An annual review of research* (Vol. 4, pp. 225–256). Chicago: University of Chicago Press.

Clarke, R. V. (1999). *Hot products: Understanding, anticipating and reducing demand for stolen goods* (Paper No. 112, Police Research Series). London: British Home Office Research Publications.

Clarke, R. V. (2002). *Shoplifting*. Washington, DC: U.S. Department of Justice, Office of Community Oriented Policing Services.

Clarke, R. V. (2008). *Improving street lighting to reduce crime in residential areas* (Problem Guide No. 8). Washington, DC: U.S. Department of Justice, Office of Community Oriented Policing Services. Retrieved July 30, 2014, from http://www.popcenter.org/Responses/pdfs/street_lighting.pdf

Clarke, R. V., & de By, R. A. (2013). Poaching, habitat loss, and the decline of neotropical parrots: A comparative spatial analysis. *Journal of Experimental Criminology, 9*(3), 333–353.

Clarke, R. V., & Eck, J. E. (Eds.). (2005). *Crime analysis for problem solvers in 60 small steps*. Washington, DC: U.S. Department of Justice, Office of Community Oriented Policing Services.

Clarke, R. V., & Eck, J. E. (2007). *Understanding risky facilities*. Washington, DC: U.S. Department of Justice, Office of Community Oriented Policing Services.

Clarke, R. V., & Goldstein, H. (2002). Reducing auto theft at construction sites: Lessons from a problem-oriented project. In N. Tilley (Ed.), *Analysis for crime prevention* (pp. 89–130). Monsey, NY: Criminal Justice Press.

Clarke, R. V., & Goldstein, H. (2003). Theft from cars in Center-City parking facilities: A case study in implementing problem-oriented policing. In J. Knutsson (Ed.), *Problem-oriented policing: From innovation to mainstream* (Crime Prevention Studies, Vol. 15). Devon, UK: Willan. Retrieved July 26, 2014, from http://www.popcenter.org/library/crimeprevention/

Clarke, R. V., & Harris, P. M. (1992). Auto theft and its prevention. In M. Tonry (Ed.), *Crime and justice: A review of research* (Vol. 16, pp. 1–54). Chicago: University of Chicago Press.

Clarke, R. V., Kemper, R., & Wyckoff, L. (2001). Controlling cell phone fraud in the US—Lessons for the UK. *Security Journal, 14*(1), 7–22.

Clarke, R., & Lester, D. (1987). Toxicity of car exhausts and opportunity for suicide: Comparison between Britain and the USA. *Journal of Epidemiology & Community Health, 41*(2), 114–120.

Clarke, R. V., & Mayhew, P. (1998). Preventing crime in parking lots: What we know and what we need to know. In M. Felson & R. B. Peiser (Eds.), *Reducing crime through real estate development and management* (pp. 125–136). Washington, DC: Urban Land Institute.

Clarke, R. V., & Newman, G. (Eds.). (2005). *Designing out crime from products and systems*. Monsey, NY: Criminal Justice Press.

Clarke, R. V., & Newman, G. (2006). *Outsmarting the terrorists*. Portsmouth, NH: Greenwood.

Clarke, R. V., & Petrossian, G. (2012). *Shoplifting* (Guide No. 11, 2nd ed.). Washington, DC: Center for Problem-Oriented Policing.

Clarke, R. V., & Smith, M. (2000). Crime and public transport. In M. Tonry (Ed.), *Crime and justice: An annual review of research* (Vol. 27, pp. 169–233). Chicago: University of Chicago Press.

Cleary, S., Shukla, R., & Felson, M. (2014). Situational crime prevention and the Wild West. In G. Braunsma & D. Weisburd (Eds.), *Encyclopedia of criminology and criminal justice* (pp. 4874–4883). New York: Springer.

Cohen, L. E., & Felson, M. (1979). Social change and crime rate trends: A routine activity approach. *American Sociological Review, 44,* 588–608.

Colquhoun, P. (1969). *A treatise on the police of the metropolis.* Montclair, NJ: Patterson Smith. (Original work published 1795)

Colvin, M. (2000). *Crime and coercion: An integrated theory of chronic criminality.* New York: St. Martin's.

Cornish, D., & Clarke, R. V. (Eds.). (1986). *The reasoning criminal.* New York: Springer-Verlag.

Crofts, P. (2003). White collar punters: Stealing from the boss to gamble. *Current Issues in Criminal Justice, 15*(1), 40–52.

Cromwell, P. (Ed.). (2012). *In their own words: Criminals on crime* (6th ed.). New York: Oxford University Press.

Cromwell, P., & Olson, J. N. (2004). *Breaking and entering: Burglars on burglary.* New York: Wadsworth.

Cromwell, P. F., Olson, J. N., & Avary, D. W. (1991). *Breaking and entering: An ethnographic analysis of burglary.* Newbury Park, CA: Sage.

Cromwell, P. F., Olson, J. N., & Avary, D. W. (1993). Who buys stolen property: A new look at criminal receiving. *Journal of Crime and Justice, 16*(1), 75–95.

Crowe, T. D., & Zahm, D. (1994). Crime prevention through environmental design. *Land Management, 7*(1), 22–27.

Cusson, M. (1993). A strategic analysis of crime: Criminal tactics as responses to precriminal situations. In R. V. Clarke & M. Felson (Eds.), *Routine activity and rational choice: Advances in criminological theory* (Vol. 5, pp. 295–304). New Brunswick, NJ: Transaction Books.

Cutler, D., & Miller, G. (2005, February). The role of public health improvements in health advances: The twentieth-century United States. *Demography, 42*(1), 1–22.

Dabney, D. A., Hollinger, R. C., & Dugan, L. (2004). Who actually steals? A study of covertly observed shoplifters. *Justice Quarterly, 21*(4), 693–728.

Davis, R. C., Maxwell, C. D., & Taylor, B. (2006). Preventing repeat incidents of family violence: Analysis of data from three field experiments. *Journal of Experimental Criminology, 2*(2), 183–210.

Davis, R., & Pease, K. (2000). Crime, technology and the future. *Security Journal, 13*(2), 59–64.

Decker, D., Shichor, D., & O'Brien, R. (1982). *Urban structure and victimization.* Lexington, MA: Lexington Books.

Decker, S., & van Winkle, B. (1996). *Life in the gang: Family, friends, and violence.* Cambridge, UK: Cambridge University Press.

Dolmen, L. (Ed.). (1990). *Crime trends in Sweden, 1988.* Stockholm: National Council for Crime Prevention.

Douvan, E., & Gold, M. (1966). Modal patterns in American adolescence. In L. W. Hoffman & M. L. Hoffman (Eds.), *Review of child development research* (Vol. 2, pp. 469–528). New York: Russell Sage Foundation.

Duffala, D. C. (1976). Convenience stores, armed robbery, and physical environmental features. *American Behavioral Scientist, 20*(2), 227–245.

Eck, J. E. (1995). A general model of the geography of illicit retail marketplaces. In J. E. Eck & D. Weisburd (Eds.), *Crime and place* (pp. 67–93). Monsey, NY: Criminal Justice Press.

Eck, J. E. (1997). Preventing crime at places. In L. W. Sherman, D. Gottfredson, D. MacKenzie, J. E. Eck, P. Reuter, & S. Bushway (Eds.), *Preventing crime: What works, what doesn't, what's promising.* Washington, DC: National Institute of Justice.

E-Fencing Enforcement Act of 2009, H.R. 1166, 111th Congress (2009–2010). Retrieved October 19, 2014, from https://www.congress.gov/bill/111th-congress/house-bill/1166

Ekblom, P. (2002). Future imperfect: Preparing for the crimes to come. *Criminal Justice Matters, 46*(Winter), 38–40. London: Kings College, Centre for Crime and Justice Studies.

Ekblom, P. (2005a). Designing products against crime. In N. Tilley (Ed.), *Handbook of crime prevention and community safety* (pp. 203–244). Cullompton, UK: Willan.

Ekblom, P. (2005b). How to police the future: Scanning for scientific and technological innovations which generate potential threats and opportunities in crime, policing and crime reduction. In M. Smith & N. Tilley (Eds.), *Crime science: New approaches to preventing and detecting crime* (pp. 27–55). Cullompton, UK: Willan.

Ekblom, P. (2008). *Gearing up against crime.* London: Design Against Crime Research Centre: http://www.designagainstcrime.com/files/crimeframeworks/11_gearing_up_against_crime.pdf

Engels, R. C. M. E., Luijpers, E., Landsheer, J., & Meeus, W. (2004). A longitudinal study of relations between attitudes and delinquent behavior in adolescents. *Criminal Justice and Behavior, 31*(2), 244–260.

Environmental Protection Agency. (2000). *The history of drinking water treatment.* Washington, DC: Environmental Protection Agency, Office of Water. Retrieved July 30, 2014, from http://www.epa.gov/safewater/consumer/pdf/hist.pdf

Farrell, G. (1995). Preventing repeat victimization. In M. Tonry & D. Farrington (Eds.), *Crime and justice: A review of research* (Vol. 19, pp. 469–534). Chicago: University of Chicago Press.

Farrell, G., Clark, K., Ellingworth, D., & Pease, K. (2005). Of targets and supertargets: A routine activity theory of high crime rates. *Internet Journal of Criminology*, www.internetjournalofcriminology.com

Fattah, E. A. (1991). *Understanding criminal victimization: An introduction to theoretical victimology.* Scarborough, Ontario, Canada: Prentice Hall.

Federal Bureau of Investigation. (2013a). *Law enforcement officers killed and assaulted.* Washington, DC: Government Printing Office.

Federal Bureau of Investigation. (2013b). *Uniform crime reports: Crime in the United States.* Washington, DC: Government Printing Office.

Feeney, F. (1986). Robbers as decision makers. In D. Cornish & R. V. Clarke (Eds.), *The reasoning criminal* (pp. 53–71). New York: Springer-Verlag.

Felson, M. (1987). Routine activities and crime prevention in the developing metropolis. *Criminology, 25,* 911–931.

Felson, M. (1998). *Crime and everyday life* (2nd ed.). Thousand Oaks, CA: Pine Forge.

Felson, M. (2003). The process of co-offending. In M. Smith & D. Cornish (Eds.), *Theory for practice in situational crime prevention* (pp. 149–167). Monsey, NY: Criminal Justice Press.

Felson, M. (2006). *Crime and nature.* Thousand Oaks, CA: Sage.

Felson, M. (2012). Crime in the broad sweep of history. In J. van Dijk, A. Tseloni, & G. Farrell (Eds.), *The international crime drop: New directions in research* (pp. 279–285). New York: Palgrave.

Felson, M. (2014). Book review of *Breaking rules: The social and situational dynamics of young people's urban crime. Journal of Criminal Justice Education, 25*(2), 254–258.

Felson, M., Belanger, M. E., Bichler, G. M., Bruzinski, C. D., Campbell, G. S., Fried, C. L., . . ., & Williams, L. M. (1996). Redesigning hell: Preventing crime and disorder at the Port Authority Bus Terminal. In R. V. Clarke (Ed.), *Preventing mass transit crime* (pp. 5–92). Monsey, NY: Criminal Justice Press.

Felson, M., Berends, R., Richardson, B., & Veno, A. (1997). Reducing pub hopping and related crime. In R. Homel (Ed.), *Policing for prevention: Reducing crime, public intoxication and injury* (Crime Prevention Studies, Vol. 7, pp. 115–132). Monsey, NY: Criminal Justice Press. Retrieved July 27, 2014, from http://www.popcenter .org/library/crimeprevention/volume_07/

Felson, M., & Clarke, R. V. (1997). The ethics of situational crime prevention. In G. Newman, R. V. Clarke, & S. G. Shoham (Eds.), Rational choice and situational crime prevention: Theoretical foundations (pp. 197–218). Dartmouth, UK: Ashgate.

Felson, M., & Clarke, R. V. (1998). *Opportunity makes the thief* (Paper No. 98, Police Research Series). London: British Home Office Research Publications.

Felson, M., & Cohen, L. E. (1980). Human ecology and crime: A routine activity approach. *Human Ecology, 8,* 389–406.

Felson, M., & Cohen, L. E. (1981). Modeling crime rate trends—A criminal opportunity perspective. *Journal of Research in Crime and Delinquency, 18,* 138–164 (as corrected, 1982, *19,* 1).

Felson, M., Dickman, D., Glenn, D., Kelly, L., Lambard, L., Maher, L., . . ., & Veil, J. (1990). Preventing crime at Newark's subway stations. *Security Journal, 1*(3), 137–142.

Felson, M., & Gottfredson, M. (1984). Adolescent activities near peers and parents. *Journal of Marriage and the Family, 46,* 709–714.

Felson, R. B. (1996). Big people hit little people: Sex differences in physical power and interpersonal violence. *Criminology, 34,* 433–452.

Felson, R. B. (2001, April 22). Blame analysis: Accounting for the behavior of protected groups. *American Sociologist, 22*(1), 5–23.

Felson, R. B. (2004). A rational choice approach to violence. In M. A. Zahn, H. H. Brownstein, & S. L. Jackson (Eds.), *Violence: From theory to research* (pp. 71–90). Cincinnati, OH: Anderson Publishing.

Felson, R. B. (2013). What are violent offenders thinking? In B. LeClerc & R. Wortley (Eds.), *Cognition and crime: Offender decision making and script analyses* (chap. 2). Crime Science Series. London, UK: Routledge.

Felson, R. B., Ackerman, J., & Yeon, S. J. (2003). The infrequency of family violence. *Journal of Marriage and Family, 65,* 622–634.

Felson, R. B., & Felson, S. (1993, September/October). Predicaments of men and women. *Society,* pp. 2016–2020.

Felson, R. B., & Outlaw, M. C. (2007). The control motive and marital violence. *Violence and Victims, 22*(4), 387–407.

Festinger, L. (1957). *Introduction to a theory of cognitive dissonance.* Evanston, IL: Row Peterson.

Finney, A., Wilson, D., Levi, M., Sutton, M., & Forest, S. (2005). *Handling stolen goods: Findings from the 2002–03 British Crime Survey and 2003 Offending, Crime and Justice Survey.* London: Home Office Online Report 38/05. Home Office Research, Development and Statistics Directorate.

Fisher, B. S., Daigle, L. E., & Cullen, F. T. (2003). Reporting sexual victimization to the police and others: Results from a national-level study of college women. *Criminal Justice and Behavior, 30*(1), 6–38.

Fisher, B. S., Daigle, L. E., & Cullen, F. T. (2007). Assessing the efficacy of the protective action-completion nexus for sexual victimizations. *Violence and Victims, 22*(1), 18–42.

Fisher, K., & Gershuny, J. (2013). Time use and time diary research. *Oxford Bibliographies.* Oxford University Press. Retrieved October 7, 2014, from http://www.oxfordbibliographies.com/view/document/obo-9780199756384/obo-9780199756384-0027.xml

Friedrichs, D. O. (2006). *Trusted criminals: White collar crime in contemporary society* (3rd ed.). Belmont, CA: Wadsworth.

Gans, H. (1962). *The urban villagers.* New York: Free Press.

Geis, G., & Meier, R. F. (1977). *White-collar crime: Classic and contemporary views.* New York: Free Press.

Gilfillan, S. C. (1935). *The sociology of invention.* Cambridge: MIT Press.

Gill, M. (2000a). *Commercial robbery: Offenders' perspectives on security and crime prevention.* London: Blackstone.

Gill, M. (2000b). *Insurance fraud: Causes, patterns, and prevention.* Unpublished doctoral dissertation, University of Leicester, England.

Glensor, R. W., & Peak, K. J. (2004). *The problem of cruising* (Guide No. 29). Washington, DC: Center for Problem Oriented Policing.

Gottfredson, D., & Soulé, D. (2005). The timing of property crime, violent crime, and substance use among juveniles. *Journal of Research In Crime and Delinquency, 42*(1), 110–120.

Gottfredson, M. R. (1984). *Victims of crime: The dimensions of risk.* London: Her Majesty's Stationery Office.

Gottfredson, M., & Hirschi, T. (1990). *A general theory of crime.* Stanford, CA: Stanford University Press.

Grabosky, P. (2001). Virtual criminality: Old wine in new bottles? *Social and Legal Studies, 10*(2), 243–249.

Graham, K., & Homel, R. (2008). *Raising the bar: Preventing aggression in and around bars, pubs and clubs.* Monsey, NY: Criminal Justice Press, and London: Willan Press.

Graycar, A., & Sidebottom, A. (2012). Corruption and control: A corruption reduction approach. *Journal of Financial Crime, 19*(4), 384–399.

Greenberg, J. (2002). Who stole the money, and when? Individual and situational determinants of employee theft. *Organizational Behavior and Human Decision Processes, 89*(1), 985–1003.

Grove, L., Farrell, G., Farrington, D. F., & Johnson, S. D. (2012). *Preventing repeat victimization: A systematic review.* Swedish National Crime Prevention Council. http://www.bra.se/bra/bra-in-english/home/publications/archive/publications/2012-06-11-preventing-repeat-victimization.html

Hammons, A. J., & Fiese, B. H. (2011). Is frequency of shared family meals related to the nutritional health of children and adolescents? *Pediatrics, 127*(6), 1565–1574.

Harding, R., Morgan, F. H., Indermaur, D., Ferrante, A. M., & Blagg, H. (1998). Road rage and the epidemiology of violence: Something old, something new. *Studies on Crime and Crime Prevention, 7*(2), 221–238.

Harries, K. (1999). *Mapping crime: Principle and practice.* Washington, DC: National Institute of Justice.

Hartshorne, H., & May, M. A. (1928). *Studies in deceit.* New York: Macmillan.

Hartshorne, H., & May, M. A. (1928–1930). *Studies in the nature of character.* New York: Macmillan.

Hawley, A. H. (1971). *Urban society: An ecological approach.* New York: Ronald Press.

Hayes, R. (1999). Shop theft: An analysis of shoplifter perceptions and situational factors. *Security Journal, 12*(2), 7–18.

Haynie, D. L., & Osgood, D. W. (2005). Reconsidering peers and delinquency: How do peers matter? *Social Forces, 84*(2), 1109–1130.

Hearnden, I., & Magill, C. (Eds.). (2004). *Decision-making by house burglars: Offenders' perspectives* (Vol. 259). London: Home Office Research, Development and Statistics Directorate.

Heinonen, J. A., & Eck, J. E. (2012). *Home invasion robbery* (Guide No. 70). Washington, DC: Center for Problem Oriented Policing. Retrieved July 25, 2014, from http://www.popcenter.org/problems/pdfs/home_invasion_robbery.pdf

Henry, B., Caspi, A., & Moffitt, T. E. (1999). Staying in school protects boys with poor self-regulation in childhood from later crime: A longitudinal study. *International Journal of Behavioral Development, 23*(4), 1049–1073.

Herrmann, C. R. (2012). *Risky businesses: A micro-level spatiotemporal analysis of crime, place, and business establishments.* Doctoral dissertation, Graduate Center, City University of New York.

Highway Loss Data Institute. (1996–2014). Injury, collision, & theft losses: By make and model, 2003–05 models. Retrieved July 9, 2014, from http://www.carsafety.org/iihs/iihs-website-search?q=injury%20collision%20theft%20losses

Hindelang, M., Gottfredson, M., & Garafolo, J. (1978). *Victims of personal crime: An empirical foundation for a theory of personal victimization.* Cambridge, MA: Ballinger.

Hipp, J. R., & Perrin, A. (2006). Nested loyalties: Local networks' effects on neighborhood and community cohesion. *Urban Studies, 43*(13), 2503–2523.

Hirschi, T., & Gottfredson, M. R. (2000). In defense of self-control. *Theoretical Criminology, 4*(1), 55–69.

Hoeben, E., & Weerman, F. (2014). Situational conditions and adolescent offending: Does the impact of unstructured socializing depend on its location? *European Journal of Criminology, 11*(4), 481–499.

Hollis-Peel, M., Welsh, B. C., & Reynald, D. M. (2012). An international comparative study of guardianship in action: A cross-cultural examination of active guardianship in the Netherlands. *Crime Law & Social Change, 58*(1), 1–14.

Holt, T. J., & Bossler, A. M. (2009a). Examining the applicability of lifestyle-routine activities theory for cybercrime victimization. *Deviant Behavior, 30*(1), 1–25.

Holt, T. J., & Bossler, A. M. (2009b). On-line activities, guardianship, and malware infection: An examination of routine activities theory. *International Journal of Cyber Criminology, 3*(1), 400–420.

Homel, R. (2001). *Preventing violence: A review of the literature on violence and violence prevention.* A Report Prepared for the Crime Prevention Division of the NSW Attorney General's Department. Sydney (Australia): NSW Department of the Attorney General.

Homel, R., & Clark, J. (1994). *The prediction and prevention of violence in pubs and clubs.* Retrieved from http://www.popcenter.org/library/crimeprevention/volume_03/01_homel.pdf

Homel, R., Hauritz, M., McIlwain, G., Wortley, R., & Carvolth, R. (1997). Preventing drunkenness and violence around nightclubs in a tourist resort. In R. V. Clarke (Ed.), *Situational crime prevention: Successful case studies* (2nd ed., pp. 263–282). New York: Harrow & Heston.

Homel, R., Hauritz, M., Wortley, R., McIlwain, G., & Carvolth, R. (2007). Preventing alcohol-related crime through community action: The Surfers Paradise safety action project. In R. Homel (Ed.), *Policing for prevention: Reducing crime, public intoxication and injury* (Vol. 7, pp. 35–90). Monsey, NY: Criminal Justice Press.

Hutchings, A., & Hayes, H. (2009). Routine activity theory and phishing victimisation: Who gets caught in the 'net'? *Current Issues in Criminal Justice, 20*(3), 1–20.

Insurance Institute for Highway Safety. (2008, April). Motorcycle helmets and helmet use laws: Research facts every rider and legislator needs to know. Retrieved July 19, 2014, from http://www.smarter-usa.org/documents/IIHS-Helmet-Q&A.pdf

iSport. (2014). Underwater tactics for water polo. Retrieved July 20, 2014, from http://waterpolo.isport.com/water-polo-guides/underwater-tactics-for-water-polo

Jacobs, B. A. (2004). Typology of street criminal retaliation. *Journal of Research in Crime and Delinquency, 41*(3), 295–323.

Jacobs, J. (1961). *Death and life of great American cities.* New York: Random House.

Jeffery, C. R. (1971). *Crime prevention through environmental design.* Beverly Hills, CA: Sage.

Johns, T., & Hayes, R. (2003). Behind the fence: Buying and selling stolen merchandise. *Security Journal, 16*(4), 29–44.

Johnson, S., & Loxley, C. (2001). *Installing alley-gates: Practical lessons from burglary prevention projects* (Home Office Bring Note 2/01). London: Home Office. Retrieved July 24, 2014, from http://www.popcenter.org/tools/implementing_responses/pdfs/johnson.pdf

Johnston, L. D., O'Malley, P. M., Bachman, J. G., & Schulenberg, J. E. (2007). *Monitoring the future national results on adolescent drug use: Overview of key findings, 2006* (NIH Publication No. 07–6202). Bethesda, MD: National Institute on Drug Abuse.

Johnston, L. D., O'Malley, P. M., Bachman, J. G., Schulenberg, J. E., & Miech, R. A. (2014). *Monitoring the future national survey results on drug use, 1975–2013: Volume I, Secondary school students.* Ann Arbor: Institute for Social Research, The University of Michigan.

Jorgenson, A. K. (2004). Global inequality, water pollution, and infant mortality. *Social Science Journal, 41*(2), 279–288.

Junger, M., & Marshall, I. H. (1997). The interethnic generalizability of social control theory: An empirical test. *Journal of Research in Crime and Delinquency, 34*(1), 79–112.

Kautt, P. M., & Roncek, D. W. (2007). Schools as criminal "hot spots": Primary, secondary and beyond. *Criminal Justice Review, 32*(4), 339–357.

Kelling, G. L. (1999). *Broken windows and police discretion* (Report No. 178259). Washington, DC: National Institute of Justice.

Kelling, G. L., Pate, T., Dieckman, D., & Brown, C. (1974). *The Kansas City preventive patrol experiment: A summary report.* Washington, DC: Police Foundation.

Kennedy, L. W., & Forde, D. R. (1990). Routine activities and crime: An analysis of victimization in Canada. *Criminology, 28*(1), 137–152.

Kidwell, R. E., & Martin, C. L. (2005). *Managing organizational deviance.* Thousand Oaks, CA: Sage.

Kleemans, E. R. (2012). Organized crime and the visible hand: A theoretical critique on the economic analysis of organized crime. *Criminology and Criminal Justice, 13*(5), 615–629.

Kleemans, E. R., Soudijn, M. R. J., & Weenink, A. W. (2012). Organized crime, situational crime prevention, and routine activity theory. *Trends in Organized Crime, 5,* 87–92.

Klein, M. W. (1971). *Street gangs and street workers.* Englewood Cliffs, NJ: Prentice Hall.

Klein, M. W. (1992). Attempting gang control by suppression: The misuse of deterrence principles. *Studies on Crime and Crime Prevention, 2,* 88–111.

Klein, M. W. (1995). *The American street gang: Its nature, prevalence, and control.* New York: Oxford University Press.

Klein, M. W. (2004). *Gang cop: The words and ways of Officer Paco Domingo.* Walnut Creek, CA: Altamira Press.

Klein, M. W. (2005). Street gangs: A cross-national perspective. In C. R. Huff (Ed.), *Gangs in America III.* Thousand Oaks, CA: Sage.

Klein, M. W., & Crawford, L. (1967). Groups, gangs and cohesiveness. *Journal of Research in Crime and Delinquency, 4,* 63–75.

Klein, M. W., & Maxson, C. L. (2006). *Street gang patterns & policies.* Oxford, UK: Oxford University Press.

Klein, M. W., Maxson, C. L., & Cunningham, L. C. (1991). "Crack," street gangs, and violence. *Criminology, 29,* 623–650.

Klockars, C. B. (1974). *The professional fence.* New York: Free Press.

Knutsson, J. (2000). Swedish drug markets and drug policy. In M. Natarajan & M. Hough (Eds.), *Illegal drug markets: From research to prevention policy* (pp. 179–201). Monsey, NY: Criminal Justice Press.

Knutsson, J., & Kuhlhorn, E. (1997). Macro measures against crime: The example of check forgeries. In R. V. Clarke (Ed.), *Situational crime prevention: Successful case studies* (2nd ed., pp. 113–121). New York: Harrow & Heston.

Kuhlhorn, E. (1997). Housing allowances in a welfare society: Reducing the temptation to cheat. In R. V. Clarke (Ed.), *Situational crime prevention: Successful case studies* (2nd ed., pp. 235–241). New York: Harrow & Heston.

Langworthy, R. (1989). Do stings control crime? An evaluation of a police fencing operation. *Justice Quarterly, 6*(1), 27–45.

Langworthy, R., & LeBeau, J. (1992). The spatial evolution of a sting clientele. *Journal of Criminal Justice, 20*(2), 135–146.

Lasley, J. (1998). *"Designing out" gang homicides and street assaults: Research in brief.* Washington, DC: National Institute of Justice.

Lasley, J. R., & Rosenbaum, J. L. (1988). Routine activities and multiple personal victimization. *Sociology and Social Research, 73*(1), 47–50.

LaVigne, N. (1996). Safe transport: Security by design on the Washington Metro. In R. V. Clarke (Ed.), *Preventing mass transit crime* (pp. 163–197). Monsey, NY: Criminal Justice Press.

LaVigne, N. (1997). Security by design on the Washington Metro. In R. V. Clarke (Ed.), *Situational crime prevention: Successful case studies* (2nd ed., pp. 283–299). New York: Harrow & Heston.

Leap, T. L. (2007). *Dishonest dollars: The dynamics of white-collar crime.* Ithaca: ILR Press.

Leap, T. L. (2011). *Phantom billing, fake prescriptions, and the high cost of medicine: Health care fraud and what to do about it.* Ithaca: ILR Press.

LeBeau, J. (1987). The journey to rape: Geographic distances and the rapist's method of approaching the victim. *Journal of Police Sciences and Administration, 15*(2), 129–136.

LeBeau, J., & Langworthy, R. (1992). The spatial distribution of sting targets. *Journal of Criminal Justice, 20,* 541–551.

LeClerc, B., & Felson, M. (2014). Routine activities preceding adolescent sexual abuse of younger children. *Sex Abuse: A Journal of Research and Treatment.* Published online, July 2014.

LeClerc, B., Wortley, R., & Smallbone, S. (2011). Getting into the script of adult child sex offenders and mapping out situational prevention measures. *Journal of Research in Crime and Delinquency, 48*(2), 209–237.

Leitenberg, H., & Henning, K. (1995). Sexual fantasy. *Psychological Bulletin, 117*(3), 469–496.

Lemieux, A. M. (2010). *Risks of violence in major daily activities, United States, 2003–2005.* Unpublished doctoral dissertation, Rutgers University, Newark, NJ.

Lemieux, A. M. (Ed.). (2014). *Situational prevention of poaching.* London: Routledge.

Lemieux, A. M., & Felson, M. (2012). Risk of violent crime victimization during major daily activities. *Violence and Victims, 27*(5), 635–655.

Llinares, F. M. (2011). La oportunidad criminal en el ciberespacio: Aplicación y desarrollo de la teoría de las actividades cotidianas para la prevención del cibercrimen. *Revista Electrónica de Ciencia Penal y Criminología, 13,* 1–7. Retrieved July 25, 2014, from http://criminet.ugr.es/recpc/13/recpc13-07.pdf

Locker, J. P., & Godfrey, B. (2006). Ontological boundaries and temporal watersheds in the development of white-collar crime. *British Journal of Criminology, 46*(6), 976–992.

Macintyre, S., & Homel, R. (1997). Danger on the dance floor: A study of interior design, crowding and aggression in nightclubs. In R. Homel (Ed.), *Policing for prevention: Reducing crime, public intoxication and injury* (pp. 91–113). Monsey, NY: Criminal Justice Press.

Madensen, T. D., & Eck, J. E. (2008). *Spectator violence in stadiums* (Guide No. 54). Washington, DC: Center for Problem Oriented Policing.

Madensen, T. D., & Knutsson, J. (Eds.). (2011). *Preventing crowd violence.* Boulder, CO: Lynne-Rienner.

Maimon, D., Kamerdze, A., Cuiker, M., & Sobesto, B. (2013). Daily trends and origin of computer-focused crimes against a large university computer network: An application of the routine activities and lifestyle perspective. *British Journal of Criminology, 53*(2), 319–343.

Main, D. (2013, May 16). Wildlife bandits: How criminology can fight poaching. *Livescience*, Planet Earth Section. Retrieved July 30, 2014, from http://www .livescience.com/32085-wildlife-crime-criminology.html

Mallett, C. A., Dare, P. S., & Seck, M. M. (2009). Predicting juvenile delinquency: The nexus of childhood maltreatment, depression and bipolar disorder. *Criminal Behaviour and Mental Health, 19*(4), 235–246.

Mannon, J. M. (1997). Domestic and intimate violence: An application of routine activities theory. *Aggression and Violent Behavior, 2*(1), 9–24.

Marcum, C. D., Ricketts, G. E., & Higgins, M. L. (2010). Potential factors of online victimization of youth: An examination of adolescent online behaviors utilizing routine activity theory. *Deviant Behavior, 31*(5), 381–410.

Masuda, B. (1993). Credit card fraud prevention: A successful retail strategy. In R. V. Clarke (Ed.), *Crime prevention studies* (Vol. 1, pp. 121–134). Monsey, NY: Criminal Justice Press.

Masuda, B. (1997). Reduction of employee theft in a retail environment: Displacement vs. diffusion of benefits. In R. V. Clarke (Ed.), *Situational crime prevention: Successful case studies* (2nd ed., pp. 183–190). New York: Harrow & Heston.

Matthews, R. (2002). *Armed robbery*. Cullompton, Devon, UK: Willan.

Maurer, M. (2010, March 3). Study conducted in Hoboken links bar servers to alcoholism, irresponsible behavior. *The Jersey Journal,* retrieved July 30, 2014, from http://www.nj.com/hobokennow/index.ssf/2010/03/study_conducted_in_ hoboken_lin.html

Mayhew, C. (2000). *Violence in the workplace—Preventing armed robbery: A practical handbook* (Public Policy Series, No. 33). Canberra: Australian Institute of Criminology.

Mayhew, P., Clarke, R. V., & Eliot, D. (1989). Motorcycle theft, helmet legislation, and displacement. *Howard Journal of Criminal Justice, 28*(1), 1–8.

Mayhew, P., Clarke, R. V., Sturman, A., & Hough, J. M. (1976). *Crime as opportunity*. London: British Home Office Research Publications.

Mazzarole, L. G., & Roehl, J. (Eds.). (1998). Civil remedies and crime prevention. In R. V. Clarke (Ed.), *Crime prevention studies* (Vol. 9, pp. 1–18). Boulder, CO: Lynne-Rienner.

Miller, W. B. (1982). Crime by youth gangs and groups in the United States. Report to the Office of Juvenile Justice and Delinquency Prevention, National Institute for Juvenile Justice and Delinquency Prevention, U.S. Department of Justice. Washington, D.C.

Mills, J. (1958). Changes in moral attitudes following temptation. *Journal of Personality, 26*, 517–531.

Mischel, W. (2014). *The marshmallow test: Mastering self-control.* New York: Little-Brown.

Mischel, W., Shoda, Y., & Rodriguez, M. L. (1989). Delay of gratification in children. *Science, 244,* 933–938.

Morselli, C., & Tremblay, P. (2004). Criminal achievement, offender networks and the benefits of low self-control. *Criminology, 42*(3), 773–804.

Morselli, C., Tremblay, P., & McCarthy, B. (2006). Mentors and criminal achievement. *Criminology, 44*(1), 17–43.

National Gang Intelligence Center. (2009). *National gang threat assessment: 2009.* Washington, DC: Federal Bureau of Investigation. Retrieved July 18, 2014, from http://www.fbi.gov/stats-services/publications/national-gang-threat-assessment-2009-pdf

Navarro, J. N., & Jasinski, J. L. (2012). Going cyber: Using routine activities theory to predict cyberbullying experiences. *Sociological Spectrum, 32*(1), 81–94.

Newman, G. (2003). *Check and card fraud.* Washington, DC: U.S. Department of Justice, Office of Community Oriented Policing Services.

Newman, G. (2004). *Identity theft.* Washington, DC: U.S. Department of Justice, Office of Community Oriented Policing Services.

Newman, G. (2007). *Sting operations.* Washington, DC: U.S. Department of Justice, Office of Community Oriented Policing Services.

Newman, G., & Clarke, R. V. (2003). *Superhighway robbery: Preventing e-commerce crime.* Cullompton, Devon, UK: Willan.

Newman, O. (1972). *Defensible space: Crime prevention through urban design.* New York: Macmillan.

Newton, A. (2014). *Activity nodes and licensed premises: Risky mixes and risky facilities.* Paper presented at the annual meeting, Environmental Criminology and Crime Analysis, Rolduc Abbey, Kerkrade, Netherlands, June 17, 2014.

Noom, M. J., Dkovic, M., & Meeus, W. (2001). Conceptual analysis and measurement of adolescent autonomy. *Journal of Youth and Adolescence, 30*(5), 577–595.

Ogburn, W. F. (1922). *Social change with respect to culture and original nature.* New York: B. W. Huebsch.

Ogburn, W. F. (1964). *On culture and social change: Selected papers of William F. Ogburn* (O. D. Duncan, Ed.). Chicago: University of Chicago Press.

Osgood, D. W., Wilson, J. K., O'Malley, P. M., Bachman, J. G., & Johnston, L. D. (1996). Routine activities and individual deviant behavior. *American Sociological Review, 61*(4), 635–655.

Painter, K., & Farrington, D. P. (1997). The crime reducing effect of improved street lighting: The Dudley Project. In R. V. Clarke (Ed.), *Situational crime prevention: Successful case studies* (2nd ed., pp. 209–226). New York: Harrow & Heston.

Painter, K., & Tilley, N. (1999). Editor's introduction: Seeing and being seen to prevent crime. In K. Painter & N. Tilley (Eds.), *Surveillance of public space: CCTV, street lighting and crime prevention* (pp. 1–13). Monsey, NY: Criminal Justice Press.

Payne, B. K., & Gainey, R. R. (2004). Ancillary consequences of employee theft. *Journal of Criminal Justice, 32*(1), 63–73.

Pease, K. (1992). Preventing burglary on a British public housing estate. In R. V. Clarke (Ed.), *Situational crime prevention: Successful case studies* (pp. 223–229). New York: Harrow & Heston.

Pease, K. (1999). A review of street lighting evaluations: Crime reduction efforts. In K. Painter & N. Tilley (Eds.), *Surveillance of public space: CCTV, street lighting and crime prevention* (pp. 47–76). Monsey, NY: Criminal Justice Press.

Pease, K., Rogerson, M., & Ellingworth, D. (2008). *Future crime trends in the United Kingdom.* Association of British Insurers, General Insurance Research Report No. 7.

Peel, M., Reynald, D. M., van Bavel, M., Elffers, H., & Welsh, B. C. (2011). Guardianship for crime prevention: A critical review of the literature. *Crime, Law & Social Change, 56*(1), 53–57.

Petrosino, A., & Brensilber, D. (2003). The motives, methods, and decision-making of convenience store robberies: Interview with 28 incarcerated offenders in Massachusetts. In M. Smith & D. Cornish (Eds.), *Theory for practice in situational crime prevention* (pp. 237–263). Monsey, NY: Criminal Justice Press.

Petrossian, G. A., & Clarke, R.V. (2014). Explaining and controlling illegal commercial fishing: An application of the CRAVED theft model. *British Journal of Criminology, 54*(1), 73–90.

Phillips, C. (2003). Who's who in the pecking order?: Aggression and "normal violence" in the lives of girls and boys. *British Journal of Criminology, 43*(4), 710–728.

Pires, S. F. (2012). Parrot poaching in the neo-tropics: A literature review. *Global Crime 13*(3), 176–190.

Pires, S. F., & Clarke, R. V. (2011). Sequential foraging, itinerant fences, and parrot poaching in Bolivia. *British Journal of Criminology, 51*(2), 314–355.

Pires, S. F., & Clarke, R. V. (2012). Are parrots CRAVED? An analysis of parrot poaching in Mexico. *Journal of Research in Crime and Delinquency, 49*(1), 122–146.

Pires, S. F., & Moreto, W. (2011). Preventing wildlife crimes: Solutions that can overcome the "tragedy of the commons." *European Journal on Criminal Policy and Research*, 17(2), 101–123.

Plant, J. B., & Scott, M. (2009). *Effective policing and crime prevention: A problem-oriented guide for mayors, city managers, and county executives.* Washington, DC: Center for Problem-Oriented Policing. Retrieved July 30, 2014, from http://www.popcenter.org/library/reading/pdfs/mayorsguide.pdf

Porterfield, A. L. (1943, November). Delinquency and outcome in court and college. *American Journal of Sociology*, 49, 199–208.

Porterfield, A. L. (1946). *Youth in trouble.* Fort Worth, TX: Leo Potishman Foundation.

Poyner, B. (1998). The case for design. In M. Felson & R. B. Peiser (Eds.), *Reducing crime through real estate development and management* (pp. 5–21). Washington, DC: Urban Land Institute.

Poyner, B., & Fawcett, W. H. (1995). *Design for inherent security: Guidance for nonresidential buildings*. London: Construction Industry Research and Information Association.

Poyner, B., & Webb, B. (1991). *Crime free housing*. Oxford, UK: Butterworth.

Pratt, T., & Cullen, F. T. (2000). The empirical status of Gottfredson and Hirschi's general theory of crime: A meta-analysis. *Criminology, 38*(3), 931–964.

Pratt, T. C., Holtfreter, K., & Reisig, M. D. (2010). Routine online activity and Internet fraud targeting: Extending the generality of routine activity theory. *Journal of Research in Crime and Delinquency, 47*(3), 267–296.

Rebellon, C. J., & Manasse, M. (2007). Tautology, reasoned action, or rationalization? Specifying the nature of the correlation between criminal attitudes and criminal behavior. In K. T. Froeling (Ed.), *Criminology: Research focus* (pp. 257–276). Hauppauge, NY: NOVA Science.

Reiss, A. (1988). Co-offending and criminal careers. In N. Morris & M. Tonry (Eds.), *Crime and Justice, Vol. 10*. Chicago: University of Chicago Press.

Rengelink, H. (2012). Tackling Somali piracy. *Trends in Organized Crime, 15*(2–3), 180–197.

Rengert, G. F., & Wasilchick, J. (2000). *Suburban burglary: A tale of two suburbs* (2nd ed.). Springfield, IL: Charles C Thomas.

Reuter, P. (1998). *The mismeasurement of illegal drug markets* (Report RP-613). Santa Monica, CA: RAND.

Reynald, D. M. (2010a). Crime prevention through environmental design. In B. Fisher & S. Lab (Eds.), *Encyclopedia of victimology and crime prevention* (pp. 221–226). Thousand Oaks, CA: Sage.

Reynald, D. M. (2010b). Defensible space. In B. Fisher & S. Lab (Eds.), *Encyclopedia of victimology and crime prevention* (pp. 272–277). Thousand Oaks, CA: Sage.

Reynald, D. M. (2010c). Guardians on guardianship: Factors affecting the willingness to monitor, the ability to detect potential offenders & the willingness to intervene. *Journal of Research in Crime and Delinquency, 47*(3), 358–390.

Reynald, D. M. (2011a). Factors associated with the guardianship of places: Assessing the relative importance of the spatio-physical and socio-demographic contexts in generating opportunities for capable guardianship. *Journal of Research in Crime & Delinquency, 48*(1), 110–142.

Reynald, D. M. (2011b). *Guarding against crime: A theoretical & empirical elaboration of the routine activity concept*. London, UK: Ashgate Publishers.

Reynald, D. M. (2014). Informal guardianship. *Encyclopedia of criminology and criminal justice* (pp. 2480–2489). New York: Springer.

Reyns, B., Henson, B., & Fisher, B. S. (2011). Applying cyberlifestyle–routine activities theory to cyberstalking victimization. *Criminal Justice and Behavior, 38*(11), 1149–1169.

Rhee, V., Mullany, L. C., Khatry, S. K., Katz, J., LeClerq, S. C., Darmstadt, G. L., & Tielsch, J. M. (2008). Maternal and birth attendant hand washing and neonatal mortality in Southern Nepal. *Archives of Pediatric and Adolescent Medicine, 162*(7), 603–608.

Rickman, N., & Witt, R. (2003). *The determinants of employee crime in the UK*. London: Center for Economic Policy Research.

Riedel, M. (1999). The decline of arrest and clearance for criminal homicide: Causes, correlates and third parties. *Criminal Justice Policy Review, 9*(3&4), 279–306.

Roncek, D. W. (1981). Dangerous places: Crime and residential environment. *Social Forces, 60,* 74–96.

Roncek, D. W., & Lobosco, A. (1983). The effect of high schools on crime in their neighborhoods. *Social Science Quarterly, 64,* 598–613.

Roncek, D. W., & Maier, P. A. (1991). Bars, blocks and crimes revisited: Linking the theory of routine activities to the empiricism of "hot spots." *Criminology, 29,* 725–754.

Ross, H. L. (1992). *Confronting drunk driving: Social policy for saving lives*. New Haven, CT: Yale University Press.

Rossmo, D. K. (2000). *Geographic profiling*. Boca Raton, FL: CRC Press.

Runyan, C. W., Bowling, J. M., & Schulman, M. (2005). Potential for violence against teenage retail workers in the United States. *Journal of Adolescent Health, 36*(3), 1–6.

Sampson, R. (2002). *Bullying in schools* (Guide No. 12). Washington, DC: Center for Problem Oriented Policing, Retrieved July 27, 2014, from http://www.popcenter .org/problems/bullying/

Sampson, R., Eck, J. E., & Dunham, J. (2010). Super controllers and crime prevention: A routine activity explanation of crime prevention success and failure. *Security Journal, 23,* 37–51.

Schneider, J. L. (2003). Prolific burglars and the role of shoplifting. *Security Journal, 16*(2), 49–59.

Scott, M. (2001). *Disorderly youths in public places* (Guide No. 6). Washington, DC: Center for Problem-Oriented Policing. Retrieved July 30, 2014, from http://www .popcenter.org/problems/disorderly_youth/

Scott, M., & Dedel, K. (2006). *Assaults in and around bars* (2nd ed.). Washington, DC: U.S. Department of Justice, Office of Community Oriented Policing Services.

Scott, M., Emerson, N. J., Antonacci, L. B., & Plant, J. B. (2006). *Drunk driving*. Washington, DC: U.S. Department of Justice, Office of Community Oriented Policing Services.

Shaw, C., & McKay, H. (1942). *Juvenile delinquency and urban areas*. Chicago: University of Chicago Press.

Shearing, C. D., & Stenning, P. C. (1997). From the Panopticon to Disney World: The development of discipline. In R. V. Clarke (Ed.), *Situational crime prevention: Successful case studies* (2nd ed., pp. 300–304). New York: Harrow & Heston.

Sherman, C. (2009, February 25). *National Retail Federation welcomes legislation to fight organized retail crime, says retailers can't afford losses from theft during recession*. News Release. Available at http://www.nrf.com

Sherman, L., Gartin, P. R., & Buerger, M. E. (1989). Hot spots of predatory crime: Routine activities and the criminology of place. *Criminology, 27*(1), 27–56.

Siennick, S. E., & Osgood, D. W. (2012). Hanging out with which friends? Friendship-level predictors of unstructured and unsupervised socializing in adolescence. *Journal of Research on Adolescence, 22*(4), 646–661.

Simon, H. A. (1957). *Models of man.* New York: Wiley.

Sloan, J. H., Kellermann, A. L., Reay, D. T., Ferris, A. J., Rice, C. L., & LoGerfo, J. (1988). Handgun regulations, crime, assaults, and homicide: A tale of two cities. *New England Journal of Medicine, 319,* 1256–1262.

Sloan-Howitt, M., & Kelling, G. D. (1997). Subway graffiti in New York City: "Gettin'up" vs. "meanin' it and cleanin' it." In R. V. Clarke (Ed.), *Situational crime prevention: Successful case studies* (2nd ed., pp. 242–249). New York: Harrow & Heston.

Smith, B. T. (2013). *Differential shoplifting risks of fast-moving consumer goods.* Unpublished doctoral dissertation, Rutgers University Graduate School of Criminal Justice.

Smith, D. J. (1995). Youth crime and conduct disorders: Trends, patterns and causal explanations. In M. Rutter & D. J. Smith (Eds.), *Psychosocial disorders in youth populations: Time trends and their causes* (pp. 389–489). Chichester, UK: Wiley.

Smith, M. (2005). *Robbery of taxi drivers.* Washington, DC: U.S. Department of Justice, Office of Community Oriented Policing Services.

Smith, M., & Cornish, D. (Eds.). (2006). *Secure and tranquil travel: Preventing crime and disorder on public transport.* Cullompton, Devon, UK: Willan.

Smith, P. K., Morita, Y., Junger-Tas, J., Olweus, D., Catalano, R., & Slee, P. (Eds.). (1999). *The nature of school bullying: A cross-national perspective.* New York: Routledge.

Snyder, H. N., & Sickmund, M. (2006). *Juvenile offenders and victims: 2006 national report* (Prepared for the Office of Juvenile Justice and Delinquency Prevention). Pittsburgh, PA: National Center for Juvenile Justice.

Soudijn, M. R. J., & Kleemans, E. R. (2009). Chinese organized crime and situational context: Comparing human smuggling and synthetic drugs trafficking. *Crime, Law and Social Change, 52,* 457–474.

Sousa, W. H., & Madensen, T. (2011). The police and major event planning: A case study in Las Vegas, Nevada. In T. C. Madensen & J. Knutsson (Eds.), *Preventing crowd violence* (Crime Prevention Studies, Vol. 26, pp. 139–158). Boulder, CO: Lynne-Rienner.

Spencer, J. (2011, May 11). Target, other stores battle theft rings fencing stolen goods on web. *Seattle Times.* Retrieved July 18, 2014, from http://seattletimes.com/html/businesstechnology/2014975231_storetheft06.html

Staff, J., & Uggen, C. (2003). The fruits of good work: Early work experiences and adolescent deviance. *Journal of Research in Crime and Delinquency, 40*(3), 263–290.

Steffensmeier, D. (1986). *The fence: In the shadow of two worlds.* Totowa, NJ: Rowman and Littlefield.

Sutherland, E. H. (1933). *The professional thief, by a professional thief.* Chicago: University of Chicago Press.

Sutherland, E. H. (1939). *Principles of criminology.* Chicago: Lippincott.

Suttles, G. D. (1968). *The social order of a slum.* Chicago: University of Chicago Press.

Sutton, M. (1995). Supply by theft: Does the market for second-hand goods play a role in keeping crime figures high? *British Journal of Criminology, 35,* 400–416.

Sutton, M. (1998). *Handling stolen goods and theft: A market reduction approach* (Home Office Research Study No. 178). London: British Home Office Research Publications.

Sutton, M. (2004). How burglars and shoplifters sell stolen goods in Derby: Describing and understanding the local illicit markets. *Internet Journal of Criminology,* pp. 1–44.

Sutton, M., Schneider, J., & Hetherington, S. (2001). *Tackling theft with the market reduction approach.* London: Policing and Reducing Crime Unit, U.K. Home Office.

Tedeschi, J., & Felson, R. B. (1994). *Violence, aggression and coercive action.* Washington, DC: American Psychological Association.

Tremblay, P. (1986). Designing crime. *British Journal of Criminology, 26,* 234–253.

Tremblay, P. (1993). Searching for suitable co-offenders. In R. V. Clarke & M. Felson (Eds.), *Routine activity and rational choice: Advances in criminological theory* (Vol. 5, pp. 17–36). New Brunswick, NJ: Transaction Books.

Tremblay, P., Clermont, Y., & Cusson, M. (1994). Jockeys and joyriders: Changing patterns in car theft opportunity structures. *British Journal of Criminology, 34,* 307–321.

Tremblay, P., & Morselli, C. (2000). Patterns in criminal achievement: Wilson and Abrahamse revisited. *Criminology, 38*(2), 633–659.

Tremblay, P., & Pare, P. (2003). Crime and destiny: Patterns in serious offenders' mortality rates. *Canadian Journal of Criminology and Criminal Justice, 45*(3), 299–326.

Truman, J., & Langton, L. (2014, September). *Criminal victimization, 2013.* Washington, DC: Bureau of Justice Statistics, Report NCJ-247648. Retrieved September 20, 2014, from http://www.bjs.gov/content/pub/pdf/cv13.pdf

van Dijk, J. J. (1994). Understanding crime rates: On interactions between rational choices of victims and offenders. *British Journal of Criminology, 34*(2), 105–121.

van Dijk, J. J. M., van Kesteren, J. N., & Smit, P. (2008). *Criminal victimization in international perspective: Key findings from the 2004–2005 ICVS and EU ICS.* The Hague, Netherlands: Boom Legal Publishers.

von Hirsch, A. (1987). *Past or future crimes: Deservedness and dangerousness in the sentencing of criminals.* New Brunswick, NJ: Rutgers University Press.

von Lampe, K. (2011). The illegal cigarette trade. In M. Natarajan (Ed.), *International criminal justice* (pp. 148–154). New York: Cambridge University Press.

Warr, M. (1988). Rape, burglary and opportunity. *Journal of Quantitative Criminology, 4*(3), 275–288.

Warr, M. (2002). *Companions in crime.* Cambridge, UK: Cambridge University Press.

Weber, M. (1978). *Economy and society: An outline of interpretive sociology.* Berkeley: University of California Press. (Original work published 1922)

Webster, S. D. (2005). Pathways to sexual offense recidivism following treatment: An examination of the Ward and Hudson self-regulation model of relapse. *Journal of Interpersonal Violence, 20*(10), 1175–1196.

Weerman, F. M., Bernasco, W., Bruinsma, G. J. N., & Pauwels, L. J. R. (2013). When is spending time with peers related to delinquency? The importance of where, what and with whom. *Crime & Delinquency.* doi: 0011128713478129

Weerman, F., Wilcox, P., & Sullivan, C. (2013, November 19). *Peers, activities and short-term changes in delinquency and substance use: An analysis of bi-weekly data.* Paper presented at the annual meeting of the ASC Annual Meeting, Palmer House Hilton, Chicago.

Weisburd, D. L., & Eck, J. (2004). What can police do to reduce crime, disorder and fear? *Annals of the American Academy of Political and Social Science, 593,* 42–65.

Weisburd, D., Telep, C. W., Hinkle, J. C., & Eck, J. E. (2008). The effects of problem-oriented policing on crime and disorder. *Campbell Systematic Reviews, 14*(14). Retrieved July 14, 2014, from http://www.campbellcollaboration.org/lib/?go=monograph&year=2008

Weisburd, D., Waring, E., & Chayet, E. (2001). *White-collar crime and criminal careers.* Cambridge, UK: Cambridge University Press.

Weisburd, D., Wyckoff, L., Ready, J., Eck, J., Hinkle, J., & Gajewski, F. (2006). Does crime just move around the corner? A controlled study of spatial displacement and diffusion of crime control benefits. *Criminology, 44,* 549–592.

Weisel, D. L. (2005). *Analyzing repeat victimization.* Washington, DC: U.S. Department of Justice, Office of Community Oriented Policing Services.

Wheeler, S. (1983). White collar crime: History of an idea. In S. H. Kadish (Ed.), *Encyclopedia of crime and justice* (pp. 1652–1656). New York: Free Press.

White, R. C. (1932). The relation of felonies to environmental factors in Indianapolis. *Social Forces, 10,* 498–513.

Wikström, P.-O. (1985). *Everyday violence in contemporary Sweden: Situational and ecological aspects* (Report No. 2015). Stockholm: National Council for Crime Prevention.

Wikström, P.-O., Oberwittler, D., Treiber, K., & Hardie, B. (2012). *Breaking rules: The social and situational dynamics of young people's urban crime.* Oxford, UK: Oxford University Press.

Winchester, S., & Jackson, H. (1982). *Residential burglary: The limits of prevention* (Research Study #74). London: British Home Office Research Publications.

Wortley, R. (1997). Reconsidering the role of opportunity in situational crime prevention. In G. Newman, R. V. Clarke, & S. G. Shoham (Eds.), *Rational choice and situational crime prevention* (pp. 65–81). Dartmouth, UK: Ashgate.

Wortley, R. (1998). A two-stage model of situational crime prevention. *Studies on Crime and Crime Prevention, 7*(2), 173–188.

Wortley, R., & Smallbone, S. (Eds.). (2006). *Situational prevention of child sexual abuse*. Monsey, NY: Criminal Justice Press.

Wright, J. P., & Cullen, F. P. (2000). Juvenile involvement in occupational delinquency. *Criminology, 38*(3), 863–896.

Wright, R. T., & Decker, S. H. (1997). *Armed robbers in action: Stickups and street culture*. Boston: Northeastern University Press.

Wrong, D. H. (1961). The oversocialized conception of man in modern sociology. *American Sociological Review, 26*, 183–193.

Yablonsky, L. (1959). The delinquent gang as a near-group. *Social Problems, 7*(2), 108–109.

Yar, M. (2005). The novelty of "cybercrime": An assessment in light of routine activity theory. *European Journal of Criminology, 2*(4), 407–427.

Zahm, D. (2007). Using crime prevention through environmental design in problem solving (Tool Guide No. 8). Washington, DC: Center for Problem Oriented Policing. Retrieved July 24, 2014, from http://www.popcenter.org/tools/cpted/

Zimring, F. F. (2001). *American youth violence*. New York: Oxford University Press.

Zimring, F. F., & Hawkins, G. (1999). *Crime is not the problem: Lethal violence in America*. New York: Oxford University Press.

Zolotor, A. J., & Runyan, D. K. (2006). Social capital, family violence and neglect. *Pediatrics, 117*(6), 1124–1131.

INDEX

⑤SAGE research**methods**

The essential online tool for researchers from the world's leading methods publisher

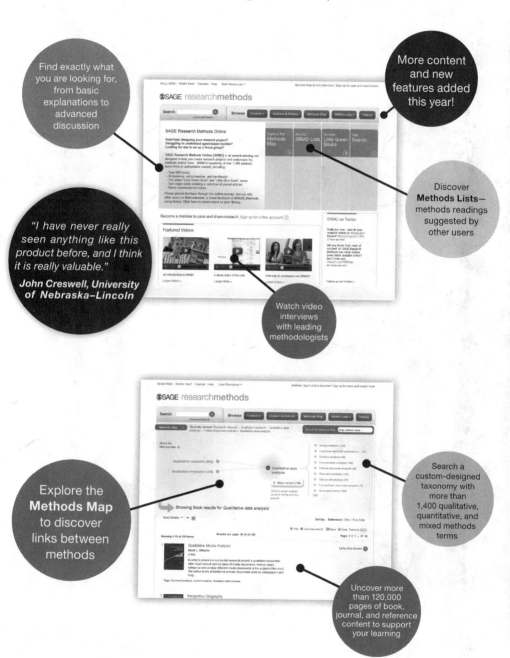

Find exactly what you are looking for, from basic explanations to advanced discussion

More content and new features added this year!

"I have never really seen anything like this product before, and I think it is really valuable."
John Creswell, University of Nebraska–Lincoln

Discover **Methods Lists**— methods readings suggested by other users

Watch video interviews with leading methodologists

Explore the **Methods Map** to discover links between methods

Search a custom-designed taxonomy with more than 1,400 qualitative, quantitative, and mixed methods terms

Uncover more than 120,000 pages of book, journal, and reference content to support your learning

Find out more at
www.sageresearchmethods.com